STAUBACH

Portrait of the Brightest Star

CARLTON STOWERS

TRIUMPH
BOOKS

Library of Congress Cataloging-in-Publication Data

Stowers, Carlton.
    Staubach : portrait of the brightest star / by Carlton Stowers.
    p. cm.
    Includes bibliographical references and index.

    1. Staubach, Roger, 1942- 2. Football players—United States—
Biography. I. Title.
    GV939.S733S76 2010
    796.323092—dc22
    [B]
                                2010026630

This book is available in quantity at special discounts for your group or organization. For further information, contact:

Triumph Books
814 North Franklin Street
Chicago, Illinois 60610
(800) 888–4741
Fax (312) 337–1807
www.triumphbooks.com

Printed in U.S.A.
ISBN: 978-1-62937-727-8
Design by Patricia Frey

For the charter members of the Old Timer's Club—
Tex Schramm, Bert Rose, Curt Mosher, Doug Todd, Pat
Summerall, Blackie Sherrod, Bob St. John, and Frank
Luksa—and those who eventually aged properly to join—
Babe Laufenberg, Brad Sham, Mickey Spagnola, Rick
Gosselin, and Hugh Aynesworth. Oh, the tales they've told.

"There is no question that Roger Staubach is this country's greatest sports hero today, maybe of our time. He is unique in that his following spans all age generations."

—Tex Schramm, 1979

CONTENTS

FOREWORD

Some 30 years after his retirement, friends and family members are still amused at how I react when the debate ensues on TV or radio concerning the greatest quarterbacks of all time. I stand up, stomp across the room, flail my arms, and shout four-letter words that do not rhyme with "ESPN." I hear commentators talk about Montana, Elway, Unitas, Bradshaw, Favre, and Marino. *"What about Staubach?"* I yell. *"You idiots can't even spell Staubach!"*

No NFL quarterback did more with less time than Roger Staubach. In 11 seasons, he compiled the highest passer rating (83.4) ever. He won two Super Bowls and led the Dallas Cowboys to 23 fourth-quarter comebacks.

Of course, he was far more than statistics, wins, and losses. I started covering the Cowboys on a daily basis as a newspaperman at age 24, and I was in awe of the man. In two decades of reporting on the NFL, I never witnessed a better leader, nor did I see anyone who could light a fire under a team like Roger did. When he swept onto the field in the fourth quarter with the game on the line and the clock ticking down, it seemed that everyone got out of his way.

I remember a trip to RFK Stadium in Washington, D.C., in 1978 when, 30 minutes before kickoff, the fans began to chant, "Roger's a sissy! Roger's a sissy!" I turned to a fellow writer and said, "These people have *really* been drinking." Roger Staubach was John Wayne in cleats, a man who possessed the nimble feet of Jimmy Connors, the guts of a warrior, and the cunning of James Bond.

Personal remembrances abound. At the age of 10, I sat with my nose about six inches from my family's black-and-white TV and watched him take Navy to a 21–7 lead over Army with wild scrambles and pinpoint passing. The Midshipmen hung on that day for a 21–15 victory that set up the national championship game on January 1, 1964, against Texas in the Cotton Bowl.

While I was in college at SMU, I spotted him one evening searching for a parking spot in front of our fraternity house as a big tennis match was about to begin over at Moody Coliseum. We made room for his car in front of the house—then somebody pulled out a football. He threw spirals to us as we ran pass patterns across the intramural field. By the way, I hear that Staubach, now in his late sixties, still carries a football in the front seat of his car.

During the final great comeback of his career against the Redskins in 1979 with the NFC title on the line in the last game of the season, he led the Cowboys to two touchdowns in the waning minutes. He arced the winning touchdown pass to Tony Hill at the back of the end zone with 1:12 left and proceeded to jump into the arms of Ron Springs. The Cowboys won 35–34, establishing Staubach once more as the greatest comeback quarterback of all time. A few minutes later, my body was so filled with nervous tension that I could not get out of my chair in the press box at the end of the game. The muscles in my legs were locked. There I was, sitting with some of the greatest sportswriters of all time—the likes of Blackie Sherrod, Carlton Stowers, Frank Luksa, and Randy Galloway—and I could not get out of my damn chair. As the others were hustling toward the elevator that would take them down to the locker room, I finally pushed myself up with my arms and stumbled down press row like a man walking on wooden stilts.

None of us will ever forget his farewell press conference in March 1980 when about 200 reporters came from all over the country and as far away as London. We were still living in the pre-ESPN age, and I can promise you that if the same event were held today, there would be 1,000 reporters coming from as far away as Tokyo.

Roger Staubach left the game at age 38. If not for all of the concussions, I swear he could have played until 48. Then there would be no debate about the greatest quarterback of all time. My great friend Carlton Stowers has written a terrific book about the most exciting player in the history of the NFL.

—Jim Dent, May 2010

PREFACE

The road that leads to the level of success you will read about in these pages is not always well marked. The route sometimes winds along strange twists and turns, down occasional blind alleys, up hills, and through valleys. A sizable portion of luck helps chart the journey. One wrong turn, even an unnecessary delay along the way, can make the destination impossible to reach.

No matter how gifted and determined, willful and stubborn-minded, the right things have to happen at the right time for life's perfect storm to occur.

In Dallas during the 1970s, such an event played out. And, woe is me, was it needed.

Though a proud city, Dallas was floundering in its effort to not only be favorably recognized as a major player on the American social and economic landscape but to erase a dark moment in history that threatened to define it forever. Dallas, for all its wealth and glitter, its high-rises and high-rollers, was losing a battle to repolish an image unfairly branded on it by the outside world.

Since a dark November day in 1963, when President John Fitzgerald Kennedy was assassinated on its streets, Dallas had been the target of blame and criticism, its every fault and shortcoming magnified. So effective had been the political piling-on that a public epidemic of self-doubt and insecurity developed. While the chamber of commerce would never admit it, many in Dallas had embraced the notion that they had precious few things about which they could legitimately boast to the outside world. And in Texas, where bragging is considered a treasured art form, the problem was devastating.

Dallas needed a champion, a hero, something or someone to emerge as a new talisman of pride and hope.

The rescue would be accomplished by an unlikely assortment of young men who had arrived in the city with varied and unusual backgrounds collected to offer themselves as the city's rallying point. They were the Dallas Cowboys, the city's still-new entry in the National Football League, and if the experts were right, they were on the verge of becoming the gold standard of professional football.

They were as colorful as they were talented—coached by a man who had been lured from his early days in the insurance business to give another career a try, and joined by an Olympic gold medalist who had claimed the title of World's Fastest Human, a rodeo star who wanted only a new horse trailer in exchange for agreeing to play pro football, castoffs from other teams, and those who had made their collegiate marks in other sports but had demonstrated the raw talent necessary to make the transition to linemen, defensive backs, and receivers. The man who sought them out and lured them to the team had previously earned his living as a baby photographer, of all things.

They had arrived from outposts well known and never before heard of. Some came from the hotbeds of collegiate football—Penn State and Oklahoma, Stanford and Ohio State. Others had played in obscurity at places like Elizabeth City College, Ouachita Baptist, and Fort Valley State. Try finding those on the collegiate map. One had even come from Yale, the Ivy League bastion where academics historically trumped athletics. They were black and white, country boys and urban dwellers—as unlikely a combination of talent and pedigree as had ever been gathered.

And understand it was all taking place in a time long before multmillion-dollar sports contracts were commonplace and end-zone celebrations were choreographed specifically for ESPN highlights shows, before games were played in billion-dollar stadiums where the cost of a couple of tickets exceeded the signing bonuses given some of the players of the era. If memory serves me correctly, I think times were also a bit more fun then for all concerned.

While those yesteryear Cowboys quickly grew into legitimate contenders during the first decade of the franchise's history, they had not yet achieved that which the city so badly needed. They had not reached the level of champions.

For that to happen, a remarkable string of circumstances would have to occur. A gifted kid playing in an all-boys Catholic high school in Cincinnati would have to be snubbed by coaches at football powerhouse Notre Dame and, instead, opt to continue his higher education at the United States Naval Academy. The Cowboys would have to ultimately take a long-shot gamble that he might still be able to make it in professional football after a four-year military obligation was completed. Then, the unexpected retirement of the team's brightest star would happen, making room on the roster for a 27-year-old rookie.

That rookie's name was Roger Staubach, and while none knew it, he brought with him the final ingredient the Cowboys and the city in which they played had been searching for.

Mike Ditka, a latter-day member of the team after years of All-Pro stardom with the Chicago Bears, was there during the transition. "When I arrived in Dallas I was impressed with the incredible talent of the Cowboys," he remembered. "And in Tom Landry they had one of the best coaches in the history of the game. The only thing that was missing was that on-the-field leader who could step up and make a good team into a great one."

The kid Notre Dame hadn't wanted, the Vietnam veteran, the rookie too old to be beginning a pro football career, was the answer. The winding road had led him to Dallas. And once there, he would not only lead the Cowboys to new heights but also help give a city a renewed reason to lift its head, to brag again, and to look ahead to a bright new future.

This, then, is the story of how that perfect storm occurred.

ACKNOWLEDGMENTS

I n the newspaper days of the Staubach era, it was, for better or worse, an all-male collection of sportswriters who were assigned to follow the team. The ladies will forgive me, I hope, when I say that I was privileged to share press-box space with some of the true legends of Texas journalism: Walter Robertson, Bob St. John, Sam Blair, David Casstevens, Steve Pate, Mike Jones, Temple Pouncey, and Randy Galloway, fellow writers at the *Dallas Morning News*; Frank Luksa and Blackie Sherrod of the *Dallas Times Herald*; Jim Dent and Gil LeBreton of the *Fort Worth Star-Telegram*; Denne Freeman and Mike Cochran of the Associated Press; Mike Rabun of United Press International; Steve Perkins of the *Times Herald* and later editor of the *Dallas Cowboys Weekly* before I took his handoff; and Jarrett Bell, who ably assisted before eventually taking the reins himself.

Long before you saw their names on dust jackets of best-selling books, they all spent years fine-tuning their craft as daily newspaper and wire service journalists. Some, to readers' good fortune, continue to do so. Their writings and the publications and organizations for which they worked also served as valuable source material.

A deep bow is also necessary to the Cowboys public relations directors of the time—Curt Mosher and Doug Todd—who not only stood ever ready to help but had the historical foresight to maintain remarkable files on all who played for the team. A grateful nod is due Anita Grisham for directing traffic.

And of course, sincere thanks to Roger Staubach. And those who coached him, played with him, and against him. On the following pages you'll read their names.

When Triumph Books offered the opportunity to revisit Roger's career, my first thought was to approach the welcomed task in a reflective manner, to have him and those who played supporting roles look back on days now long past. Ultimately, it occurred to me that the road best taken might be that which, whenever possible, dealt in the moment, capturing events as they occurred rather than how they are later remembered.

To that end I could finally give some degree of logic to a notion that visited me years ago. For reasons I can't recall, I dutifully began storing away articles I wrote for newspapers and magazines and notes for my own books in an old filing cabinet that the lady of the house argued did absolutely nothing to improve the décor of my cluttered office. In it I found a wealth of material I had long forgotten—yellowed game accounts, more newspaper and magazine stories about Staubach than I'd remembered writing, countless profiles of teammates, columns in which I'd offered up my own two-cent evaluations, even ghost writings later done for Tom Landry and Tex Schramm. Herein, you'll find revised bits and pieces from articles that I originally wrote for such publications as the *Dallas Morning News*, *Dallas Cowboys Weekly*, *Football Digest*, *The Sporting News*, *College & Pro Football Weekly*, the *Dallas Observer*, *Sports Illustrated*, *GameDay*, *Country Rambler*, and even *D-FW Home & Garden*.

And while I must admit the prose was sometimes a bit clunky, I did like the spontaneity of the quotes the pieces included, the immediacy of the scenes and events they described. They told how it was at the time in Thousand Oaks, the Cotton Bowl, Texas Stadium, the old practice field on Forrest Lane, and sites of Super Bowls, not how today's faulted memory too often colors people, places, and events.

And that, I decided, was the best way to tell the story of a quarterback and a team that finally escaped a legacy of yearly shortcomings and disappointment to become one of the most celebrated in the history of professional sports.

Like Roger, who has admirably reflected on his life and playing days not once but twice in book form, said when I alerted him to my task, "Hey, you know nothing has changed." He was right.

And I didn't wish it to.

—Carlton Stowers

CHAPTER 1

"When you think about the Cowboys' success in the '70s, you've got to look directly at Roger. He's the epitome of a competitor, the leader of leaders."
Charlie Waters, All-Pro defensive back

In the hush of the Dallas Cowboys practice facility, somber players and assistant coaches sat listening to a live radio broadcast of an announcement that was being made several miles away in Texas Stadium. It was not news to them, really, since the man who was winding up an 11-year career as one of the National Football League's most gifted and celebrated athletes had met with them earlier in the day to tell them of his decision.

Still, they strained to hear every word spoken by the teammate who had for so long been their guiding force, the spiritual embodiment of what the Cowboys of the '70s had become.

Roger Staubach was calling it quits.

Though anticipated by most who knew the 38-year-old quarterback well, the reality was a jolt. Speculation had become irrefutable fact. Rumors that had circulated since the sudden end of the 1979 season had finally been proven true. While still at the top of his game and ranked No. 1 among the league's all-time passers, he was making it official.

He did so with tears in his eyes and a smile on his face. Twice during the early stages of his announcement, made before one of the largest media gatherings in Dallas history, his voice broke as he paused to regain

1

the typical Staubach composure. He saluted the Cowboys organization, his coaches, and his teammates, reflected on past glories and memorable moments, and then finally uttered the words so many dreaded to hear, "I'm retired."

And with that he brought to an end a career unrivaled in the 20-year history of the Dallas franchise; one highlighted by two Super Bowl victories, four NFL passing titles, five Pro Bowl appearances, and ownership of every passing record in the Cowboys book. There had been the repeated come-from-behind victories that had become his trademark—23 fourth-quarter wins, 14 in the final minutes of play or overtime. During his eight years as Dallas' starting quarterback Staubach had won 85 games and lost 29.

Fielding questions from the 200 members of the media on hand, he spoke of a "gut feeling" that had ultimately proved to be the deciding factor in his decision. "It was based on several things," he said. "I want to spend more time, more quality time, with my family. Then, there was just the feeling that it was the right time to retire."

Only when a reporter asked did he admit the underlying reason he had decided to play no more. The five concussions he had suffered in the previous season alone had given him, and medical experts with whom he had consulted, pause.

Still, he insisted, "If that had been the only thing, I think I would still be playing." Standing at his side, wife Marianne knew better.

Neither, he pointed out, would it have made any difference had head coach Tom Landry softened his stance on the oft-argued play-calling situation and relinquished the responsibility to him. "I was successful because the system we had was successful," Staubach said. "It was successful before I got here, and it will be successful long after I'm gone."

Following Staubach to the podium, Landry said that he had not tried too hard to convince his quarterback to prolong his career. "When it became obvious that he had made up his mind, I didn't press it too much. I respect his decision." Still, Landry could not help but add a footnote. He had seen no indication that Roger's performance in the '79 season had signaled any drop-off in ability. "He was as good last year as he was five years ago. I made him aware of how much we wanted him to continue playing, but beyond that I didn't try to talk him out of his decision."

What the central figure of the occasion had anticipated as nothing more than a small press conference turned into a happening. Journalists from throughout the United States and as far away as London were on hand to chronicle the end of an era. Local television and radio stations broke away from normal programming to carry the event live, one providing a feed to a Washington affiliate eager to alert its viewers to the fact one of its greatest football adversaries was finally leaving the game.

NFL Films was on hand to record the announcement, and local newspapers dispatched teams of reporters to chronicle the event's every aspect. Teammates would soon be interviewed, as was the man on the street.

By nightfall, all three TV networks had devoted major portions of their evening news broadcasts to Staubach's leave-taking. Local stations were hurriedly piecing together primetime specials on his career. The *Dallas Times Herald* was busily preparing a special section for the next day's edition. Several Dallas businesses had placed "Good-bye Roger" signs on their marquees.

Staubach himself was surprised by the overflow of attention. "One day," he said, "I'll look back on all this and appreciate it. But right now, it has made me very uncomfortable." Perhaps the longtime Cowboys offensive captain did not fully realize the lofty stature he had gained, not only in Dallas but throughout the world of sports.

"It is going to be difficult without him," Landry noted. "The Dallas Cowboys as well as the entire game of professional football are going to miss him. We don't have enough Roger Staubachs in this league."

The man of the hour, meanwhile, maintained his characteristic modesty. "I'd like to be remembered," he said, "as a pretty darned consistent performer."

Truth is, he was *damned* consistent.

As he ended his career, Staubach had an 83.4 quarterback rating, easily placing him ahead of former Washington standout Sonny Jurgensen's 82.6 on the all-time passing list. He threw for 22,700 yards and 153 regular season touchdowns. The statistical achievements go on and on.

As did the nationwide praise following his announcement. Coaches and players from throughout the league unanimously cited him as one of the game's greatest quarterbacks.

The special plaudits, however, came from his immediate football family, teammates who greatly admired him personally as well as professionally.

Said longtime road roommate Bob Breunig, "I've got nothing but superlatives for a guy who is truly what an all-pro quarterback represents to me. He's one of those people who has all his priorities in order. He has a great sensitivity for people and gives so much. No one will ever know how much, really."

"The thing that will always stand out in my mind," Billy Joe DuPree said, "is that he never knew when it was over. At the end of the game, even if we were down by 20 points, he'd be standing there by himself, trying to figure out some way we could still win."

"What really said it all about Roger for me," Larry Cole added, "was that picture of him jumping into Ron Springs' arms in excitement when we beat Washington. It captured what he's all about—a fierce, fierce competitor."

"You know," offensive guard Tom Rafferty said, "I'll never forget staring into his eyes in the huddle. When he wanted something, his eyes would get this flaming, intense look. I just couldn't believe that someone could be that incredibly competitive."

Applause also came from the opposition. "During my career," added Los Angeles Rams defensive end Fred Dryer, "I've seen that guy do some incredible things. There is no one in professional sports who has been able to achieve what he has. He so symbolized the Dallas Cowboys that it will be difficult for anyone to identify with another quarterback for a while."

St. Louis Cardinals coach Jim Hanifan agreed. "There wasn't a player on the Cowboys offense or defense who didn't look at him and think, 'As long as we have Roger, we have a chance to win.' That's a real tribute to him. And I know this: The opposition thought that way, too."

Seated in one corner of the Cowboys dressing room, reflecting on the announcement, linebacker coach Jerry Tubbs, offered some idea of what Staubach was feeling. A player for the early Cowboys, Tubbs said, "Once you do retire and realize it is over, it can be a traumatic experience. It's a tough adjustment to go through. I don't know anyone who can honestly say he's not going to miss it. Roger will. I know that.

"And we'll miss him."

For several days following his farewell, the popular Willie Nelson ballad, "My Heroes Have Always Been Cowboys," was played repeatedly on Dallas radio stations. TV producers, not generally fans of country and western music, used the song as background music for their tributes.

"There for a couple of days," Roger would later recall, "I got the strange feeling that I had died rather than simply retired from football. It was a little discomforting."

In time, NFL Films released a highlight film of Staubach's career, the first it had ever produced that focused on a single player. The voice-over that accompanied the closing moment, the subject in dramatic freeze frame, summed up his career in one perfectly chosen sentence,

"For everyone touched by Roger Staubach, say a fond farewell. For you and the game of football will be diminished by his absence."

And none would realize that comment's truth more than the Dallas Cowboys. It would be 13 years before the team would again appear in a Super Bowl. And even now, his remarkable accomplishments during a magical decade long past have not been forgotten.

In truth, it had begun long before his arrival in Dallas.

CHAPTER 2

"We have only one child. God gave us a good one."

Robert Staubach

Though Silverton, Ohio, was his childhood home and the founding place of so many youthful memories, Roger Staubach most often tells those who ask that he's from Cincinnati. It's just easier than explaining the location of the suburban community that sits in the eastern shadows of the larger, better-known city.

Old Dallas Cowboys teammate Bob Lilly would understand. Rather than saying that he grew up in the West Texas hamlet of Throckmorton, the geographical description he most often uses for his childhood heartland is "a hundred or so miles east of Fort Worth."

In neither case are they short-changing their roots. For both, the places of their upbringing were where special guidance was delivered, life paths were set, and dreams took early shape.

It was in backyards along Silverton's South Berkley Avenue and the vacant lot down at the corner of Ohio and Webster that Roger and his Pleasant Ridge neighborhood friends were playing their games long before reaching the age when they were welcomed into organized sports.

While his parents didn't push him to focus his budding talent and energy on a particular extracurricular activity, each had an idea about the opportunities to which their son should be exposed. Betty Staubach, a secretary at General Motors, enrolled her boy in piano lessons. His dad

Robert, a sales manager for a local shoe company, served as volunteer coach of a local pee-wee baseball team that Roger played for. In time, music's loss would become athletics' gain as Roger quickly gravitated to whichever sport was in season. He played catcher for a Knothole League team of grade schoolers that won 39 consecutive games and the Ohio state championship.

At St. John's grade school in neighboring Deer Park, he was a guard on the Catholic Youth Organization basketball team and a halfback in football.

While it appeared any real future he might have as an athlete was most likely as a baseball player, his fascination with football continued to grow.

Though his team failed to win a single game during his seventh-grade season, it would go undefeated the following year. Against rival Assumption Junior High, the St. John's Eagles were considered overwhelming underdogs. Still, so anticipated was the game that Robert Staubach took off work to be certain he was in the stands. And with his son playing halfback and end, St. John's scored a 21–20 upset victory. Roger ran back the opening kickoff for one touchdown, caught a 50-yard pass for another, and then ran for the third.

During the 10-game season, he scored 17 touchdowns.

In basketball he and his St. John's teammates came within a game of winning the CYO league championship, and in baseball they reached the semifinals of the city tournament.

Already, coaches at Cincinnati's all-boys Purcell High, a parochial school that looked to the Catholic Youth Organization as something of a feeder system for its athletic teams, were familiar with the 6', 160-pound Silverton youngster who would soon be coming their way.

In the time-honored debate over where the best high school football in the country is played, the state of Ohio has historically ranked among the best, along with Texas, Florida, California, and Pennsylvania. In the late '50s, Purcell, with its 1,200-student enrollment and tradition of academic and athletic excellence, was looked on as a football powerhouse.

When Staubach reported for the team as a freshman, more than 100 candidates were on hand.

Though he aspired to continue playing halfback, he took note of the lengthy line of players with the same notion and gave his future a second thought. The line for candidates hoping to earn a place on the team as receivers was shorter, thus he moved into it in an effort to ensure a better chance of making the squad.

Not only did he earn a place on the team but had soon advanced to the starting lineup—until one day when he ran onto the practice field a few minutes after calisthenics were already underway.

He recalled the incident in his autobiography, *First Down, Lifetime to Go*, "The freshman coach was a dynamic guy named Bernie Sinchek. He certainly helped me learn discipline. One day I was late for practice. 'Staubach, you're late and now you're on the last string,' he said. It would take a week for me to work my way back up."

Such was the depth of the Purcell talent pool that underclassmen had little choice but to perform on the freshman and junior varsity teams, awaiting their chance to ultimately graduate to the varsity by the time they were juniors or seniors. That is not to say, however, that head coach Jim McCarthy wasn't constantly looking to the future.

When he asked his assistants about younger players with potential to eventually become a varsity quarterback, they had to admit that their current roster had none who would develop into the kind of player necessary to ultimately become the young man to direct the varsity's T-formation offense.

Who, then, was the best athlete, the best leader among the young players? Staubach's named was the first mentioned. In that case, McCarthy responded, convert him to quarterback.

Even as he learned a new position, however, there was a pecking order to Purcell High football that the coach held stubbornly to. His starting offensive players were, historically, seniors who demonstrated experience and poise gained as back-up players and members of the defense during their first years on the varsity.

Thus by his junior year, most of the playing time Staubach saw was in the defensive secondary. On the roster he was listed as the second string quarterback, allowed to play only in the latter stages of a few games that Purcell was well on its way to winning.

Which, in truth, wasn't a great disappointment. The team's offense looked as if it had been taken from the playbook of Ohio State; a pounding ground attack that featured quick handoffs to the running backs who plowed their way to short, time-consuming gains. Passing was rarely an option. And the idea of a quarterback who ran the ball himself was unheard of. Thrilling, the Purcell offense wasn't. But who was to argue with the year-after-year record of winning the school accomplished?

Being a starter on defense, with an opportunity to make tackles and perhaps an occasional interception, Roger judged, was far more exciting than calling signals and simply handing off the ball.

Still, by his senior season he was the team's co-captain and first team quarterback. And one of the assistant coaches, keenly aware of the unique running ability he'd shown during his days as a halfback, persuaded McCarthy to expand the playbook to include an occasional quarterback roll-out. The halfbacks and fullbacks would do nicely, pounding up the middle, but with the threat of Staubach faking a handoff before sprinting to the outside on end runs, a new dimension could be added to the Cavaliers' attack.

In the fall of 1959, then, fans were introduced to a new style of Purcell football. The three-yards-and-a-cloud-of-dust offense was still in place, but it was suddenly being spiced with an occasional open-field run by the new quarterback.

Author Joe Gergen cites the Purcell-Elder High game as an example of the excitement Staubach brought to the team:

"The two teams were stalled when Roger stepped into the huddle with the ball at the Purcell 40-yard line. He called a '28 Power Sweep Right,' which would send [Vince] Eysoldt on a power sweep to the right. As the team moved up to the line of scrimmage, Roger lingered for a word with his halfback. 'Vince,' he said, 'don't grab for the ball. I'm going to keep it.'

"Sure enough, Roger took the ball from center, faked a handoff to Eysoldt going right, tucked the ball behind his left hip, and sprinted around left end. He didn't stop until he reached the goal line."

That late-game 60-yard touchdown run proved to be the difference in a 20–14 win.

By season's end the Cavaliers were 8–2 and shared the Greater Cincinnati League championship. Of the 18 seniors on the team, 16 of them, including All-City selection Staubach, would be offered college scholarships.

None, however, came from Notre Dame, the storied university where most young Catholic schoolboys dreamed of one day playing.

For Staubach, thoughts of college became complicated during his senior year. His father had been diagnosed with diabetes and was in and out of the hospital. Robert was forced to miss the historic victory over Elder because of surgery to remove toes from an infected foot. Following the game, Roger took a film of the game to his dad's hospital room in an effort to lift his spirits.

With the University of Cincinnati and Xavier both showing interest, the young Staubach considered choosing a school close to home so that he might help with the care of his father. His mother, a strong and persuasive woman, explained to her son that she could take care of things on the home front quite well. What's more, she believed that an important part of a youngster's education was best served by experiencing a new environment. The time was soon coming, she knew, for her son to see what the world beyond Silverton and Cincinnati had to offer.

Among the colleges eager to offer scholarships were several in the football rich Big Ten conference. Woody Hayes, the legendary coach of the Buckeyes, was particularly persistent, insisting that a running quarterback would fit perfectly into his system. He not only stayed in constant touch with young Roger but his parents, as well. When he learned that Betty Staubach was concerned that Ohio State might be too big, Hayes invited her to accompany her son on a visit to the campus. In short order, she was sold.

Roger, meanwhile, remained undecided. He visited the campuses of Michigan, Purdue, and the Naval Academy. Finally, during spring baseball season, he informed the coaches at Purdue that he had liked all he'd seen, including the small-town atmosphere of the Lafayette, Indiana, campus. Additionally, he liked the idea that Purdue had a wide-open style of offense that would allow him the opportunity to prove himself as a passer. If he did attend a Big Ten school, he promised, he would be enrolling there in the fall.

Privately, he remained disappointed that Notre Dame had shown him no interest. If he couldn't play *for* the Fighting Irish, he wanted to attend a school that would allow him the opportunity to play *against* them.

And his visit to the Naval Academy kept coming to mind. He'd been impressed with the emphasis placed on academics, the camaraderie he'd seen, and he liked the coaches and the players who had shown him around the campus. And, lest he forget, Midshipman assistant coach Rick Forzano, assigned to recruit in the Cincinnati area, had stayed in touch to regularly remind him that he would be welcomed to Annapolis. So did Cincinnati businessman Richard Kleinfeldt, a former Midshipman halfback who had been the first to alert the Navy coaches to the Purcell athlete's potential.

By the time his senior year was coming to an end, Staubach had decided he would attend the Naval Academy.

The relief of having made the commitment was, however, short-lived when it was discovered that the English grade Roger had received on his College Board exam fell short of Naval Academy requirements. Disappointed, Roger hoped that the offer from Purdue was still in place.

Forzano, however, offered an unusual alternative: He suggested that Staubach consider spending a year at the New Mexico Military Institute in Roswell where a number of other student athletes had attended before moving on to the military academies. At NMMI, Forzano said, a freshman could not only improve his grades but play a year of junior college football. And in doing so, the Navy assistant pointed out, Roger would in no way be making a binding agreement to eventually play for the

Midshipmen. After a year in junior college, he would still be able to choose any four-year college he wished to attend.

Roger agreed to think about it.

Meanwhile, Forzano contacted new NMMI football coach Bob Shaw to sing Staubach's praises. When Shaw said he had no more athletic scholarships available, Forzano replied, "Find one; you won't be sorry."

By early summer, as Roger prepared to participate in the annual North-South All-Star game, which showcased Ohio's premier graduating seniors, he had reached his decision. He would spend a year in Roswell, improve his grades, and then enroll at the Naval Academy.

His reason was simple and beyond his teenage years, "I want to do more with my life than just play football," he told his parents.

When the all-star players gathered in Canton, Ohio, it became immediately obvious to Roger that he would likely play little at quarterback. The South team was being coached by Dayton's Pete Ankney, and his nephew, Mo Ankney, also an outstanding quarterback, had been named to the team. Thus, for most of the game, Roger played safety on defense and receiver on offense.

Starring for the North team was Warren High School running back Paul Warfield. Repeatedly, he broke into the South secondary before being tackled by Staubach. On a dozen occasions, it was Roger's tackles that prevented the fleet Warfield from even longer gains.

Only after the game was out of hand in the final period did Staubach finally come on for a brief appearance at quarterback, completing a couple of passes and running for the team's longest gain of the night.

Afterwards, Warfield, headed for future stardom at nearby Ohio State, was named the North's Most Valuable Player. Staubach, soon to travel off to a junior college in a part of the country he knew nothing about, received the MVP honor for the losing South squad.

And, even as he prepared for his trip to Roswell, a call he'd once so hoped to receive finally came. Among the numerous college scouts who had attended the All-Star game had been members of the Notre Dame coaching staff. Told of his impressive performance, the Fighting

Irish head coach Joe Kuharich was calling to offer him a four-year scholarship.

Roger thanked the coach politely and declined.

As he traveled to Roswell and New Mexico Military Institute, Staubach was leaving an almost idyllic life behind. Concerns for his father's declining health aside, the two-story house on South Berkley Avenue had been a wonderful place to grow up. Now, 1,300 miles away, a new adventure, a new experience, waited. Gone would be the lazy summer afternoons when old friends and teammates would meet to play pick-up games on the Disabled American Veterans' softball field, attending Saturday night dances at Castle Farms with girlfriend Marianne Hoobler, and listening as favorite deejay Jim LaBarbara, "The Music Professor," played the hit songs of the day.

Roger Staubach, three-sport letterman, Student Council and senior class president, and altar boy at St. John's Evangelist, was leaving behind a world in which he had long found great comfort.

The city of Roswell sits in the arid, mesquite- and cactus-dotted eastern region of New Mexico, a single main street running through its downtown and out to the NMMI campus. For many of the youngsters who arrive to enroll in the town's four-year high school or two-year college, the culture shock is two-fold. The geography lends an air of isolation to the community and the campus; the strict military lifestyle is light years removed from carefree public school days.

For Roger, the regimentation was, at least in some ways, familiar. At Purcell High, there had been strict rules that students were required to follow. Slacks, not jeans, a dress shirt, and tie were part of the day-to-day dress code. Tardiness and bad behavior had not been tolerated by school administrators, and teachers were quick to punish. Discipline had been an important part of his high school curriculum.

NMMI simply took matters up a notch or two. Uniforms, spit polishing shoes, saluting upper classmen, and hours of marching were routine. So was being awakened daily by the break-of-dawn sounds of Revielle.

For a youngster whose family tree included no one with any military background, it was a jarring awakening.

Still, despite occasional bouts with homesickness, he found himself adjusting to his new lifestyle and surroundings. He was learning proper study habits and making good grades, had found new friends, and was fast developing a fondness for the region known as the Land of Enchantment.

It didn't hurt that Bob Shaw, the former All-American end at Ohio State and a standout receiver for the NFL Cleveland and Los Angeles Rams and Chicago Cardinals, was an outstanding coach who favored the kind of offensive attack that fit Staubach's skills perfectly. The NMMI Broncos played a wide-open, free-wheeling kind of game that featured a complicated playbook of passes, reverses, and quarterback options.

Aware that Roger had thrown the ball very little in high school but had a strong arm, Shaw constantly drilled him on the passing techniques that had been successful for Baltimore Colts legend Johnny Unitas.

Shaw was also a master at psychology. Picking up early on signs that his quarterback was homesick and questioning his decision to attend NMMI, the coach summoned him to his office on the pretext that he was in need of help. There were some players, Shaw explained, who were pretty down about being so far from home and away from family for the first time. What he needed was for Roger to put his unique leadership skills to work and help them get past it and focus on their studies and football.

Staubach quickly accepted the challenge and spent so much time encouraging others than in time his own concerns faded.

Only once did he seriously consider leaving school to return home. Following the team's third game of the season, a narrow win over Trinidad, Colorado Junior College, Roger had phoned home immediately after-ward to share the good news. What he learned was that his father was back in the hospital where he would have more foot surgery. During the team's all-night bus ride back to the Roswell campus, Staubach decided that he should drop out of school and return home to help care for his dad.

On that occasion, no Shaw psychological ploy was necessary. Betty Staubach sternly reemphasized to her son that all was under control on the home front and that his help was not needed. It would, she added, break his father's heart to feel he had been the reason for his son turning his back on the academic and athletic opportunity he'd been given.

As the season progressed, the Broncos climbed in the national junior college rankings with a series of come-from-behind, last-minute wins. Against the Air Force Academy junior varsity, Staubach threw for a touchdown with just 20 seconds remaining to lift NMMI to a 19–18 victory.

The Homecoming game against San Angelo Junior College was even more dramatic. Down by two touchdowns with only four minutes left to play, NMMI scored, quickly got the ball back, and needed to move 64 yards for a tying touchdown. Before being forced to come out of the game for a play after being dazed by a jarring tackle, Staubach had advanced the Broncos to the San Angelo 20. He returned to complete a 19-yard pass to the San Angelo 1-yard line. From there he scored on a quarterback sneak and the extra-point kick gave his team a 35–34 victory.

The Broncos finished the season with a 9–1 record and were ranked fourth in the national junior college poll. Their quarterback was named to the Junior College All-America team, his skills remarkably expanded under Shaw's guidance. Working in a pro set offense, Roger had completed 60 percent of his passes. Among those congratulating him was Navy assistant Rick Forzano who sent a telegram that read, "Before you leave the Naval Academy you will make All-America and win the Heisman Trophy."

Even the positive-thinking Staubach considered such a forecast a bit optimistic.

The remainder of the school year passed quickly as Roger became increasingly comfortable in his new environment, performing well in the classroom and in other sports. As an All-Conference guard on the basketball team, he averaged 16 points per game on a team that advanced to the regional finals. Playing center field on the baseball team, he hit for a .385 average and attracted the attention of several pro scouts.

And throughout the spring, a steady stream of college football recruiters were again in touch, hoping to persuade him to put aside his plan to attend the Naval Academy.

Roger wasn't interested. He'd charted his course and was comfortable in the knowledge that it pointed in the right direction. At Purcell High, McCarthy had taught him how to play as a running quarterback. At NMMI, Shaw had developed him into a passer. At Navy he hoped to combine all he had learned.

CHAPTER 3

"When it comes to reacting under pressure, I like to place Roger in the category of an Arnold Palmer, Jack Nicklaus, or Ben Hogan. Roger has a sixth sense that makes it possible for him to do the right thing at the right time."

Navy coach Wayne Hardin

The U.S. Naval Academy's Plebe Summer is a July-to-September period that offers a demanding, warp-speed indoctrination into the military lifestyle. New enrollees are barraged with rules and regulations they are required to memorize and adhere to before the full brigade returns for fall classes. They march to and from the dining hall, attend classes to learn everything from the proud history of the Academy to the proper care of their uniforms and the strict sanctity of the school's Honor Code, maintain rigid posture whether standing or seated, and speak only when spoken to. Regardless of the destination, Plebes move in double-time. Discipline is the order of the day, from sunrise to sunset, and military jargon becomes a new language.

The regimented atmosphere of New Mexico Military Institute had provided Staubach only a hint of life at Annapolis. Plebe Summer, he learned, was a time when a number of his fellow teenage candidates quickly realized that a serious mistake had been made and that life on a laid-back campus of a state university back home would, after all, be a better academic choice. One of the primary functions of having Plebes arrive on campus during the summer is to weed out those who prove not to be Naval Academy material before the first semester officially gets underway.

Physical and mental demands aside, the setting is picturesque and campus traditions run deep and are carefully guarded. The Academy is bordered on one side by the Severn River, which flows gently into Chesapeake Bay, and the city of Annapolis, with its cobblestone streets and buildings that date as far back as the 1700s, on the other. At the center of the tree-lined campus is Bancroft Hall, the immense granite-faced dormitory where all Midshipmen are housed. At its entrance is a statue of legendary Indian warrior Tecumseh, standing as a talisman of good fortune for those seeking academic and athletic success. It is tradition for a Midshipman en route to a test to toss a penny at the warrior for luck; in advance of sporting events, he is bathed in war paint. Nearby is a replica of the Gokoku-ji Bell brought to the U.S. by Commodore Matthew Perry following an 1853 mission to Japan during which he succeeded in having Japanese ports opened to American ships, there to be rung by team members following all football victories over arch rival Army.

At the Academy, history abounds. In Memorial Hall, the faded flag with the inscription "Don't Give Up The Ship" that flew above the USS *Chesapeake* during the War of 1812, is on display.

The spires of the campus chapel, where the crypt containing the body of legendary sailor John Paul Jones is displayed, tower above a maze of pristine academic buildings. And in the distance is the 25,000-seat Navy–Marine Corps Memorial Stadium, completed just two years before Staubach and his Plebe class arrived.

Throughout the campus there are reminders to passersby of just how many days, hours, and minutes remain before the kickoff of the next Army-Navy football game. "Beat Army" is part of every Midshipman's vocabulary.

Even before Staubach reported for the first day of Plebe football practice, he had already experienced his first collegiate injury. During a physical education class boxing tournament, he had reached the finals but during the third round of the championship fight delivered a roundhouse left that completely missed its mark. He felt a sudden sharp pain in his shoulder that immediately told him it had been dislocated. As he rested against the ropes while the referee signaled the end of the bout, it popped back into place.

It would be one of no less than 18 times that he would suffer a shoulder separation over the course of his athletic career.

When he joined the other 300 candidates for the football team, the shoulder was still sore and Staubach worried that it might be reinjured and hinder his performance. But with no less than 25 quarterbacks among those hoping to earn a place on the team, he chose to downplay the problem. Instead, he quietly asked one of the team trainers if he could provide him with a harness that would assure that the shoulder stayed in place during practices.

And in short order, he was the first string quarterback.

It was a time before the NCAA allowed first-year players to participate on the varsity, thus the primary purpose of the Plebe team was to serve as practice fodder for the upperclassmen, helping Navy to prepare for its next game each week while still playing its own schedule against other freshman teams.

Author Joe Gergen, in his book *Roger Staubach of the Dallas Cowboys*, recalled a series of practices as Navy readied for its 1961 opener against Penn State. "As far as head coach Wayne Hardin was concerned, the first scrimmage between the varsity and the Plebes proved the varsity wasn't ready. It seemed the Plebe quarterback was doing pretty much as he pleased against Hardin's best defenders.

"The coach ordered hard tackling practice for the varsity the following day, but the next scrimmage was no more satisfying than the first. The coach got the message this time. 'It's not their fault,' he told an assistant. 'It's Staubach. He's amazing.'"

In an oral history prepared for the Naval Institute by Captain Charles Minter Jr., the former commandant recalled the degree of frustration Plebe Staubach dealt his elders. Running and passing at will during a practice session, the angered varsity defenders began to gang tackle Roger on every play.

Said Minter, "I finally walked right out in the middle of the field and got a hold of [Coach] Hardin and said, 'Hey, [Plebe coach Dick] Durden needs this kid. Call off your dogs.' And he did...though he seemed dumbstruck that I had the audacity to tell him how to run his football practices."

It was fast becoming clear that those followers of Midshipmen football eagerly awaited the day when the young quarterback from Ohio would be eligible to play for the varsity.

While Navy would post a 7–3 record in '61, including victories over Notre Dame and Army, Roger was directing the Plebes to an 8–1 mark, their only loss to the University of Maryland freshman team, which kicked a field goal with 15 seconds remaining to score a 29–27 victory.

By the time he returned home during the Christmas break, Staubach began to feel increasingly comfortable in his new environment, adapting to the military lifestyle, generally performing well in the classroom despite a struggle with mechanical drawing, and he was looking forward to spring football practice.

Navy coach Wayne Hardin, a native of the small Arkansas town of Smackover, had played his collegiate football for the legendary Amos Alonzo Stagg at College of Pacific. He had spent his early days of coaching at the high school and junior college level before being hired as an assistant on the Navy staff in 1955. Four years later, at age 32, he was elevated to the position of head coach. Sharp-tongued, demanding, and possessing an innovative football mind, Hardin was also famously stubborn.

Among his credos was the firm belief that experienced players offered his team the best opportunity to win.

Thus, as spring training got underway, Staubach, despite his impressive high school and junior college pedigree and performance on the Plebe team, was far down the depth chart. Fifth-string some days, sixth on others. There was no question that senior-to-be Ron Klemick, who had finished the previous season highly ranked among the nation's passers, would again be Navy's starting quarterback. The only question in Roger's mind was how many of the other upperclassmen he might be able to move past before the spring practices ended.

Eventually he made it up to the third string.

And a new determination set in. Throughout the summer, he worked constantly to improve his passing skills. Even when assigned cruise duty on an aircraft carrier, he found time to throw to fellow seamen on the football field-sized flight deck of the USS *Forrestal*. Also, there was a weight room below deck that he visited regularly.

As the Midshipmen gathered at Quonset Point, Rhode Island, in late summer to begin preparation for the 1962 season, Hardin issued a word of caution to fans, members of the media, and even the nation's Commander-in-Chief. When President John Kennedy, a Navy veteran and longtime fan of the Academy's team, stopped by to visit practice, Hardin confided to him that Navy could well be an even better team yet not have as good a record as it had the previous year. The schedule his team would face, he said, offered a serious challenge.

The opener against a powerful Penn State team proved his point. The Nittany Lions defeated the Midshipmen 41–7, the most one-sided loss in Hardin's brief tenure. Staubach entered the game only after the outcome was determined, playing the final four minutes. His varsity debut was hardly dramatic as he threw two passes, one of which was intercepted.

The following Saturday, he never left the sidelines as Klemick quarterbacked Navy to a lackluster 20–16 win over William and Mary.

And there was, across the campus and throughout the Navy community, growing concern that if Hardin didn't soon make drastic changes the season might be lost. It was an open secret that many believed the most talented quarterback on the team was Staubach.

Still, Hardin started Klemick against a University of Minnesota team that featured the likes of NFL-bound defensive standouts Carl Eller and Bobby Bell. Klemick, a drop-back passer with limited mobility, was sacked repeatedly as the Gophers won 21–0.

Again, Staubach was little more than an afterthought, playing just the final few minutes of the game.

The following week an abnormally quiet crowd watched as Navy struggled through the first quarter against visiting underdog Cornell. Finally, when a short punt gave the Midshipmen the ball at their opponent's 39-yard line, Hardin sent in his sophomore quarterback to replace Klemick who was still groggy from a hit he'd received on an earlier series.

For the first couple of plays, it didn't appear that the new quarterback would make much difference. Then, however, as he faced a third-and-7 situation, Staubach threw to flanker Jim Stewart for a 13-yard gain. Two plays later, Roger ran for his first touchdown as a Midshipman.

During just 23 minutes of playing time he directed Navy to a 41–0 victory, completing 9-of-11 passes for 99 yards. His most impressive moment came late in the afternoon when he scrambled through the Cornell defense, reversing his field and eluding tackles on a 68-yard touchdown run that brought a roar from the Memorial Stadium crowd.

The opposition, in all honesty, was hardly the toughest on Navy's schedule, but the manner in which Roger had taken control was cause for renewed enthusiasm for the remainder of the season.

Hardin was convinced it was time for a change.

Staubach was in the starting lineup the following week against a highly favored Boston College team that was being quarterbacked by All-American candidate Jack Concannon. Despite constant pressure, Staubach eluded the relentless Boston College rush enough to complete 14-of-20 passes for 165 yards and two touchdowns. With the addition of a couple of scrambles for first downs, his offensive output for the day was 182 yards, just two shy of what the entire Boston offense managed. The Midshipmen won 26–6, and Roger had earned the starting job.

A week later Navy defeated the University of Pittsburgh 32–9, as he completed all eight of his passes for 192 yards and a touchdown, and he ran 22 yards for another. Roger's performance, however, would not be the chief topic of postgame discussion. Rather, it would be a call that Hardin, long a fan of gimmick plays, had made early in the game.

In his *First Down, Lifetime to Go*, Staubach recalled the controversy:

"The officials were told about the 'sleeper' play before the game so they would understand what we were doing when we pulled it. After Pitt kicked off to us, one of our tackles faked a block near the sideline and rolled off the field, leaving us with ten players. Then while we huddled, one of our receivers, Jimmy Stewart, went limping toward our bench, and Dick Ernst ran on to the field. Of course, what the Pitt players thought they saw was one guy limp off and another replace him. But Ernst lined up at tackle, and Stewart stopped on the edge of the playing field. He stayed close enough to the huddle to be legal, though, and we had the standard eleven players on the field.

"The Pitt defense paid no attention to Stewart. I took the snap, dropped back, and watched Stewart sprint down the sideline. The Pitt safety just stood there staring at me. He couldn't believe that I was throwing the ball. It was the weirdest thing in the world. Stewart was all alone, and he caught the pass for 66 yards and a touchdown.

"Pitt thought the play was unethical, and Hardin caught a lot of criticism after the game."

It wasn't, however, just the controversial gadget play that the media focused on in the aftermath of the one-sided Navy victory. Praises were being sung for its new quarterback. *New York World Telegram* sportswriter Lawrence Robinson went so far as to proclaim that Staubach, after only two starts, promised to soon become the best quarterback in Navy football history.

Still, the demands of the schedule that Hardin had earlier warned about became evident as Navy lost to Notre Dame in a driving rain, then to Syracuse. And the immediate future looked no brighter. Next up was a trip to Los Angeles to face unbeaten and No. 1–ranked Southern Cal.

While the eventual national champions would win 13–6, it was Staubach's performance in the storied LA Coliseum that firmly established him as college football's rising star.

Against the Trojans, he completed 11-of-17 passes for 106 yards and ran for an additional 113 and the Midshipmen's lone touchdown. And in the waning seconds of the game, Navy had driven to the USC 4-yard line. Fullback Pat Donnelly, who had run well against the Trojans defense all afternoon, took a handoff from Staubach and was nearing the goal line when the ball was jarred from his grasp. USC recovered in its end zone to avoid the potential upset.

Afterward, colorful USC coach John McKay analyzed his team's narrow escape. "What hurt us," he said, "was not the plays they worked on, but the ones where they were trapped. When he couldn't pass and had to run, Staubach looked like Red Grange. I don't think they could have practiced that play too much."

Already, Navy coach Hardin had begun making plans to alter his offense for the following season. Long a believer in a drop-back passing style of offense, he was ready to make a change that would provide his agile and strong-armed quarterback the freedom to leave the protection of the pocket and sprint out with an option to pass or run. He would allow Staubach to do those things that, while not coachable, seemingly came naturally for him.

First, however, there was his team's season-ending date in Philadelphia with Army.

Legend has it that prior to the 1893 Army-Navy game, an admiral and a general met for lunch at New York's Army-Navy Club to discuss the merits of their respective teams. The conversation deteriorated quickly as each officer boasted that his alma mater was superior. Finally, the argument escalated to the point where it was suggested that differences be settled by a duel. Fortunately, cooler heads ultimately prevailed.

Still, the anecdote, while extreme, serves as an indication of the importance placed on the game.

By the early 1960s, the rivalry remained one of sports' most intense despite the fact the pregame activities got no more dramatic than the occasional prank like kidnapping of one another's mascots or sneak attacks on campuses to leave behind hand-painted signs. Army Cadets went one up on the Midshipmen when they rowed out to a destroyer anchored in Hudson Bay and painted "Beat Navy" on its starboard side. Later, a hired plane flew over the U.S. Military Academy campus and dropped thousands of "Beat Army" leaflets.

Though he'd witnessed the pageantry and excitement that preceded the game firsthand as a Plebe, it was nothing like the anticipation of being a participant. Throughout the week there were constant pep rallies and bonfires. Tecumseh's war paint had been applied. Banners of encouragement hung from windows of virtually every building on campus. Across the front of Bancroft Hall, a large sign proclaimed it the "Home of Roger Staubach."

The colorful Hardin got into the spirit of the occasion by announcing at a pep rally that his underdog team, despite entering the game with a 4–5 record, would not only defeat Army but "run up the score." He had also designed a new decal—a tiny skull and crossbones—that would be worn on each Navy player's helmet. He had borrowed the symbol from the legendary Jolly Roger flag that had, according to Navy mythology, flown above a phantom ship that came out of nowhere and never lost a battle.

Some wondered if perhaps it was actually a not-too-subtle nod to the talents of the Midshipmen's quarterback.

Never in his athletic career had Staubach experienced difficulty sleeping before a game. The electric atmosphere of the Army-Navy build-up, however, was unlike anything he'd ever been involved in. It was impossible not to think of what would transpire the following day. A hundred charter busses would soon be transporting the entire Naval Academy battalion to Philadelphia. The President of the United States had announced his plan to be on hand. Roger's parents and girlfriend, Marianne, who had not seen him play since his senior year at Purcell High, would be in the stands. And the game would be broadcast to a national television audience.

On Friday night, sequestered in a Philadelphia hotel with fellow team members, he tossed and turned as time slowly crept by. Finally getting up at first light, he dressed and attended Mass before joining his teammates for the pregame meal.

And on that November Saturday afternoon he had one of the most remarkable games of his career.

Early in the game an errant snap from the Army center resulted in a two-point safety for the Midshipmen. Thereafter, it was one long, time-consuming Navy drive after another that marked the path to a 34–14 victory. Eluding an Army rush, Staubach threw 12 yards to end Neil Henderson for Navy's first touchdown. Then he ended a 63-yard drive with a 21-yard scoring run that saw him break free of a half dozen attempted tackles.

On the first play of the second half, Roger completed a 65-yard pass to fullback Nick Markoff to up the lead to 22–6. Early in the fourth quarter, he ended an 89-yard drive with a two-yard run for his second touchdown of the day.

Late in the game, Navy's Walt Pierce intercepted a desperation Army pass and returned it to the opponent's 5-yard line. At that point, Coach Hardin sent senior quarterback Ron Klemick into the game for his fare-well appearance as a Midshipman.

None cheered louder than Staubach when the upperclassman he had replaced in the starting lineup threw a pass for Navy's final touchdown of the season.

For the afternoon, Staubach had completed 10-of-12 passes for 204 yards and rushed for 34, his performance earning him college football's National Back of the Week award.

And, while the victory allowed the Midshipmen to complete the year with a 5–5 record, it also served as a beacon of optimism for the 1963 season. With a talented and experienced team returning and Hardin planning to retool his offense to better exploit his quarterback's unique abilities, chances seemed good that Navy might soon compete for a national championship.

Though Roger had not planned to play basketball, Midshipmen coach Ben Carnevale, in need of additional depth, asked that he join the team. Though he played sparingly through much of the season, he was in the starting lineup when the team hosted Army, assigned to guard the Cadets' leading scorer and All-American candidate, Joe Kosciusko.

Carnevale, certain Army would remember how dominating Staubach had been against its football team, was exercising his own brand of psychology.

Roger's aggressive defensive play not only held Kosciusko to just six points but completely disrupted the Army's offense as Navy scored a 55–48 upset.

Author Joe Gergen recalled that General William Westmoreland, then superintendent of the Military Academy, had been on hand in the Navy field house for the game:

"'Why did you use that guy?' General Westmoreland asked Coach Carnevale later in the locker room. 'He's no basketball player.'

"Carnevale smiled. 'He may not be a basketball player, General,' the coach replied, 'but he's a winner.'"

During the baseball season there were no questions about why Staubach was in the lineup. Reporting to the team following spring football practice, he started regularly in center field and posted a .421 batting average.

And at year's end, the three-sport letterman achieved another milestone in his athletic career. He was awarded the Academy's Thompson Trophy, which annually went to the athlete who had done the most for Navy sports during the school year. Staubach was the first sophomore ever to receive the award.

CHAPTER 4

"Staubach has gotten every award but the Good Housekeeping seal this season.
He can run, pass, catch, kick, cook, and sew. He plays basketball, football,
and baseball, and would be a threat in any contest up to and including the
Pillsbury bake-off."

Jim Murray, *Los Angeles Times* columnist

A s the 1963 college football season approached, sportswriters across the nation were boldly predicting that it would be the Year of the Quarterback. The lengthy and glittering list included Alabama's Joe Namath, Southern Cal's Pete Beathard, University of Miami's George Mira, Baylor's Don Trull, Georgia Tech's Billy Lothridge, Boston College's Jack Concannon, and Staubach's former Cincinnati schoolboy rival Steve Tensi, who was playing exceptionally well at Florida State.

Wayne Hardin wanted to be certain that his quarterback was not overlooked.

Anticipating a successful season during which Roger would be the Midshipmen's guiding force, he met with Naval Academy public relations director Budd Thalman and made a suggestion. Hardin urged Thalman to travel to New York each Monday during the season to attend the New York sportswriters' luncheon, to keep them updated on Staubach's accomplishments. Thalman not only embraced the idea but went a step further, preparing a four-page brochure titled "Meet Roger Staubach" and mailing it to sportswriters and sportscasters throughout the United States before the season got underway.

"In 1963," Thalman told author Mike Towle for his book, *Roger Staubach: Captain America*, "New York was the center of the universe, and that's where all the wire services were based, where the television networks were headquartered, and they had six or eight newspapers in town in those days. So on every Monday during the '63 season, I boarded a train in Baltimore and went to the writers' luncheon in New York."

In retrospect, Thalman was setting a precedent that would grow wildly in years to come. With his modest brochure, weekly mailings of Staubach's ever-growing statistics, and visits to New York, he became the founding father of the concept of actively promoting a candidate for college football's ultimate award, the Heisman Trophy.

And Roger obliged with a season for the ages.

In the opener against West Virginia, he completed 17 passes and accounted for 185 yards of total offense as Navy won 51–7. A week later against William and Mary, he established a school record with 297 yards, passing for 206 and running for 91 despite playing only three quarters as the Midshipmen scored a 28–0 victory.

Thalman had plenty of ammunition for his Monday meetings with the New York writers, including glowing quotes from opposing coaches. West Virginia coach Gene Corum, for instance, had suggested that Staubach was "already as good as most NFL quarterbacks" he'd seen.

A sellout Ann Arbor crowd, which included Attorney General Robert Kennedy and his family, watched in amazement as Navy handily defeated Michigan 26–13. And, while Staubach completed 14-of-16 passes for 237 yards and ran for 70 more, it was not his 307 total yards that was the prime subject of postgame interviews. Rather, it was a second-quarter play where his elusiveness had been perfectly displayed.

Fading to pass, he had found himself surrounded by three defensive linemen. Spinning away, he broke a tackle while continuing to give ground. Finally, 25 yards behind the line of scrimmage, he was hit again. As he was falling to the ground, he finally threw to fullback Pat Donnelly—for a one-yard gain.

It had not been the only play that drew a collective gasp from the crowd. As time was winding down in the first half with Navy at mid-field and holding a two-touchdown lead, it appeared that Navy would be content to run off the remaining seconds on the clock. On first down, Staubach called for a run up the middle; same on second down. On third down, however, he surprised the Wolverines defense by sending halfback Johnny Sai on a deep pass pattern and connecting with him for a 54-yard touchdown.

Afterward, Michigan coach Bump Elliot called Staubach "the greatest quarterback I've ever seen."

The nation's media was beginning to share his opinion. *Time* magazine informed Thalman that it was preparing a cover story that would feature the Navy quarterback.

Undefeated and moving up in the national rankings, the Midshipmen's next stop would be an unusual Friday night game against Southern Methodist University in Dallas' famed Cotton Bowl. And though Navy was an overwhelming favorite, the team quickly found itself involved in an offensive shootout.

Twice Staubach had to be helped to the sidelines, his bothersome left shoulder dislocated. The first came on a brutal blindside tackle early in the first quarter, forcing Roger to the training room for a harness that would allow him to continue. Only five minutes had elapsed before he was back on the field to score on a quarterback sneak. As he lay beneath the pile in the end zone, an SMU player managed to pull off his helmet and scratch at his face. By the time Navy linebacker Nick Markoff was kicked by a male SMU cheerleader following a sideline tackle, the game had taken on the ugly tenor of a Texas bar brawl.

By halftime Navy held to an 18–13 lead yet was still desperately trying to figure out how to slow a swift-running Mustangs halfback named John Roderick. A 9.4 sprinter for the SMU track team, he was enjoying the game of his life.

Again in the third quarter, Staubach's shoulder was injured, but instead of leaving the game, he responded with a touchdown pass that appeared to finally put Navy into a comfortable lead. However, SMU responded quickly with two touchdowns, one coming on a 45-yard run by the 168-pound Roderick, and SMU was suddenly ahead, 26–25.

Soon thereafter Staubach lay on the turf again following a short gain. Addled by yet another gang tackle, he was given smelling salts by the Navy trainer and insisted he could continue to play. And with just three minutes left, the Midshipmen kicked a field goal to regain the lead.

SMU again responded, needing only four plays to score on the exhausted Navy defense.

With two minutes remaining, Navy had the ball at its own 40, and the 37,000 Mustangs supporters on hand fell silent in fear of a final Staubach miracle. On fourth down, he found room around right end for a 17-yard gain that kept the drive alive. Then he completed passes for 14 and 12 yards and ran out of the grasp of two SMU defenders for another 15. With just five seconds remaining and the ball at the Mustangs 8-yard line, the battered Staubach sent halfback Skip Orr on a pass route across the back of the end zone. As the game clock showed 0:00, the ball sailed off the tip of the receiver's fingers as SMU preserved its 32–28 victory, one that would later be cited by the Associated Press as college football's Upset of the Year. Navy coach Hardin would remember it differently. Years later, as he looked back on that disappointing night in Dallas, he would call it the "dirtiest" game he'd seen during his 25-year coaching career.

The day following its loss to SMU, the Navy team remained in Dallas and returned to the Cotton Bowl to watch as the undefeated University of Texas, using a stubborn defense and a powerful running game, defeated No. 1–ranked Oklahoma.

Defeated Sooners players aside, the most despondent person in the stadium that afternoon might have been the badly battered Staubach. His injured shoulder pained him so that he could barely lift his arm. The preliminary diagnosis of a team doctor who traveled with the Midshipmen was that season-ending surgery would likely be required.

Fortunately, further examination upon his return to Annapolis was a bit more optimistic. A new kind of harness, doctors felt, would hold the shoulder in place. If, however, it didn't work and another separation occurred, the only option left would be to operate.

Against Virginia Military Institute the following Saturday, Roger played the most cautious game of his football career, running sparingly and avoiding collisions with defenders. Still, Navy easily won 21–12 and began looking ahead to hosting No. 3–ranked Pittsburgh.

The pain in Staubach's shoulder had subsided, and he put concerns of additional injury behind him. The game was to be televised nationally and temporary seats were being added to Navy–Marine Corps Memorial Stadium to accommodate the anticipated crowd.

Pittsburgh, still seething over the controversial "sleeper play" that Navy has successfully used the previous season, made no secret of the fact it had to stop the elusive Staubach if it was to remain unbeaten. And to some degree, its defense succeeded. On no less than seven occasions it trapped the Midshipmen quarterback for a total loss of 93 yards. Yet it wasn't enough. Navy's defense matched the visitors' effort, forcing five turnovers and holding the Panthers running attack to just 76 yards.

Staubach, meanwhile, completed 14-of-19 passes for 168 yards as Navy scored a 24–12 victory and found itself back in the race for the national title.

If any question remained that he was the marquee college player of the season, Roger and his teammates put the issue to rest as Navy faced Notre Dame.

With the game tied 7–7 at halftime, center and team captain Tom Lynch asked Staubach to briefly excuse himself from the locker room. With Roger out of earshot, Lynch burst into a tirade, pointing out the importance of a victory. He retold the story of how the Irish had disappointed Roger by not offering him a scholarship, reminded everyone in the room what he had meant to the team, how he had played through injury to bring them to this point in the season. He noted that writers would soon be casting their ballots for the Heisman Trophy and that it was the responsibility of everyone in the room to see to it that their quarterback was the winner.

The Midshipmen responded by scoring three touchdowns in the third quarter en route to a 35–14 win. Afterward, the ever-outspoken Hardin pointed out to members of the media that his quarterback had just established a new Navy single-season record with 1,420 yards of total offense in only seven games. "If Roger doesn't win the Heisman this year," the coach said, "the game is crooked."

Apparently many agreed. Constant requests for interviews were being received by Thalman despite Hardin's dictate that none would be allowed during the week. And the public relations director noted that Staubach had begun stopping by his office regularly to ask for publicity photos. When he finally questioned Roger about what he was doing with them, Staubach explained that he was replying to mail he was receiving, much of it from youngsters asking for a signed picture. Learning that requests had grown to several dozen per day, Thalman quickly assigned a secretary to help Staubach with his mail. What pleased Roger even more was Thalman telling him that the public relations department would immediately begin paying the cost of the postage.

It was small compensation for the amount of publicity that Staubach was generating for the Naval Academy. After *Time* had published its cover story, *Sports Illustrated* followed suit. And soon, he was told, he would appear on the cover of *Life* magazine.

Meanwhile, the Midshipmen kept winning. In a 42–7 victory over Maryland, an early scoring series was vintage Staubach. Facing fourth-and-7 at the opposition's 18-yard line, he dropped back to pass, found no open receivers, and wound his way through the Terrapin defense for an apparent touchdown. A 15-yard penalty nullified the play, however, and moved Navy back to the 33. Roger again faded to pass, broke into a scramble when his protection collapsed, avoided several tacklers, and then passed complete for a first down at the Maryland 6-yard line. Two plays later, he ran in for a touchdown.

On the following Saturday, Navy defeated Duke 38–25 with Roger wearing a knee brace to protect a slight injury he'd received the previous week. Still, he passed for 122 yards and rushed for 73 on the day the year's first All-America team was announced. The Midshipmen's quarterback was named to the first team.

Unlike today's holiday frenzy wherein virtually every college team that wins a minimum of six games is invited to play in one of the more than 30 postseason bowl games, such honor was restricted to an elite few in 1963. There was the Rose Bowl, Cotton Bowl, Sugar Bowl, Orange Bowl, and Liberty Bowl, all played on New Year's Day. Rumors had begun to spread that the Midshipmen might be asked back to Dallas and the Cotton Bowl to face the No. 1–ranked University of Texas.

All it needed to do was close out its season with a fifth straight victory over Army.

By mid-November, life at the U.S. Naval Academy was good. Its football team had, despite the all-but-dismissed loss to SMU, climbed to No. 2 in the national rankings, its quarterback was an All-American, and the annual season-ending trip to Philadelphia for the Army-Navy game was on the near horizon.

During the off-week that traditionally preceded the game, Hardin had traveled to New York to speak at the sportswriters' luncheon and made his final pitch on Staubach's behalf. He insisted to the writers that his quarterback was the best he'd ever seen, including professional greats Y.A. Tittle and Johnny Unitas.

On his return to Annapolis, Hardin confided to Roger that he was certain he was going to be named the winner of the Heisman.

Then, on the afternoon of Friday, November 22, all excitement and anticipation faded to black.

Staubach remembered the day in his *First Down, Lifetime to Go*, "I was between classes and had gone back to my room. I was stretched out on my bed, half asleep and half awake, just resting a few minutes before I went to thermodynamics class. I heard some commotion in the hall, which was quite unusual in the middle of the day when it normally is quiet, so I got up and walked out.

"The hall was filled with a strange emotional electricity. Guys were running back and forth yelling. I said, 'Hey, what's going on?'

"Someone yelled, "The president has been shot!" I couldn't believe what I was hearing. I asked again. 'The president's been shot!'

"I started asking how badly he was wounded. One guy said it was critical but another guy said he thought he was going to be okay. At that moment no one knew. The only thing anyone knew was the news that had been flashed across the country, that President Kennedy had been shot in Dallas and was being rushed to a hospital.

"I was in a state of shock. I walked down a couple of flights of stairs, left Bancroft Hall, and started to class. Everybody was yelling back and forth about President Kennedy, but no one knew anything definite about his condition.

"Everyone in thermodynamics class just sat and stared. The professor wasn't there. He was somewhere listening to a radio. Finally he came in and announced the president was dead. I got a terrible sick feeling in my stomach. I remembered how I had seen him at Quonset Point, so happy and full of life. I just couldn't believe it had happened."

That afternoon, as a pall spread across the nation, a badly shaken Hardin gathered his team, led it in a brief prayer, and then canceled practice. He told the players that a memorial service was scheduled for later in the evening. The much-anticipated game against Army, he said, might well be canceled. It appeared that the assassination of the president, one of the most terrible tragedies in American history, might end what had been a glorious season.

The following Tuesday, however, word came from the Pentagon that the grieving Kennedy family had requested that the game not be canceled. Instead, it would be delayed for a week of mourning and played in the president's memory.

On that same day, Staubach received a telegram informing him that he had been named the winner of the Heisman Trophy. While his teammates gathered with him to applaud the news, there was a bittersweet mood to the celebration. Everything, even winning college football's highest individual honor, was overshadowed by the unthinkable event that had occurred in Dallas.

At the last minute, editors at *Life* magazine chose to replace its planned cover photo of Staubach with a memorial portrait of President Kennedy.

A million copies of the magazine with Roger on its cover had already been printed and were ready for distribution when the assassination occurred and plans abruptly changed. The original cover was scrapped and shredded, except for three copies. One was sent to the superintendent of the Naval Academy, one to Thalman and one to Staubach.

The week leading up to the Army-Navy game was unlike any ever experienced on the Academy campus. There were no banners, no bonfires. Tecumseh's traditional war paint had been scrubbed away. In Philadelphia Stadium, the presidential boxes on each side of the field would be empty, draped with black rosettes. For the first time in history, Army Cadets and Navy Midshipmen would not make separate pregame entrances but instead march silently into the stadium side by side. The coin toss, which traditionally involved the Commander-in-Chief, was unceremoniously done by one of the game officials.

Then on a crisp, cloudless afternoon, a game that would have delighted the fallen president and ex-Navy officer was finally played.

Army coach Paul Dietzel's game plan was quickly apparent. With a deliberate, time-consuming style of offense, grinding out first downs and taking as much time as possible to run each play, he hoped to drastically reduce the time Staubach and his potent Navy offense would spend on the field.

And it very nearly worked. So effective was Cadets quarterback Rollie Stichweh at directing long drives that Navy's offense would have the ball for only five drives during the entire game.

The underdog Cadets scored first as Stichweh ran in from the 10 following a lengthy opening drive. Navy responded in just six plays, highlighted by the running of Pat Donnelly and the passing of Staubach. A 27-yard completion to Johnny Sai had moved the Midshipmen deep into Army's end of the field before Donnelly scored on a three-yard run.

At halftime the score was tied 7–7.

In the third quarter, Donnelly, enjoying the best game of his Navy career, continued to pound the Army defense for sizable gains, scoring his second and third touchdowns of the afternoon to put the Midshipmen into a 21–7 lead.

Yet even as many of the 100,000 on hand felt that Navy had finally gained control of the game, Army came back with a vengeance. Stichweh directed another scoring drive and ran for a two-point conversion that cut Navy's lead to 21–15 with six minutes left to play.

The versatile Cadets quarterback then covered an onside kick at midfield to give his team a chance to drive for the winning score.

As Army began moving the ball, Hardin called Staubach to his side and told him to be ready to put the two-minute offense into play when he returned to the game. Watching the fast-moving clock, Roger wondered if he would get that chance. With just more than a minute to play, the Cadets were still taking their time in the huddle, still using long counts to set plays in motion.

By the time Army advanced to the Midshipmen's 7-yard line, it was clear that if the game was to be won, it would not be by any late Staubach heroics but, instead, by a final defensive stand.

Author Jack Clary described those frantic final seconds in his *Navy Football: Gridiron Legends and Fighting Heroes*:

"The noise was deafening. Several times, Stichweh stepped back from center because his team could not hear him call signals. Each time, referee Barney Finn stopped the clock until the noise subsided. On the first play, Ray Paske got two yards to the Navy 5-yard line. Navy's players dawdled as they unpiled and Army [which had no time outs left] couldn't stop the clock, so there was less than a minute to play when Ken Waldrop gained a single yard at the middle of Navy's defense on second down.

"Lined up to run a third-down play without huddling, his teammates could not hear Stichweh. He backed away and Finn stopped the clock. Stichweh then huddled his team, costing it a dozen seconds, before running a third-down play on which Waldrip was smothered at the 2-yard line.

"It all came down to one last play. There were twenty-two seconds left as Army quickly lined up and Navy's defense set itself. Again, the crowd noise was too much for Stichweh, and he got a clock stoppage from Finn. Again he took his team back into the huddle. Finn restarted the clock while Army's players huddled, seemingly unaware that the last few seconds were ticking away.

"The Army players seemed oblivious to the urgency as they broke from their huddle and lined up. Again, the noise made it impossible for the players to hear the signals, so Stichweh turned to Finn for another stoppage. But Finn ignored him, and the clock ticked off the final seconds."

Thus, Army's chance for the upset died on the 2-yard line. Navy, with its 21–15 victory, was extended an invitation to play the unbeaten University of Texas in the Cotton Bowl. Matching the No. 1 and No. 2 teams in the nation, it was certain to be the spotlight game on January 1.

With almost a month before serious preparation for the bowl game would get underway, Staubach hit the road to collect the rewards of his remarkable season. There were banquets to attend, interviews to give, and trophies to accept. In New York, he joined other All-Americans on the prime time *Ed Sullivan Show*, then was hosted by the Downtown Athletic Club, which presented him with the Heisman Trophy. On hand for the presentation were his parents as well as longtime girlfriend Marianne Hoobler. When asked to say a few words at the ceremony, the proud Robert Staubach said, "I'll make this short. We've only got one child. And God gave us a good one."

Soon his son would visit Philadelphia to add the Maxwell Trophy, annually awarded to the nation's top college football player, to his glittering collection.

All but lost in the endless celebration was a small news item that appeared on sports pages around the country. The National Football League and the new-born American Football League had made their respective player drafts, and hidden far down both lists was Staubach's name. Because he had played a year of junior college football before entering the Naval Academy and was thus four years removed from his high school graduation, he was eligible to be drafted as a future choice at the completion of his junior season. Though aware that he had another year of college eligibility remaining, then a four-year military commitment, the NFL Dallas Cowboys gambled their tenth-round choice on him while the Kansas City Chiefs selected him in the fifteenth round of the AFL draft.

To those few in the media who even bothered to ask Roger about the possibility of one day playing pro football, he insisted that he hadn't given the idea much thought. At the time it was difficult to think past the upcoming bowl game, much less what might take place five years in the future.

Having spent the season promoting his quarterback for the Heisman, Hardin turned his attentions to a new cause as he prepared to face Texas coaching legend Darrell Royal in the Cotton Bowl. Though the final Associated Press and United Press International polls had already crowned the Longhorns as mythical national champions with Navy finishing second, Hardin argued that the issue remained unsettled. To all who would listen he strongly suggested that if his Midshipmen defeated Texas on New Year's Day, they should be declared national champions.

It was difficult not to see his logic.

Texas' Royal, as folksy as Hardin was fiery, had earned his National Coach of the Year acclaim at the end of the '63 season primarily by sticking with the hardcore basics. A team with a strong defense and a three-yards-and-a-cloud-of-dust offense might not draw oohs and ahhs from the crowd, but it was a tried-and-tested formula that had resulted in an undefeated season for his Longhorns. Explaining that "three things can happen when you throw the ball, and two of them are bad," his playbook was noticeably shy on passing routes.

It was, then, easy to predict the offensive approaches the two teams would favor. Navy would bring its wide-open, scramble-and-throw attack to Dallas. Texas would arrive with a depth chart filled with big and swift backs ready to pound out short gains.

Or so the experts believed.

The sun-warmed crowd of 76,000 had hardly settled into its seats before Texas quarterback Duke Carlisle, better known to Longhorns followers as a standout defensive back, had launched touchdown passes of 58 and 63 yards to wingback Phil Harris. On each occasion, Harris had managed to exploit the fact that Navy defender Donnelly was slowed by an injured thigh muscle he'd suffered a week earlier in practice.

By the end of the first half, Texas enjoyed a three-touchdown lead, and Staubach and the Navy offense were being smothered. All-American Scott Appleton, winner of the Outland Trophy as the nation's premier defensive lineman, repeatedly muscled into the Midshipmen's backfield to throw Roger and the hobbled Pat Donnelly for losses. When it wasn't Appleton, it was sophomore linebacker Tommy Nobis. New York Jets–bound Jim Hudson led the way as the Texas secondary kept Staubach's receivers in check early in the game.

By the end of the third quarter, Texas' margin had expanded to 28–0 and Navy's only chance to narrow the gap was to dismiss its futile attempt to run the ball. Staubach began throwing, often having to avoid several defenders just to get the ball away.

In the final period, he connected on four consecutive passes to advance to the Texas 2-yard line and then ran in for Navy's lone touchdown.

Despite the decisive 28–6 Texas victory, Roger had established a new Cotton Bowl record, completing 21-of-31 passes, for 228 yards. Carlisle, meanwhile, had completed only seven passes, yet they had accounted for an amazing 213 yards.

Afterward, Staubach admitted he'd never faced a team as talented and dominating as Texas. It was, he said, "like they knew what we were going to do on every play."

And perhaps the Longhorns did. In time, rumors circulated that Army coach Dietzel, still bitter about the manner in which his team's game with Navy ended, had lent Texas a helping hand. Years later, former Midshipmen assistant coach Steve Belichick would tell author Towle that he was told by a UT ex who had played in the game that Dietzel had given the Texas coaching staff all of Navy's defensive signals.

"What Darrell Royal would do," Belichick explained, "was that as soon as he saw the defensive signal from our sideline, he would tell his quarterback what was coming, and then they would call a play to go away from what they knew we were going to do."

True or not, there was no questioning the fact that Texas had been superior. "They did everything that a No. 1 team is supposed to do," Hardin said.

Only when the extended football season and the travels to awards banquets finally ended did Staubach realize how demanding and exhausting the fall had been. Adding to his mental fatigue were the constant reminders of President Kennedy's shocking death. Yet even the lingering sadness over the loss of his Commander-in-Chief, and even the Cotton Bowl defeat, decisive though it was, could not erase the fact that it had been the most exciting time of his still-young football career.

It would, however, be nice to return to a slower pace for a time, catching up on studies that had suffered, allowing his tired body to heal. He would skip basketball, but by the time baseball season neared, the competitive juices began to flow again and he was back in centerfield for the Midshipmen.

And, too, there was spring football practice. Already Hardin was telling members of the press that he fully expected his quarterback, now more experienced and more confident in his rare abilities, to be even better in his senior season.

For a Heisman Trophy winner who had already revised the Navy football record book and led his team to the No. 2 spot in the national polls, it seemed a most ambitious prediction.

CHATER

"He's the greatest third-down-and-long-yardage quarterback the college game has ever seen. His poise under pressure is amazing."

Joe Paterno, Penn State coach

For those anticipating another glorious run at a national championship, a sixth consecutive victory over Army, and a second Heisman Trophy for Staubach, the 1964 Navy season was a thundering disappointment that started badly and got progressively worse. A long-simmering conflict between coach Hardin and the Academy administration was coming to full boil, and a mounting list of injuries took its toll on a team that had already been depleted by the graduation of several of its starters from the '63 team.

Author Clary noted that some officials at the Naval Academy had long believed that Hardin sought to isolate members of his team from many of the traditional demands of student life. He would schedule team game film reviews that conflicted with the arrival of distinguished visiting lecturers whose talks required attendance of the entire brigade. His players ate in their own dining room, removed from other midshipmen who took their meals in Bancroft Hall. There was a perception by some that Hardin viewed the Academy's military-driven system of education with a certain degree of disdain. And his penchant for speaking his mind in public, often providing controversial quotes to members of the media, went against what many considered to be the Navy way. Even as Hardin had lobbied to be promoted to the powerful position of assistant athletic director at the Naval Academy, rumors were spreading that a move was afoot to dismiss him from his duties.

While all of the nation's high-profile college coaches serve at the whim of school administrators, a board of regents, and wealthy alumni, Hardin faced the constant reminder that his fate could ultimately be decided by men so powerful that they had offices in the Pentagon.

And it didn't help matters that his quarterback was injured in the season opener.

While the Midshipmen defeated Penn State 21–8, Staubach had limped to the sidelines before the game ended. Scrambling to find time to throw in the second quarter, he was hit by a Nittany Lions defender who had eluded the block of center Bruce Kenton. As all three fell to the turf, Roger heard something snap.

His ankle had been badly sprained and his Achilles tendon strained. And from that moment, the high expectations for his final season as a collegian turned into a frustrating week-to-week struggle just to play.

Even with the damaged ankle heavily taped, he was unable to run during the week of practice preceding the William and Mary game. Hardin started sophomore quarterback Bruce Bickel, hoping a week of rest might allow Roger's injury to heal. Late in the game, however, Navy was leading by only 14–6 when Bickel suffered a broken nose. Hardin called on Staubach to take over the struggling Midshipmen offense.

Virtually immobile, he simply handed off to Kip Paskewich on his first play and the Navy halfback ran for a 71-yard touchdown. Following a William and Mary fumble, Roger limped back onto the field and threw three straight completions, the third to John Michelson for a score. In just four plays, he had directed Navy to two touchdowns as the team went on to win, 35–6.

With Michigan next on the schedule, trainers and team doctors worked feverishly to make Staubach ready to play. Different types of tapings were experimented with, and an ankle brace was ordered. Still the pain remained. Finally, it was decided that injections of Cortisone and Novocaine might speed the healing process while posing no threat to cause further damage. With the pain killing shots, Roger was able to run more normally.

But in a 21–0 loss to the Wolverines, he was injured again. With the ankle numbed before game time, he played well in the first half, twice moving the ball deep into Michigan's end of the field before fumbles ended the drives.

By halftime, the effect of the painkilling injection had worn off, and Roger received another shot. But when Wolverine All-American tackle Bill Yearby fell on the injured ankle in the third quarter, Staubach was finished for the afternoon.

Immediately following the team's return to Annapolis, he was hospitalized and his entire leg placed in a cast. Doctors insisted that the ankle be immobilized for at least ten days, perhaps longer.

Navy, then, would travel to its date against Georgia Tech without him. Back in Annapolis, a distraught Staubach watched on closed-circuit television as the Midshipmen were again shut out, losing 17–0. Ignoring doctors' orders, he slipped from his hospital room into a nearby courtyard where, balancing on his cast, he practiced throwing.

On the day before the team was to travel to the West Coast and play the University of California, Roger was released from the hospital and told that while there were no plans for him to play, he would be allowed to accompany the team. Still, the Navy equipment manager packed a pair of high-topped football shoes with Staubach's uniform.

Roger tested the ankle during a brief Friday afternoon practice following the team's arrival in California and found that the tightly laced new shoe seemed to serve its supportive purpose. Though stiff and weakened by his hospital stay, he was pleased to note that he felt no pain. Still, he didn't anticipate leaving the sidelines on Saturday.

But as the game got underway and the Navy defense repeatedly dropped Cal's heralded quarterback Craig Morton for losses, it appeared the Midshipmen might have a chance to score an upset. Hardin began sending Staubach into the game in situations where the opportunity for a touchdown presented itself. The best Roger could do was get Navy close enough for a field goal.

He would be on the field for only 12 plays, completing six passes and suffering four interceptions. Meanwhile, Morton, who was being hailed as one of the leading candidates in the new season's Heisman race, threw for two touchdowns as Cal easily won 27–13.

Back at the Academy, Hardin's decision to allow Staubach to play so soon after being released from the hospital was being roundly criticized. And adding to the team's growing list of misfortunes was the fact that fullback Pat Donnelly had suffered what appeared to be a season-ending knee injury during the game.

Against the University of Pittsburgh, Roger was finally able to play an entire game, rallying Navy from a 14–0 first quarter deficit into a 14–14 tie. However, the injury list continued to grow as flanker back Skip Orr was helped from the field, lost for the season.

Navy faced Notre Dame with a quarterback still playing with a limp and without its fullback, flanker, and starting end Neil Henderson, who had been sidelined with a pulled hamstring muscle. And though Staubach would complete 19 passes, the Fighting Irish soundly defeated the depleted Midshipmen 40–0. A week later he threw for 231 yards and three touchdowns, yet Maryland extended the Navy downslide with a 27–22 victory.

Finally, as the dismal season began to wind down, Roger managed a record-setting game in his final appearance in Navy–Marine Corps Memorial Stadium. Against Duke he broke his own record for total yardage in a game as he passed for 217 yards and ran for 91 in a 27–14 Navy victory.

The record, however, almost didn't come. Late in the fourth quarter, Hardin, wishing to allow his quarterback a proper farewell from the brigade and Navy fans, summoned Roger to the sidelines. Even as he was receiving a thundering wave of applause, public relations director Thalman was hurrying toward the booth from which Navy assistant coaches called down plays. There, he told them to alert Hardin to the fact Staubach was still 10 yards shy of the record.

A timeout was called and Roger returned to the game, completed one more pass for 11 yards, and again retired to the sidelines as a second ovation erupted.

With Staubach returning to form and the surprise announcement that Donnelly was expected to rejoin the Midshipmen backfield, there was renewed hope that the disappointing season might be salvaged with a victory over Army.

It was not to be.

Determined to avenge the previous season's narrow defeat, Army's defense was clearly designed to control Staubach. On Navy's first series, he was trapped in the end zone for a safety. Then quarterback Rollie Stichweh methodically marched the Cadets for an early touchdown.

Only a few seconds remained in the first half when Navy scored and Staubach threw for a two-point conversion to tie the game. The play was reminiscent of so many he had performed over the course of his career. Facing an all-out blitz from the Cadets, he was forced to scramble and had retreated back to the 15-yard line before being cornered by two Army defenders. Yet in the grasp of the would-be tacklers, he managed to complete the pass to Phil Norton in the end zone.

It was one of his few successful escapes of the day, however, as Army shut out the Midshipmen in the second half. Navy's defense was equally impressive, holding Army to only a field goal in the final two quarters. That, however, would be enough as the Cadets ended their five-game losing streak with an 11–8 victory.

For Navy in the fall of 1964, there would be no national ranking, no bowl invitation, no joyful ringing of the Gokoku-ji Bell. Roger Staubach's storybook college football career had come to an end with the 3–6–1 season record. And soon, as many had expected, Wayne Hardin was dismissed as coach.

In their absence, Navy football would never again enjoy the remarkable heights and memorable magic the pair had helped produce.

Adding to Staubach's senior-year frustration was the fact he'd only begun to feel good physically as the season was winding down. The ankle had finally healed, and his conditioning, lost with so many missed practices early in the year, had begun to return.

For those reasons he was pleased to be invited to play in a couple of postseason All-Star games. If his life in football was indeed nearing an end, he wanted to go out on a higher note than walking off the renamed JFK Stadium in Philadelphia following a heartbreaking loss to Army.

At the North-South Shrine game, played on Christmas Day in Miami, Staubach shared the quarterbacking duties with the University of Tulsa's record-setting Jerry Rhome, who had just starred in the Bluebonnet Bowl. Also on his South squad was Olympic gold medal–winning sprinter Bob Hayes of Florida A&M.

At quarterback for the North was Notre Dame's John Huarte, the recently announced winner of the 1964 Heisman Trophy.

After three quarters, the North held a 30–6 lead. But, under the unique All-Star Game rule, the team that trailed would receive the kickoff, even after it scored. The South took full advantage, and with Staubach putting on a dazzling passing display, it moved into a 30–30 tie as only a couple of minutes remained. Huarte finally put the issue to rest as he threw for the winning North touchdown with just seconds left to play.

For Staubach it had been an invigorating experience. Practicing with and playing against many of the nation's premier college athletes had been fun. And he'd been honored earlier in the week when his new teammates had voted him captain of the South squad.

From Miami, Roger immediately headed to San Francisco to participate in the East-West Shrine game where he was again named captain and starter for the East All-Stars. California's Craig Morton quarterbacked the West.

Played in a downpour, it was hardly the scoring donnybrook fans in Miami had enjoyed, yet Staubach ran and passed well all day despite the conditions. In the third quarter he completed a 38-yard pass to Michigan State's Dick Gordon, a native of Cincinnati, to set up the East's only score. With just two minutes left in the game, Morton connected with Cal teammate Jack Schraub for a touchdown that gave the West an 11–7 victory.

Despite his team's loss, Staubach was voted the Most Valuable Player.

To all concerned, who won and who lost was secondary to the camaraderie and competition. For Staubach, football had again become fun.

Staubach's final semester as a student at the Naval Academy was spent focusing on studies, and looking ahead to June Week graduation and his active duty assignment. And he would earn his last letter as a Midshipman in his final season as a member of the baseball team.

He bade his athletic days at the Academy a dramatic farewell with a towering home run that lifted Navy to a 5–4 victory over Brown.

And as the semester neared an end, the Academy saluted him. For the third consecutive year, he was presented with the Thompson Trophy as Navy's top athlete, then a sword that honored the senior "who has excelled in athletics during his years of varsity competition." Then, as the awards banquet was nearing an end, he was called back to the stage. His fellow Midshipmen had, he later learned, petitioned the Naval Academy Athletic Association to make a final and special presentation.

With Roger standing by his side, Academy superintendent Admiral Charles Minter told the audience, "Such a young man comes along only once in a great while in the life of an institution. A superb athlete and a complete gentleman, his performance, both on and off the field, reflecting great credit on the institution he represents and on college athletics in general."

And with that, it was announced that Staubach's jersey No. 12 was being retired. Along with 1960 Heisman Trophy winner Joe Bellino's number 27, it would forever be on display in the Naval Academy field house.

By the time his parents and girlfriend Marianne arrived in Annapolis for the June Week graduation ceremonies, Roger was looking back on his time spent at the Academy as the greatest experience of his young life.

And his future offered a new and exciting range of possibilities and decisions as he prepared to begin life as Ensign Roger Staubach.

First, however, there was still more football to be played. Officials of the Coaches All-American game, to be played in Buffalo, had invited him to participate; so had the organizers of the late summer College All-Star game, which matched the best collegians against the reigning champion of professional football.

In Buffalo, the team was being coached by Notre Dame's Ara Parseghian. From the day the players arrived to begin practice, it was no secret that Parseghian favored his Heisman-winning quarterback Huarte as the starter. Staubach and Army rival Stichweh, the other quarterbacks on the roster, would make their appearances as defensive backs.

For the ever-competitive Staubach, the limited playing time was only a mild disappointment. In truth, he had more important things on his mind.

Following the game, he traveled to Cincinnati where late on a Saturday evening he nervously waited for Marianne Hoobler, his long-time girlfriend whom he had known since elementary school days, to finish her nursing shift in the intensive care unit of Good Samaritan Hospital.

With an engagement ring in his pocket, he was planning to ask her to marry him. She accepted his proposal, and they began planning for a September wedding.

Roger returned to Annapolis where he had been assigned six months of duty as an Academy physical education instructor and assistant coach of the Plebe football team. And he had one final all-star game to prepare for.

When he joined the college squad that would face the Cleveland Browns in Chicago's Soldier Field, Staubach was amazed at the array of talent on hand. There were running backs like Gale Sayers, Tucker Frederickson, and Junior Coffey; receivers Bob Hayes, Fred Biletnikoff, Jack Snow, and Roy Jefferson; and defensive standouts like linebacker Dick Butkus, and outstanding linemen like Ralph Neely and Malcolm Walker. It was a virtual who's who of college football.

With the exception of Roger and Navy teammate Pat Donnelly, all were on their way to professional training camps as soon as the game was played.

The quarterbacks that All-Star coach Otto Graham had to choose from included Staubach, Notre Dame's Huarte, California's Craig Morton, and Michigan's Bob Timberlake. Following a close competition with Huarte, Roger was named the starting quarterback. And once again, he was elected team captain.

While the world champion Browns, as expected, won the game 24–16, Staubach came away from the experience having learned two things. First was the belief that he had demonstrated to the numerous scouts attending workouts and the game that he was capable of playing football at the professional level. Second, he should have listened to Coach Graham.

Throughout the all-star practices, the legendary former Cleveland quarterback had warned Staubach against leaving his feet as he threw the ball. The jump-pass might have worked against college competition, he said, but against the defense he was soon to face, it could be disastrous. It took a blow from blitzing Browns linebacker Galen Fiss to prove the point. As he hit Staubach just as he jumped to throw, Roger's left shoulder was again knocked out of place.

With the game only half over, Roger was en route to a Chicago hospital where, after a couple of hours, the shoulder went back into place.

Upon his return to the Academy he finally agreed to an operation that would permanently resolve the long-troubling problem.

Throughout his senior year at the Academy, Roger had received a steady stream of questionnaires from professional teams but had never bothered to reply to any of them. Despite having been drafted by the Cowboys and Chiefs, he hadn't seriously considered the far-fetched possibility that he might still have a future as a pro player after the four years of service that awaited him.

He and Marianne had settled into a small cottage near the Academy, awaiting word when they would be moving to Athens, Georgia, where

Roger would begin training as a Naval supply officer, when Lamar Hunt, owner of the Kansas City Chiefs, phoned.

He wanted to visit Annapolis and discuss signing Staubach to a contract.

A few days later, the multimillionaire Texan was sitting in their modest home, extolling the bright future of the newly formed American Football League and expressing his belief that Roger would still be able to play at the professional level once his Navy commitment was fulfilled.

The unique contract that Hunt had brought with him promised a bonus of $5,000 simply for signing and a monthly payment of $300 during the entire time Roger was on active duty. In the event he decided to make a career of the Navy and play no more football, he would not be required to return the signing bonus or monthly payments. On the other hand, if he did choose to join the Chiefs after his four-year tour of duty was over, a three-year contract that would pay him $25,000 per season awaited.

Excited by the offer, Roger explained that he would need to check with Captain Paul Borden, legal officer for the Academy, to make sure he wouldn't be violating any Navy regulations should he sign the agreement.

Word spread quickly through the athletic department that Staubach was soon to sign an agreement to one day play for the Chiefs. And almost immediately, Captain Borden received a call from Dallas Cowboys personnel director Gil Brandt, urging him to tell Roger not to sign anything until he'd heard Dallas' offer.

At the time Staubach had no knowledge of the longstanding battle that had been waged between Kansas City owner Hunt and Dallas Cowboys owner Clint Murchison.

In the first few years of the 1960s, one too many pro football teams called Dallas home. Murchison and the Cowboys had been granted an NFL franchise that was to begin play in the 1961 season, but when Hunt, the driving force behind the establishment of the renegade AFL, announced that his team, the Dallas Texans, would start competing for the city's entertainment dollar in '60, the NFL rushed the Cowboys into being. Just six months after Hunt announced he was bringing his Texans to town, the Cowboys were introduced.

To say that neither team flourished would be an understatement. Finally, Murchison had even offered a mock arrangement whereby the problems of both teams could be resolved. "Let's flip a coin," he suggested to Hunt, "and the *winner* gets to leave town."

While no such gamble ever occurred, Hunt did finally choose to move to Kansas City where he renamed his team the Chiefs and immediately captured the imagination of the city. The Cowboys, with the Dallas market to themselves, also began to thrive.

Still, there were those who suspected that Hunt's decision to visit Staubach personally rather than send a coach or team scout was prompted by a lingering competitive mindset he had toward the Cowboys.

When Dallas traveled to Philadelphia to play the Eagles, Captain Borden was invited to be the team's guest for the game. There, he met with owner Murchison, general manager Tex Schramm and Brandt, and explained that Roger had no interest in any form of back-and-forth bidding and had instructed him to entertain only one offer from both of the teams that had drafted him. The Cowboys, aware of the terms Hunt had suggested, upped the signing bonus to $10,000 and the monthly payments Roger would receive while in the service to $500. They too agreed that in the event he should decide to remain in the Navy, he would not be obligated to return the money paid him.

Captain Borden phoned Staubach to tell him the terms of the Cowboys' offer, and Roger accepted. When Borden offered to contact Hunt and pass along his decision, Roger chose to do so himself.

In his *First Down, Lifetime to Go*, he recalled the conversation.

"I felt bad about Lamar because he was such a tremendous man and had thought of the plan in the first place. But the Cowboys had offered me more money, had drafted me higher, and the NFL just had more charisma at the time. I phoned him and broke the news.

"'I don't want to haggle over this and for each side to keep making counteroffers,' I told Lamar. 'I'm sorry but I just took what I felt was the best offer for me.'

"'I wish you hadn't agreed to their offer,' Hunt said. 'I'd like to have made a counteroffer, but I guess it's settled now.'"

If and when Staubach decided to give professional football a try, it would be as a member of the Dallas Cowboys. First, however, there were other obligations to address.

CHAPTER 6

"This guy can play in our league. He reminds me of Fran Tarkenton, except he has a stronger arm."

George Allen

The military options available to Naval Academy graduates included sea duty, flight training, joining the Marines, or serving in the supply corps. Since it had been discovered when Staubach arrived at Annapolis that he was slightly color blind, and unable to distinguish dark shades at long distances, the idea of becoming a pilot was immediately ruled out. Choosing to serve aboard a ship would require an automatic two years at sea. Briefly, Roger considered the Marines before deciding to volunteer to go to Vietnam where he would serve a 12–month tour as an officer in the supply corps before being reassigned stateside.

With a new daughter and Marianne pregnant with their second child, a tour of duty in Vietnam would mean that he could return to his family more quickly.

Following attendance at supply corps school, intense weapons and survival training, including a brief stay in a mock prisoner-of-war camp, Staubach was flown to Vietnam in August 1966 and assigned to the Naval airbase supply depot at Danang. Soon, however, he was promoted to the rank of lieutenant and moved 60 miles to the south to command pier operations at the Chu Lai supply terminal.

Among the few personal items he took to his new location was a football.

While he was never directly involved in the day-to-day battles, it was the responsibility of Staubach and the 130 enlisted men and 60 Vietnamese civilians under his command to see that equipment and ammunition flowed steadily to the Army and Marines who were engaged in the fighting.

Off-loading ships that arrived from the South China Sea and distributing cargo were routine but important parts of the war effort. So, too, Staubach quickly learned, was the depressing responsibility of shipping the personal effects of soldiers killed in action to families back home.

Reminders of the dark cruelty of war were everywhere and hit home most dramatically when he received news that Naval Academy friend and teammate Tommy Holden, a Marine platoon leader, had been killed during a firefight with the Vietcong. Later, he would learn that Mike Grammer, who had been a member of his Plebe class at the Academy, had been captured by the enemy and executed. His body had been found in a South Vietnamese church, hands tied behind his back and a single gunshot wound in the back of his head.

"Death was always there," Staubach wrote in his autobiography. "There would be twenty or thirty ambulances lined up near the helicopter pad, waiting to put the dead in bags to be shipped back to the United States. We volunteered to help. It just tore our guts out. These had been human beings and now they had become just bodies, or pieces of bodies, wrapped in cloth for shipment."

It was, despite all of his training, preparation and eagerness to serve his country, a world foreign and frightening to one who, as a child, had never even been allowed to own a BB gun. Now, however, he reported for his daily duties with a .45 automatic holstered to his hip, fully trained to use it.

Regardless of one's assignment or location, peril was a constant companion.

One night Staubach was awakened by the distinctive sound of approaching mortar fire that was being launched from a nearby offshore island. Jumping from his cot, he roused his roommates, instructing them to rush to the safety of a nearby bunker. No sooner had they reached it when explosions erupted less than 100 yards away from the hut where they had slept.

While Roger and his roommates were unharmed, the attack claimed the lives of four and wounded a number of others.

Even in wartime, however, there are often long stretches of quiet, particularly for those distanced from the front lines. Once work assignments were competed, some of those stationed in Chu Lai occasionally attended movies shipped from the U.S., others lingered in the mess hall to play cards or dominoes long after their meals were completed, some read, wrote letters or listened to Armed Services Radio.

Staubach threw his football—to anyone, American or South Vietnamese, who was willing to play the role of receiver.

In time, a hand-painted sign was placed on the edge of a grassless, rock-strewn open space where he ran endless wind sprints and threw passes in an effort to stay in football shape. It read, "Staubach Stadium."

When the rough ground had finally chewed the football so badly that it had become difficult to grip, Roger wrote to Cowboys player personnel director Gil Brandt, asking to purchase a new NFL regulation ball. Brandt immediately shipped one, accompanied by a note assuring that there was "no charge for our quarterback of the future."

As his stay in Vietnam wound down, Staubach found himself counting the days until he would be back in the United States, reunited with his family and several thousand miles closer to a goal that had begun to border on an obsession. It had been with him, growing in intensity, since the day he had signed his contract with the Dallas Cowboys.

By the time his year-long tour of duty in Vietnam ended in August 1967, Staubach was more certain than ever that he wanted to continue playing football. He was actually a bit surprised by how much he missed the game as he'd sat up late into the night, listening to the Armed Forces Radio broadcast of the Army-Navy game, then the Dallas–Green Bay championship game. And, while always brief, each note Cowboys player personnel director Gil Brandt had sent along with the footballs he'd requested had been encouraging reminders. From thousands of miles away, he was hearing a call that seemed to grow increasingly urgent. He was convinced that his life as an athlete was not over.

That became even more obvious to him when he briefly visited the Cowboys' training camp in California during the last few days of his rest and relaxation leave. Landry had watched him throw and suggested techniques he might work on.

First, however, there were two more years of military service to fulfill. Following the R&R stop in Hawaii, where he was reunited with Marianne and his daughters, and the short visit to the Cowboys training camp, the entire family moved to the Pensacola Naval Air Station where Staubach's new assignment would be to oversee the base's shipping and receiving.

Life had returned to a welcomed sense of the normal. He and his family were back together, new friends were made, pristine beaches awaited nearby, and his daily duties were accomplished without the threat of mortar attacks.

Plus, the base had a football team.

The Pensocola Goshawks, made up primarily of pilots in training, weren't likely to ever receive any bowl invitation, nor did pro scouts swarm to watch their games, but they were organized and played a regular schedule against small college teams like Middle Tennessee State, Northeast Louisiana, and McNeese State. And there was always the annual bragging-rights match with the Quantico Marines. It was no-frills football of hand-me-down uniforms, flying out to games on a C-47 and eating box lunches for pregame meals, but for Staubach it was a Godsend, an opportunity to warm old skills and work himself back into playing condition.

It did not bother him that his linemen were far smaller than those who had provided him protection at Annapolis or that some of his teammates had an "I'll be at practice if I don't have anything better to do" attitude. Due to the fact that players were constantly being transferred in and out, the starting lineup from week to week was seldom the same.

When Roger reported to Pensacola, the season was already underway. Immediately, however, he began attending afternoon practices. "I found out, for the first time, how much you could lose being away from the game for a couple of years," he wrote in *First Down, Lifetime to Go*. "I could throw the ball and had pretty good movement, but I just didn't feel comfortable. It was difficult getting used to wearing the equipment again, to setting up to throw and working against defenses."

Still, the Goshawks ended the season with a 5–4 record and, for the first time in Pensacola history, defeated Quantico. As a reward, the team was flown to Mexico City to play a team of Mexican All-Stars.

The game, played on a soccer field, was a four-star farce. The host team arrived on the field with the same color jerseys as those worn by the Goshawks. On some plays the hosts would have 10 men on the field, 12 or 13 the next. It quickly became obvious that the Mexican referees had little working knowledge of the rules. After each of the first three or four Goshawk touchdowns, officials threw flags, negating the score with little explanation of what infraction had occurred. As the game went on, it wasn't unusual to see a fan wander from the sidelines and join in the huddle just to offer a friendly, if slightly inebriated, *hola*.

Finally, after a half dozen touchdowns by the Americans were allowed to stand, Goshawks coach Bob Moss instructed the team not to score again. Some players simply headed to the dressing room for a hot shower, others began choosing which position they would like to play. One of the ends, Bill Zloch, wanted to try his hand at quarterback and traded spots with Staubach. Taking advantage of the fact the Mexican All-Stars had no concept of pass defense, Zloch disregarded his coach's no-more scoring instructions and immediately hurled a 60-yard bomb to Staubach for a touchdown.

A few months later, however, the Goshawk's quarterback would encounter a vastly different—and far more sane—level of competition.

Well after the Pensacola season had ended, Roger continued to train with a vengeance. He ran, lifted weights, and threw the ball to anyone he could persuade to serve as a receiver. And there was method to what some felt was his madness.

The Dallas Cowboys rookies, Staubach knew, were due to report for training camp in July, and he planned to spend his two-week leave with them.

On the campus of California Lutheran in picturesque Thousand Oaks, hopeful young draft choices and free agents had two weeks of morning and afternoon practices to impress Cowboys coaches before the veteran members of the team arrived to begin preparations for the upcoming season. Like all NFL training camps, there was an intense, boot camp-like focus on purpose. Virtually every waking minute was devoted to the highly competitive workouts and endless meetings wherein the complexities of the Dallas offense and defense were taught. Quartered in dormitory rooms and subjected to curfews, it was a Spartan setting whose purpose was to avoid all outside distractions so that a tunnel-vision focus was maintained. While the warm and sunny beaches of Malibu were just over the mountains and the bright glitter of Los Angeles and Hollywood a quick 45-minute drive away, players soon learned that even if time permitted visits, they would simply be too tired to make the trip.

A number of players, learning that Staubach had reported without any hope of immediately making the team, wondered about the sanity of his volunteering to spend his brief vacation time in such a grim environment. What didn't occur to most was that at the Naval Academy and in the military, he'd lived a life that made the rules and regulations of a pro football training camp look tame by comparison.

For Roger, the Cowboys training camp offered a two-week opportunity to prove that his skills had not deteriorated and to remind the coaching staff that he had become serious about his intent to one day be an NFL quarterback.

What Landry and his staff saw was a young man who was in excellent condition. Roger's passes, if anything, were thrown too hard. There was little indication that the time that had elapsed since his final collegiate game had any ill effects on the talent that had won him All-America honors and the Heisman.

In two scrimmages he was impressive. Against the San Francisco 49ers rookies he threw for three touchdowns; against George Allen's Los Angeles Rams, he completed 10-of-14 passes for 161 yards and two touchdowns. He also ran for several impressive gains.

Staubach returned to Pensacola feeling he had taken an important step toward proving himself, certain that he had left a good impression during his short visit. And he had with him something that Landry rarely parted with—a voluminous Dallas Cowboys playbook.

That fall, the Pensocola Goshawks, led by player-coach Staubach, would incorporate the Cowboys' offense. Or, at least, something that vaguely resembled it.

If there had ever been any doubt that he would make a full-fledged attempt at playing professional football, it was resolved in the final year of his obligatory military service. Lieutenant Staubach submitted his resignation papers and began counting the 12 months before his discharge would be official.

"If Tom Landry was going to create a perfect quarterback for his system, it would be Roger. He has great character, which Tom loves, and the intensity and dedication to give that 110 percent, go that extra hundred yards."

Don Meredith

For even the greatest of achievers, regardless of their talent or field of endeavor, there is some isolated moment in time, unplanned and unexpected, that paved their way, and removed some final barrier to allow a full-out pursuit of their goal.

For Roger Staubach, 27-year-old rookie-to-be, that opportunity came in the form of a phone call in the summer of 1969.

As he counted the days before reporting for his first full exposure to the Cowboys training camp, he thought of little else but his chances of earning a place on the roster. Don Meredith, at age 31, was entrenched as the starter, entering the prime of his professional career. Backing him up was Craig Morton, a year younger than Staubach but preparing for his fifth season in the NFL. The only positive Roger could see in his situation was the fact Jerry Rhome, weary of the going-nowhere role as Dallas' No. 3 quarterback, had asked to be traded. When the Cowboys granted Rhome's wish, dealing him to Cleveland, it provided Staubach his first glimmer of hope that a place might be available to him.

If the team was to continue its tradition of carrying three quarterbacks on its roster, he believed he had a legitimate chance to earn the final spot. Landry, he felt, had been favorably impressed with his abbreviated performances in his two visits to Thousand Oaks and had given him a welcomed number of repetitions during the early summer quarterback camp in Dallas.

Still, he was not convinced that whatever pro football life awaited him would be as a longtime member of the Cowboys. Even if he did make the team, it would be difficult to find satisfaction standing on the sidelines as a seldom-used backup player. If he was to ultimately achieve his goal of actually *playing* in the NFL, there was a good possibility that it might eventually be with some other team. Staubach fully understood the competitive nature that had driven Rhome to ask that he be traded to a team where he might have a better chance to play regularly. The same possibility was mixed into Roger's long-range career plan.

Then, on July 5, the day he was officially discharged from the Navy and just five days before the players were scheduled to report to camp, the Cowboys publicity director called. "You may be hearing from some sportswriters," Curt Mosher said. "Meredith has just retired."

In the short months that preceded his rookie season, Staubach had climbed the depth chart to become the likely backup for newly designated starter Morton.

As he would later write in his *Time Enough to Win*, "I even joked to Marianne about the situation by telling her, 'Pro football isn't so tough. I've gone from No.4 to No. 2 quarterback without doing a thing.'"

Roger Staubach was no longer a mere curiosity.

While he contemplated his future, the city of Dallas collectively shook its head over the loss of its greatest sports celebrity since the post-World War II days when Southern Methodist University icon Doak Walker had won hearts as a three-time All-American and Heisman Trophy winner.

Meredith, too, had played his college football at SMU, twice earning All-American acclaim. Before the Dallas Cowboys even had a nickname, a coach, or the official franchise blessing of the NFL, owner-to-be Murchison had signed the country music–loving quarterback to a four-year personal services contract for fear some other team might steal away the marquee player who could provide his team instant appeal.

As the Cowboys had grown from an expansion doormat, failing to win a single game in its 1960 debut season, into a contender, twice losing to Vince Lombardi's Green Bay Packers in the NFL championship game, it was Meredith who was the driving force. In the infancy of the franchise, he was good, bad, and ugly—sometimes during the course of a single game. Though often battered and bruised, cheered and booed, Meredith had endured the team's growing pains to emerge as one of the league's premier quarterbacks. Three times selected to play in the Pro Bowl, he had been honored as the NFL Player of the Year in 1966 after leading the Cowboys to their first winning season.

And even as he did so, he continued to be the fun-loving East Texas country boy who seemed oblivious to the widely held Dallas notion that winning football games was every bit as important as world peace and eliminating hunger.

The previous year, the Cowboys appeared to have its finest team, cruising through the regular season with a 12–2 record as the highest-scoring team in the NFL. Finally, the prognosticators were saying, the Cowboys would take their place as league champions. Instead, they played poorly on a frigid playoff Saturday in Cleveland and were defeated 31–20 by the underdog Browns. A frustrated Landry had benched his starting quarterback following two costly third-quarter interceptions.

Outwardly, the young man nicknamed Dandy Don seemed to just grin and bear it, moving on to the next good time, feeding more quarters into the jukebox. In truth, the constant criticisms, the injuries, and what he had come to perceive as unjust public criticism from Landry was more than he wanted to deal with. Explaining to his coach that he had simply lost his enthusiasm for the game, that football was no longer fun, he had made the decision to walk away.

Landry was taken aback not only at Meredith's timing but at his reason for quitting the game. The idea that football was supposed to be "fun" had never occurred to the coach, who for years had fretted over his quarterback's casual approach and unrealized potential.

Years later, teammate Lee Roy Jordan would reflect on the team's early-day shortfalls and Meredith's premature retirement, telling the *Dallas Morning News*' Brad Townsend, "He took too much of the blame."

"The thing was," Meredith would later explain, "the better we got, the more serious everyone became. Back when we were 1–11, everybody was singing. Everybody was loose and having a good time. Then, after a few years, we started putting it together. By the time we were going 11–1, I looked around and suddenly realized that I was the only one still singing. That should have told me something right there."

Thus, as preparation began for the '69 season, it was Craig Morton directing the Dallas offense with Staubach as his understudy. And Landry left no doubt about the pecking order. When members of the media asked about the possibility of Roger competing for the starting job, he responded, "Let me put it this way: If late in the season Staubach is our starting quarterback, it will mean this was a lost season. He has no experience. It will take him time to learn our system and be able to read defenses."

For all his gaudy collegiate accomplishments and awards, Roger was viewed as an unknown quantity, just another player trying to earn a place on the roster.

As he worked toward that goal, he found himself in an athletic netherworld. Married, father of a growing family—daughter Jennifer was three, Michelle one, and Stephanie a newborn—and four years removed from his last college game, Roger had little in common with most of his fellow rookies. Inexperienced and unproven, he was yet to be welcomed into the fraternity of veterans. In time, however, he did develop a kinship with a couple of hopefuls whose backgrounds also defied the pro football norm.

His roommate was wide receiver Richmond Flowers, a University of Tennessee ex whose greatest collegiate athletic accomplishments had come as a world class hurdler. The other was Calvin Hill, the No. 1 draft choice running back from Yale, the Ivy League school with absolutely no reputation for being a football powerhouse.

Staubach and Hill were drawn to each other by more than their determination to earn a place on the Cowboys roster. Roger's Christian faith remained a powerful force in his life and, had Hill not been afforded the opportunity to try pro ball, he had planned to enroll in divinity school.

In quiet times away from twice-daily practices and constant meetings, the three rookies shared their concerns. Flowers confided that he knew his only realistic chance lay in a reckless pursuit of a place on the Cowboys specialty teams. Hill privately acknowledged the pressure of being a surprise first-round selection. So determined had he been to prove himself that he had literally spent months training for the running of the dreaded Landry Mile that was traditionally the first order of business when camp opened.

Staubach's challenge was equally demanding. He, too, felt he had to excel at even the most obscure tests. When players lined up for end-of-practice 40-yard sprints, he strained to always beat Morton to the finish line. It was essential that he prove that his long layoff had not diminished his skills. Even routine scrimmages took on a new importance.

Roger was hardly an instant success.

Landry's playbook included more than two dozen formations from which the offense could be run. From each set there were a seemingly endless number of plays, passes, and runs to choose from. Additionally, in the Cowboys' scheme, the quarterback was expected to even call blocking assignments. Then there were myriad defenses to be read. Staubach was often hesitant and confused.

In a rookie scrimmage against the Oakland Raiders, Staubach completed only 1-of-13 passes. Roommate Flowers had several drops. And Hill missed a blitz that resulted in Roger being hit so hard that a bone in his lower back was cracked and a kidney bruised.

All three returned to the Cal Lutheran dorm that evening, wondering how severely they had damaged their professional football futures.

Things didn't get much better as the preseason schedule got underway. Normally, key starters play only sparingly during the exhibitions with backup veterans, and rookies were provided extended opportunities to impress the coaching staff. But, in the sudden absence of Meredith,

Landry wanted to be certain that Morton and an all-new Cowboys back-field were fully prepared for the upcoming season. Walt Garrison had moved into the fullback spot, replacing the retired Don Perkins, and rookie Hill was learning his way at running back while veteran starter Dan Reeves was still slowed by off-season knee surgery.

In his first appearance as a professional, albeit it in a preseason game, Staubach never left the sideline as he watched the Los Angeles Rams defeat Dallas.

It wasn't until the fourth quarter against the San Francisco 49ers that Landry finally signaled Staubach into the game. His first pass, aimed at an open tight end Mike Ditka, spiraled into the ground five yards in front of the receiver.

Roger's passing, however, wasn't Landry's primary concern. Too often during scrimmages, he had given up on pass plays too quickly and run. It was a habit Landry wanted to break quickly, one that had already gener-ated a standing joke among defensive veterans: If you break through and miss a shot at him, the story went, just lay there and wait. Sooner or later he would come back your way.

By the time the Cowboys hosted the New York Jets in the fifth exhi-bition game, Staubach was resigned to seeing only brief end-of-the-game duty. But late in the first half, Morton suffered a dislocated finger and Landry summoned Staubach.

With Dallas on its own 24-yard line and 1:19 on the clock, he advanced the offense to the Jets 17 in nine plays before completing an impromptu run that caused the Cotton Bowl crowd to cheer—and Landry to cringe. Fading to pass, Staubach was unable to find an open receiver and quickly left the protection of the pocket. Running down the sidelines, he avoided two Jets tacklers as he neared the goal. Then, from the one, he leaped over a waiting defender and scored to lift Dallas into a 10–9 lead with just four seconds remaining in the half.

By game's end, he had led the Cowboys to a 25–9 victory, completing 10-of-16 passes for 160 yards.

The following week, with Morton still unable to play, Staubach's performance was far less impressive. Aware of the obvious difficulty he was having picking up keys and his tendency to run if receivers weren't immediately open, the Baltimore Colts defense blitzed repeatedly. He was trapped six times, threw four interceptions, and scrambled 12 times for 118 yards as the Cowboys lost 23–7.

Members of an exhausted Colts defense collectively agreed they had never run so much in an effort to stop an opposing quarterback.

Landry's postgame evaluation of Staubach's performance was hardly gushing. "He'll learn," he said. Some wondered if it was a valid prediction or just wishful thinking.

As Dallas prepared to open the regular season, it was a team still getting acquainted with its new members. Ditka, the legendary Chicago Bears All-Pro who had gone on to two disappointing seasons in Philadelphia, had come to Dallas in a trade and moved into the tight end position. Linebacker D.D. Lewis was fulfilling his military obligation and would not be available. Neither would defensive lineman Willie Townes who had been lost for the year with a leg injury. There was a question of how long wide receiver Bob Hayes, who had suffered a shoulder injury in pre-season, would be sidelined.

And as a date with St. Louis neared, Morton's injured thumb had not yet healed. Reluctantly, Landry announced that Staubach would be his starting quarterback against the Cardinals. "Going into the season with a rookie quarterback," he told members of the press, "isn't an ideal situation." Then, almost as an afterthought, he added, "I have a lot of confidence in Roger. He'll do well Sunday."

"I was excited about the opportunity," Staubach recalled, "but I found myself thinking about my track record as a starting quarterback in the Cotton Bowl. I'd played there twice and had lost to SMU, then Texas in the Cotton Bowl game." He decided not to mention the trend to his coach.

Keeping with tradition, the team was sequestered in a Dallas hotel on the eve of the game. As players gathered for an evening meal, Landry spoke briefly and moved to a spot against a nearby wall as players eagerly fell into a buffet line. Staubach, encouraged by Landry's earlier observation to the press, joined the coach. "Do you realized just a year ago today," he said, "I was the starting quarterback of the Pensacola Navy Goshawks against Middle Tennessee State in Murfreesboro, Tennessee? And just think, now I'm getting ready to start for the Dallas Cowboys in the Cotton Bowl against the St. Louis Cardinals."

It was obvious that Landry appreciated neither the irony nor the humor of Staubach's observation. Without a word of acknowledgment, he turned and walked away.

Against the Cardinals, Staubach was determined to hold his ground, to adhere to the game plan Landry and his staff had designed. Nowhere in it was a single play that called for the quarterback to run the ball.

It was late in a scoreless first quarter with the Cowboys at their own 25 when Roger dropped into the pocket and patiently waited while receiver Lance Rentzel broke to the outside, a step ahead of Cardinals defender Lonnie Sanders. Rentzel ran under a well-thrown pass at the 30 and sprinted untouched to complete the 75-yard scoring play.

By intermission, Staubach had not scrambled a single time and the Cowboys led, 7–3.

In the third quarter, Dallas took command as the defense held the Cardinals in check. Calvin Hill, who had been running well all afternoon, threw a 53-yard halfback pass to Rentzel for his second touchdown. Late in the fourth, the Cowboys drove into field goal range for kicker Mike Clark and he upped the margin to 17–3.

After St. Louis fumbled the kickoff, Staubach's primary objective was to take as much time off the clock as possible. Methodically, he moved the team to the Cardinals' 4. On third down, the play sent in by Landry called for reserve running back Les Shy to take a handoff and run to his right. Shy, however, went in the wrong direction, leaving a surprised Staubach holding the ball as blockers moved to his right. Instinctively, he began running to his left, away from the pursuing St. Louis defense. He reached the 2 before avoiding the unsuccessful lunge of Cardinals linebacker Rocky Rosema and fell into the end zone. Staubach had scrambled for the first running touchdown of his pro career. And he had quarterbacked Dallas to a 24–3 victory.

His place in the spotlight would be short-lived, however, as Morton was cleared to play against New Orleans the following week and was named by Landry as the starter. For the remainder of the season, the team belonged to the veteran, while Staubach's role became that of a stand-and-wait student.

And as Dallas strung together six consecutive victories, there was little cause to fault Landry's decision.

If ever there was question about the value the Cowboys coach placed on experience, it became obvious by mid-season. In a 24–17 win over Atlanta, Morton had injured his shoulder. Team doctors examined the damage and suggested that surgery might be necessary. But, told that there was little reason to believe the injury might become more serious if the operation was put off until season's end, Morton opted to continue playing.

While the Cowboys continued to win, Morton's effectiveness tailed off considerably. After completing 70 percent of his passes through the early stages of the year, that number fell dramatically. He rarely threw in practices; in games his once-smooth delivery motion became jerky. Yet it was Morton whom the coach and members of the team felt most comfortable with. And who could argue? The regular season ended with the Cowboys winning the division title as they posted an 11–2–1 record, second best in the NFL.

During the 14 games, Staubach threw a total of only 47 passes.

Despite Morton's growing ineffectiveness, new hope for a championship bloomed. The defense had played exceptionally well, allowing two touchdowns or less in 10 games. And the running game, led by newly crowned Rookie of the Year Hill and the veteran Garrison, had more than compensated for the decline in Morton's passing statistics.

It was a confident Dallas team that prepared to face the Cleveland Browns for the conference championship.

And in front of a sellout crowd that had gathered in a rain-soaked Cotton Bowl three days after Christmas, the Cowboys played their poorest game since the early days of the franchise. When Morton wasn't being intercepted, he was being sacked for huge losses by the Browns' rush. The running game stalled. The proud Dallas defense was riddled by the near-perfect Browns attack. There were fumbles and mishandled punts. In a moment that perfectly captured the Cowboys' futility, Mike Clark advanced on the ball to attempt an on-side kick and completely missed the ball. From the sidelines a Browns player yelled, "Can't you guys do *anything* right?"

The Cleveland margin had grown to 38–7 by the time Landry determined that Morton had had enough and sent Staubach in to finish out the game. Though he was able to connect with Rentzel for a late touchdown, Cleveland won 38–14.

No one was more devastated by the embarrassing loss than Landry. In the postgame dressing room, he looked as if he'd just witnessed a multicar accident, his voice breaking as he spoke. He attempted to assure his players that the team was still on the right course, that there remained cause for an optimistic view of the future. Many listening to the brief speech wondered if the coach was trying to convince them or himself.

"I've never seen anybody so down in my life as Coach Landry was after that game," Staubach later observed in his *First Down, Lifetime to Go*.

All that remained of the shattered season was a required trip to Miami for a game being promoted as the Playoff Bowl, a match-up of the two conference championship losers. The experiment was, in reality, nothing more than the league's boorish attempt to siphon a few more dollars from fans and the broadcast networks. Players were quick to call it what it was—the Loser's Bowl.

Sharing the quarterbacking duties, neither Morton nor Staubach could muster a single score as the lackadaisical Cowboys lost 31–0 to Los Angeles.

Disenchanted Dallas fans were voicing their concern that the only salvation available to the faltering Cowboys hopes was to be quickly rid of its coach and find someone who could win the big game.

Among those who recognized the pain being suffered by Landry was former quarterback Don Meredith. "It was so sad for such a dedicated, disciplined man to wind up in such a situation," he later told the *Fort Worth Star-Telegram*. "Here was a man who devoted ten years to this game, and his philosophy was being challenged and all but destroyed."

Meredith phoned Landry and, for the first time in their lengthy relationship, asked if he might stop by his home for a talk.

The advice he wanted to pass along to Landry was that he "hang it up, forget it, get out."

In truth, it was not something Meredith expected the Cowboys coach to even consider. Landry still had goals to accomplish and, with the manpower he had in place, stubbornly believed they could be reached.

CHAPTER 8

"Craig, I'm glad it's you instead of me going against this guy because anyone who would take a vacation and come to two-a-days has got to be a little weird. He's going to get your job."

Don Meredith

The outcry of disgruntled fans that echoed long after the 1969 season ended might just as well have been yelled down an abandoned tunnel. Owner Clint Murchison had put the issue of who would coach his team to rest back in 1963 when general manager Tex Schramm had come to him with concerns that people were displeased with the progress being made by Landry and the Cowboys. When asked what he felt might be done to calm matters, Murchison's response was quick and definitive. "Let's just give Tom a 10-year contract," he said.

Like it or not, Dallas fans were stuck with Tom Landry. In many football-crazed cities, that would not have been a bad thing. From 1966 through the '69 season, the Cowboys had posted a 42–12–2 record while winning four straight division championships. In Dallas, however, that wasn't good enough.

Landry, meanwhile, had put the disappointing end to the '60s aside and was laying plans for a new decade. Changes were on the way.

During the off-season, he had sent out letters to each member of the team, asking their input on matters ranging from practice procedures to game plans. In an effort to assure candor, a cover letter from the coach requested that all replies be made anonymously.

Staubach, still unfamiliar with many of the traditions of the team, felt unqualified to respond to many of the coach's questions. He did, however, strongly suggest that all players, regardless of position or tenure, be given an opportunity to compete for a starting job.

If the Cowboys were to rebound from the disappointing end of the previous season, changes were necessary in everything from coaching staff responsibilities to revised game plans. High on Landry's list was a new emphasis on a controlling rushing attack that would feature Calvin Hill and Walt Garrison. Gone were many of the deep pass routes previously assigned to Hayes and Rentzel.

Many of the changes encountered by players as they reported to training camp in the summer of 1970 were subtle efforts to ensure a more disciplined approach—fines for not wearing a helmet at all times during practice, etc. One, however, was clearly designed to promote an intensified effort from the players: If, in the opinion of members of the coaching staff, any starter was performing below expectations in practices or games, he could expect to be replaced.

To those who struggled constantly to interpret the subtleties of Landry-speak, it was the answer Staubach had hoped for.

Earlier during a pretraining camp team gathering, he had listened as Landry explained his belief that only veteran quarterbacks could expect to consistently win in the NFL. No one with less than three years experience, he pointed out, had ever won any kind of championship. In response, the impatient Staubach spoke his mind. How, he wanted to know, could Landry judge everyone by the same yardstick? "If you do that, I don't have a chance because I'm just in my second year. You've got to judge everyone individually," he argued.

Later, in private, Landry elaborated on his philosophy of developing a quarterback, explaining the importance of the mental growth necessary to reach a point where reading defenses and getting the most from an offense's potential became second nature.

Staubach remained convinced that he could make up for any short-comings of knowledge with his athletic ability. And, he reasoned, the more he played, the more quickly he would learn.

The preseason performance of the Cowboys, again favored to breeze through their division, fell far shy of expectations. By the time they had struggled through four consecutive exhibition defeats, many of the experts were altering their predictions.

And Landry, true to his promise, was revising his lineup.

Morton had undergone off-season surgery to repair the damage to his shoulder, having a tendon from his ankle transplanted to the area where the separation had occurred, but he was still having difficulties with his delivery. In the process of altering his throwing motion, he had developed a knee problem. His training camp and preseason performance had fallen shy of Landry's expectations.

Thus, as Dallas prepared to open the regular season against Philadelphia, it would be Staubach starting at quarterback. Also temporarily benched was veteran guard Ralph Neely, who was having difficulties adjusting to his move from tackle to guard, and receiver Hayes, who had reported to Thousand Oaks in less-than-peak condition. They were replaced in the starting lineup by Blaine Nye and Dennis Homan, respectively.

When asked about his quarterbacking decision, Landry's comments focused as much on Morton's struggles as Roger's potential. "Craig," he said, "is in a slump. Because of the difficulties he's been having throwing the ball, the pressure has been building for him. Roger's been throwing well, so he'll start in Philadelphia."

Landry gave no indication, however, that the switch would be permanent.

Staubach responded to his opportunity by leading the Cowboys to a 17–7 victory. En route to completing 11-of-15 passes, he had connected with Rentzel for a 31-yard touchdown in the third quarter to break a 7–7 tie. Balancing the offensive attack had been Hill's 117-yard rushing performance.

Roger would remain in the starting job the following week as the Cowboys came from a 10-point halftime deficit to defeat the Giants 28–10. He remembered the day in his autobiography: "I just knew Coach Landry was going to take me out of the game as we walked up the ramp at halftime. 'Coach, please let me play the second half,' I told him. He didn't say a word, but he didn't replace me either.... We came back to win, and I began to think I was on solid ground."

A week later in Busch Memorial Stadium, that perceived solid footing caved in.

After throwing two interceptions against St. Louis in the opening quarter, Staubach was replaced by Morton who, in truth, fared no better. It wasn't until late in the final period that Dallas finally scored. The 20–7 Cardinals victory was more one-sided than the score indicated, raising renewed questions about the direction in which the talented but obviously troubled Cowboys might be headed.

Those questions would grow in volume two weeks later. After Morton had quarterbacked Dallas to a 13–0 victory over Atlanta, the Minnesota Vikings handed the Cowboys their worst loss in the franchise's history.

On an afternoon in Bloomington when everything the Vikings did was right and everything the Cowboys did was wrong, Morton suffered a brutal beating at the hands of the Minnesota front four. By halftime the Cowboys trailed 34–6 and showed no signs of making it a game.

Staubach, who had developed a swelling in his elbow, the result of a series of earlier turf burns, had spent several days in the hospital during the previous week in an effort to control the infection and was not expected to play. With his throwing arm still swollen and heavily taped, he was resigned to watch as the debacle played out.

In the third quarter, however, Morton limped to the sidelines and Staubach entered the game.

His presence made no difference as the Vikings went on to defeat the Cowboys 54–13. In the postgame locker room there was a quiet but growing sense that the season, once so promising, was slipping away.

Four weeks later, it seemed a certainty.

In its never-ending effort to lure more fans to its game, the NFL had joined into a partnership with ABC-TV to break away from the long-standing tradition of Sunday afternoon games and try a revolutionary experiment. The network announced that it would televise a featured game each Monday night, providing a national audience another day of professional football. It would be called *Monday Night Football* and the hype suggested that the folks at home would be treated to a carefully selected championship-caliber match-up each week.

Football-hungry fans immediately embraced the idea. So did players who recognized the opportunity to display their talents in prime time. In the cities where the game would be played, a holiday atmosphere developed as normally blue Mondays were replaced by daylong anticipation. So dedicated would be the audience that restaurants wearied of trying to lure customers from their TV sets and began closing their doors on Monday evenings.

The Cowboys made their debut in the Cotton Bowl with a resounding thud. The St. Louis Cardinals scored a 38–0 victory as Morton, his continuing arm problem obvious, was ineffective. Long before Staubach participated in the final stages of the lost cause, a chant had erupted.

ABC color commentator Don Meredith, joining Keith Jackson and Howard Cosell back in the stadium where he'd played his collegiate and professional football, suffered mightily through the telecast. He still had close friends on the team who were being humiliated and had openly shared in their agony. Then, late in the game, 60,000 disappointed fans turned their eyes toward the press box and began chanting "We want Meredith… we want Meredith."

The signal they were sending was clear. The Cowboys had become a train wreck—a hopelessly lost cause.

Even the eternally optimistic Tom Landry seemed to agree. With a 5–4 record and no sign that improvement was on the way, he all but wrote off the remainder of the season during his short and somber postgame talk with the team. Bob Lilly, in his autobiography, *A Cowboy's Life*, recalled Landry's words, "Maybe this was my fault, I don't know; but it was the worst performance by a Cowboys team that I've ever seen."

On the field the Cowboys were an ongoing disaster; off the field they dissolving into a bad soap opera.

Longtime fans of Bob Hayes had made no secret of their anger over the fact the Cowboys receiver had been benched. Angry calls and letters arrived at team headquarters, demanding that the Olympic champion, the man who had single-handedly caused NFL defenses to change their approach, be given back his rightful place in the lineup. Some even read racial overtones into the fact that the African American Hayes had been replaced by Dennis Homan, a white from Alabama.

Hayes' wife, Altamese, could not even avoid the controversy during short visits to the grocery store.

Eventually, callers found Hayes' home number. At first, they offered messages of sympathetic support. In time, however, the voices became angry.

One evening Hayes listened as several people took turns talking with him. "We're big Cowboys fans," one caller said, "and we're going to get even with Tom Landry for you. We're going to bomb his house. If that doesn't work, we'll bomb his car. Maybe we'll even bomb Tex Schramm's house."

Stunned by the threats, Hayes attempted without success to reason with the callers. He phoned player personnel director Gil Brandt to inform him of the situation and ask what he should do. Brandt said he would alert the Cowboys organization, then voiced his opinion that the callers were most likely just blowing off steam. He suggested that Hayes not mention the incident to anyone else. "But," Brandt added, "if you hear from them again, let me know right away."

A few days later, another voice on the phone made it clear that Hayes was to make a decision to "either be with us or against us." If the latter was the case, he was told, his wife and newly adopted daughter might even be kidnapped.

And the caller warned that under no circumstances was Hayes to alert the Cowboys or contact the police.

Thinking that it might well be extortionists rather than fans with whom he was dealing, Hayes asked if the callers would take some money in exchange for leaving him and the Cowboys organization alone.

"How much?" one of the callers asked.

Hayes responded that he had only $200 cash at his house.

He was instructed where to leave the money, and just before midnight, took it to the playground of a nearby elementary school. It was the last he would ever hear from them. While the FBI would later look into the matter, it was never able to determine the identity of the anonymous callers.

Law enforcement officials were, however, to discover a tormenting problem that Hayes' fellow receiver Rentzel had been secretly living with for years. Following the earlier loss to Minnesota, he had driven to the campus of a Dallas girls school and waited until the children came into the playground for recess. There, he had exposed himself to a 10-year-old girl. The child was able to provide authorities with a description of her assailant and the car he had driven away in.

In the weeks that followed, the police carried out their investigation and finally arrested Rentzel, charging him with indecent exposure.

During a team meeting, he tearfully stood before his teammates and admitted his problem and described the event that had led to his arrest. While the players voted to allow him to remain with the team, Schramm and Landry overruled the decision and placed Rentzel on the inactive reserve list.

Ultimately, he would plead guilty to his crime and receive a five-year probated sentence and agree to court-ordered psychiatric counseling. Before the next season, he would be traded to the Los Angeles Rams.

Following the devastating loss to the Cardinals, the players held a meeting of a different sort. With no coaches in attendance, they openly discussed their dilemma. Ralph Neely described the event for *Cowboys Have Always Been My Heroes* author Peter Golenbock:

"We got together and I said, 'Hey guys, there is no one pulling for us but us, the guys right here in this room. Hell, the coaches aren't pulling for us. They've already given up. Most of the wives have given up. We know damn well the press has been against us forever, so they're not pulling for us. And most of the fans are not excited about us anymore.' I said, 'Guys, it's going to happen right here in this room, or it's not going to happen.' Several of us talked. We said, 'We are going to do it for us, not for anybody else, not for the coaches or the fans or Tex or anybody else.' We were going to do it for us."

In the aftermath of the Monday night disaster, there was no talk of the importance of making stretch drives, no visible urgency to set things right. The players, it appeared, were correct: All but them had given up on the season. Landry, apparently feeling that his hardnosed approach to preparation had backfired badly, eased off considerably.

And why not? His team's hopes were circling the drain, his quarterback's physical problems seemed only to get worse with each passing week, and Calvin Hill, the heart of the running game, had injured his back. Garrison was limping. Landry's Flex defense was being called into question even by those assigned to carry out its complicated requirements. On and on the negatives went.

As the team met to begin preparation for a visit to RFK Stadium to face the Redskins, Landry informed them that the order of the day would be a free-for-all game of pass-touch. For the remainder of the season, he promised, practices and meetings would be drastically shortened.

And to take some game-day pressure off Morton, Landry announced he would call the quarterback's plays for the remainder of the season, shuttling them to the huddle with tight ends Ditka and Pettis Norman.

The given-up-for-dead Cowboys responded with a 45–21 victory over Washington. Thereafter they stunned the critics with a string of five consecutive victories that enabled them to finish the regular season at 10–4. Their record was one win better than the Giants and two better than the Cardinals who had gone into an unexplained nosedive in the final weeks of the season.

By the time Dallas defeated the Houston Oilers 52–10 in the game that clinched the division championship, Cotton Bowl fans were again cheering. Morton, despite his physical problems, threw for 349 yards and five touchdowns, four of them caught by a forgiven Bob Hayes.

Equally important, the defense had come back to life, giving up only 15 points in Dallas' final four games.

And there was a new face that gave new cause for excitement. Rookie Duane Thomas, a moody but talented running back who had played his college ball in the obscurity of little West Texas State University, had filled in for the injured Hill and gained more than 800 yards after having become a starter in the fifth game of the season.

Staubach, meanwhile, fretted as a bystander throughout the remarkable Cowboys comeback. One of the few things Landry had not reevaluated during those dark mid-season days was his firm belief that the team's best chance of victory was with an experienced quarterback directing the offense.

The old football axiom that a superior defense wins championships was never more true than in Dallas' playoff win over wildcard Detroit. On a rain-soaked Cotton Bowl turf, the Cowboys held the Lions to only 156 total yards as quarterback Greg Landry was constantly hurried by the Dallas front four. And with Morton unable to throw effectively, the Cowboys offense controlled the ball with Thomas runs.

The hosts took a three-point lead on a 26-yard Mike Clark field goal in the first quarter and were unable to add to their point total until the final period when George Andrie and Jethro Pugh tackled Landry in his own end zone for a safety.

Detroit's lone threat came in the final minutes of the game as Bill Munson, substituting for the badly beaten Landry, drove the visitors to the Dallas 29 with 54 seconds remaining before Mel Renfro made a game-ending interception.

The Cowboys' 5–0 victory marked the first time in NFL playoff history than neither team had scored a single touchdown.

A week later in San Francisco's Kezar Stadium, it was strong-armed John Brodie and the 49ers, the NFL's top scoring team, who felt the wrath of the revitalized Dallas defense. The media was predicting a game that would match Brodie's passing strength against a Cowboys running game that featured Thomas and Garrison. What it didn't know was that

Garrison, suffering with back spasms, cracked ribs, and a badly swollen ankle, was a doubtful participant until insisting to Landry just minutes before kickoff that he was ready to play.

While it was the Dallas ground attack that would ultimately win the day, it was the defense that again paved the way. With the score tied at 3–3 at halftime, the Cowboys had played 23 consecutive quarters without giving up a single touchdown.

In the second half, linebacker Lee Roy Jordan intercepted Brodie and returned the ball to the 49ers 13-yard line. From there Thomas ran it in for the day's first touchdown. Later, following a grinding Dallas drive, Garrison scored on a five-yard pass from Morton. By the time Brodie finally threw for a score to narrow the margin to 17–10, the game was decided.

For the afternoon, Thomas had rushed for 143 yards, and Garrison added 71. The battered Cowboys fullback was in such pain by the time the game ended that he needed the assistance of teammates and trainers to get to the dressing room.

Staubach had entered the game for only one play while Morton was briefly sidelined following a jarring tackle. Roger handed off the ball to Thomas for a short gain and returned to the sidelines to await the celebration.

The Cowboys, after a long and winding season of frustration, doubt, and controversy, were finally going to the Super Bowl.

Unusually emotional after the game, Landry broke into a broad smile. "You don't know how good this feels," he said.

Though swept along in the celebration of the milestone accomplishment, Staubach could not help but judge his personal achievements during the season a disappointment. As the team prepared to leave for Miami and the Orange Bowl, he knew full well that he would just be along for the ride.

There remained no question that Landry had decided that the Cowboys would end the season as Craig Morton's team.

Few knew the stubborn determination Morton had invested in the season better than Staubach. To keep his job, he had put off needed surgery on his elbow, had suffered the boos in the Cotton Bowl, endured embarrassing defeats, and directed wins for which the defense got far more credit than he did. More than once he had excused himself from the weekly film reviews of the previous Sunday's game, his stomach in knots, feeling a rush of nausea coming on. So desperate was he to improve that he would eventually visit a Dallas hypnotist in an effort to retain a positive mindset.

Although Morton stood in the way of his goal to become the Cowboys' quarterback, Staubach had great admiration for his rival. Despite his public image as a man-about-town playboy, Morton was a fierce competitor. And he knew Roger, family man and straight-laced, was a competitor as well. From their mutual admiration had grown a genuine friendship.

When *Sports Illustrated*, in its preview of Super Bowl V, labeled the Cowboys as "a team without a quarterback," Roger found the assessment insulting on several levels. First, it overlooked the fact Craig had played through pain and injury to get Dallas into the championship game. Second, it completely overlooked the fact that he was the backup, fully capable of leading the team.

Still, in the minds of most, the game would be a duel between legendary Baltimore quarterback Johnny Unitas and Dallas' newly respected defense. Morton, the experts had decided, would not likely be a factor.

For all the hype and hoopla that preceded the game, it was left to Cowboys rookie Thomas to put things into perspective. When a member of the media asked how he felt about playing in football's ultimate game, he responded with a quizzical look. "The ultimate game?" he said. "They're playing it again next year, aren't they?"

Predictably, Dallas opened the game with a ball-control running attack that featured Thomas, advancing to the Colts' 14-yard line before Mike Clark came on to kick a field goal. Unitas, meanwhile, was having difficulties with the Cowboys defense during the early going and gave up an early interception to linebacker Chuck Howley.

As the first quarter drew to an end, Morton connected with Hayes on an unexpected deep pass to the Baltimore 12. There, however, the drive stalled, and as the second quarter got underway, Clark came on to kick his second field goal of the afternoon.

Then things would take a zany turn that would last throughout the remainder of the game. Facing a third-and-10 situation, Unitas dropped into the pocket and threw over the middle in the direction of wide receiver Eddie Hinton. Breaking in front of free safety Mel Renfro and cornerback Cornell Green, Hinton managed to get a hand on the overthrown ball but couldn't make the catch. Instead, it caromed in the direction of the Cowboys defenders and ultimately into the hands of Colts tight end John Mackey. Mackey raced to the end zone untouched for a 75-yard touchdown.

Field judge Fritz Graf ruled that Renfro had tipped the ball before it reached Mackey's arms, thus making it a legal catch. Without success, a furious Renfro argued that he never touched the ball and thus the pass should have been ruled incomplete. (Rules then stated that a ball tipped directly from one offensive player to another is to be ruled incomplete. If, on the other hand, an offensive players tips a ball and it is then touched by a member of the defense, it again is judged a "live" ball that can be caught by a second member of the offense.)

Mackey's bizarre catch-and-run score stood. Cowboys defender Mark Washington then blocked the Colts' extra-point attempt to leave the score tied at 6–6.

Misfortune next visited Baltimore as the 37-year-old Unitas was hit by Lee Roy Jordan and Howley, fumbling at his own 28. Morton completed a 17-yard pass to running back Dan Reeves, then on a similar play connected with Thomas for a touchdown. Clark's conversion put Dallas into a 13–6 lead.

Then in the bizarre routine that was fast being established, the Colts suffered a blow that seemed to turn things in the Cowboys' favor. In the second quarter, Unitas' protection broke down again and he was hit by George Andrie just as he released the ball. As his pass was being intercepted, the Colts quarterback lay on the ground, the victim of a cracked rib that would force him to the sidelines for the remainder of the game.

And with Earl Morrall in for Unitas, the crazy bounces continued in the early stages of the second half. The Colts' return specialist Jim Duncan fumbled the kickoff, and Richmond Flowers recovered for Dallas at Baltimore's 31.

The Cowboys quickly began driving toward a touchdown that would, in all likelihood, settle the issue. From the Colts 1-yard line, Thomas was straining to make his way into the end zone when linebacker Mike Curtis managed to pull the ball from his grasp. Suddenly there was a mass of bodies frantically fighting for possession of the ball. Colts tackle Billy Ray Smith began yelling, "Our ball!" Referee Jack Fette agreed.

Ironically, it was Duncan, who had earlier fumbled the kickoff, who was officially credited with the crucial recovery despite the fact he was nowhere near the ball when it occurred.

Films and still photographs that were viewed days later showed an entirely different sequence of events. As Curtis pulled the ball from Thomas, it had hit the ground and bounced directly into the arms of Cowboys center Dave Manders who had quickly disappeared into the melee. Once officials untangled the players, it had been Manders who handed the ball to the referee.

Baltimore's phantom recovery would change the tenor of the game as the Colts had soon pulled into a 13–13 tie late in the game.

With just over a minute remaining, Morton was forced to abandon the running game and attempt to pass the Cowboys into field-goal range. A throw to running back Reeves glanced off the receiver's hands and into the arms of Baltimore middle linebacker Curtis. He returned it to the Dallas 28, and with the final seconds ticking away, Jim O'Brien kicked a field goal that provided the Colts a 16–13 victory.

Bob Lilly, who had endured the early dog days of the franchise, then the disappointments against Green Bay and Cleveland, removed his helmet and launched it halfway down the field in frustration.

There had been 11 turnovers during the course of the game—five lost fumbles, six interceptions—that some media cynics would call it the Blooper Bowl.

Landry didn't agree. "We're disappointed," he acknowledged afterward, "But you can't play much better defense than we did." The fact that linebacker Howley, who had made two interceptions and recovered a fumble, was named the game's Most Valuable Player—the first member of a losing team ever to receive the award—strongly punctuated Landry's assessment.

Standing in front of his locker, Jordan's head was high as he spoke with *Dallas Times Herald* beat writer Steve Perkins. "We're coming back," Jordan said. "We've got a great bunch of people. We're playing defense. All we need is a passing game."

Author Joe Gergen would later note that of the 40 players on Dallas' roster that day, only two did not get into the game. One was backup quarterback Roger Staubach.

As the team charter made its way back to Dallas, Landry briefly mingled among the players. He suggested to Staubach that he work particularly hard during the off-season. "I think," the coach said, "you can make your move this coming year."

The following day, just 48 hours after Super Bowl V had ended, Roger was the lone player on the Cowboys practice field, the solitary quiet broken only by the constant thud of a football as it repeatedly hit a large target board.

CHAPTER 9

"Talk about American heroes, this was direct from Central Casting in Hollywood. This was Ronald Reagan, James Cagney, Fred Astaire, and John Wayne wrapped up, bundled, given athletic skills beyond imagination of scriptwriters, and renamed. After all, he couldn't be Ron-Jim-Fred-John, not even in Texas, where the legend was going to reach full fruition. So they called him Roger Staubach."

Author Dave Klein

It was mid-summer when sportswriter Steve Perkins visited the office of Tom Landry to listen to the coach's thoughts about the Cowboys' fast-approaching return to training camp. Generally, Landry said, he was pleased with the look of his team that had come together in the final stages of the previous season. His defense, he acknowledged, should again be outstanding. It was the offense that had obviously occupied much of his thought during the off-season.

"This year," Landry told Perkins, who was gathering material for a *Dallas Times Herald* story as well as a book he was planning to write, "we'll concentrate on the passing game. Mainly because of Craig's arm trouble, it was below par last season, though that wasn't all of it. We have to reestablish a leader at quarterback, like Meredith was on this team. A leader has to be a performer. Craig hung in there tough in a trying situation last season, which was a big plus for him. But he has to deliver, as he's capable of doing. I have to assume he'll be 100 percent physically, but I know only the throwing demands of training camp will answer that.

"It's not that clear cut. If Roger is ever going to do it, he'll make a go of it this year. I said three years ago that this is the year he could make his move to take over as starting quarterback, and let me tell you—he dies hard. When he competes, he really competes. The only thing to do is let them prove it on the field. I've planned all winter to alternate them as starters in the preseason, leading off with Morton against the Rams. You just hope that somebody will move the other guy out and establish himself as number one without question."

Landry, then, was acknowledging what many longtime Cowboys followers had come to believe. As the team would soon begin preparing for yet another try at football's brass ring, it remained, in the mind of many, the eternal Next Year's Champion—a team of rare promise and unique talent but with some magical ingredient still missing.

That missing magic was at the quarterback position.

In the imperfect world of professional football, however, things are never as simple as choosing the starter at a single position, even quarterback. The Cowboys had much more than a Morton-Staubach face-off to consider.

While the quarterback situation was paramount, the question of just who Morton and/or Staubach would have as targets was equally interesting. Rentzel was off to the Rams to attempt to rebuild his life and football career, and Hayes, still unhappy over having spent so much time in Landry's doghouse in 1970, was seeking a new and better contract if he was to remain in Dallas.

In an effort to resolve the problems, Dallas went into what, for it, was a shopping frenzy. A trade with San Diego sent tight end Pettis Norman and linemen Ron East and Tony Liscio west in exchange for Chargers wide receiver Lance Alworth. From Kansas City they got flanker Gloster Richardson. The Rams had sent tight end Billy Truax in exchange for Rentzel. And the Cowboys ultimately made Hayes one of the highest-paid receivers in the NFL.

That was the easy part.

Petulant running back Duane Thomas, honored as the National Football Conference Rookie of the Year at the end of the 1970 season, was unhappy with the three-year contract he'd signed after being the team's No. 1 draft selection and threatening not to play if it was not torn up and renegotiated. During a July press conference, he lashed out at the Cowboys organization, calling Landry "a plastic man, no man at all," Gil Brandt a "liar," and Schramm "sick, demented, and completely dishonest." Schramm, hearing how he had been described, smiled and replied, "That's not bad. He got two out of three."

The battle between Thomas and the Cowboys, however, was far from a laughing matter. Once the brightest new star in the Dallas galaxy, a player with unlimited potential, he had alienated all around him except for a cadre of "advisors" who had managed to succeed in turning not only Dallas fans but many of his own teammates against him.

By the time training camp was underway, Thomas was still a holdout and Schramm, weary of the distraction, traded the discontented player to New England. In exchange, Dallas would get Patriots running back Carl Garrett.

Garrett was thrilled. Upon his arrival in Thousand Oaks, he told members of the media that he was delighted. "This year," he said, "I'll finally have some blocking in front of me."

Thomas, meanwhile, was not nearly so happy in his new surroundings. When the Patriots coaches attempted to alter his stance, he walked out of training camp, making it clear he was no happier as a Patriot than he'd been as a Cowboy. The trade was negated, and Garrett went back to New England to apologize to his offensive linemen. Thomas, bitter and non-communicative, first declared himself retired, then with the season already underway he reluctantly agreed to return to the Cowboys.

Once he did, he refused to speak with the press and isolated himself from his teammates.

Staubach later reflected on Thomas' strange behavior in his autobiography, *Time Enough to Win*, "He just withdrew from everybody. He simply went into a private shell that no one could penetrate. I tried. So did others. None of us got through."

What was most perplexing to Roger was the fact that Thomas had what he sorely wanted—a starting role, the rare opportunity to showcase his talent every Sunday afternoon.

Throughout training camp, it was clear that Staubach had prepared himself for the challenge. His passes had a zip and accuracy that Morton's lacked. And during scrimmages, he demonstrated that he had made considerable progress in recognizing defenses. Yet if Landry had chosen a favorite, he wasn't letting on, staying with his plan to alternate the quarterbacks in each of the preseason games before making a decision.

Those exhibitions, routinely dreaded by most players, would, Roger felt, be the most important of his brief professional career.

Dallas went through the six-game preseason schedule undefeated as both quarterbacks played well, with Staubach maintaining a slight statistical edge over Morton. In his three games, Roger completed 53 percent of his passes for 714 yards and six touchdowns. Morton's score sheet showed a 50.6 percent completion rate for 618 yards and two touchdowns.

In his regular Tuesday press conference before the opening of the regular season, Landry finally announced his decision.

"When we opened training camp," he told the collection of writers and media reporters, "each quarterback had something to accomplish. Morton took a lot of criticism last year because he couldn't throw. He had to reestablish his confidence, and I'm very satisfied that he has.

"Staubach had to make great strides in experience and know-how to offset Morton's experience. He doesn't yet have Morton's grasp, but he has enough for us to win. He can read defenses, doesn't scramble as much, and shows poise.

"On a competitive basis, Roger has a slight edge in the categories we consider most important. But he doesn't have a clear-cut advantage."

With that Landry announced a decision no one, including the two contenders for the job, had anticipated. The '71 Cowboys, Landry said, would have *two* starting quarterbacks. The preseason routine of one playing one week, the other the next, would continue.

Morton, who felt he had shown himself to be back to the form of his preinjury days, judged the idea unfair and a demotion. Staubach, privately feeling he had won the job under the rules Landry had set forth before training camp, wasn't much happier.

The reaction of the team, meanwhile, was mixed. Some favored the experienced Morton, others felt Staubach would breathe new life into the offense. Virtually everyone was surprised at Landry's hesitancy to make a more definitive decision. Among the most outspoken critics of the announcement was former Cowboys quarterback Don Meredith. "It's Landry's responsibility as head coach to pick a quarterback," the ABC commentator later told a nationwide audience. "After all this time, if he has no idea which one is best, then get another coach."

As the team prepared to visit Buffalo for the regular-season opener against the Bills, Landry's plan for Staubach to start the game was changed at the last minute. Roger had suffered a broken blood vessel in his right leg during the final preseason game with Kansas City and was still limping slightly during the first of the week's practices. Explaining that the problem appeared to be minor, Landry said he still didn't want to risk the possibility that the injury might develop into something that could sideline his quarterback for several weeks. The prudent thing would be to flip-flop his order, letting Morton open against the Bills. Staubach would get his chance the following week against Philadelphia.

The coach reemphasized that he was only being cautious. Some, however, viewed the decision as a lingering reluctance to take the offensive reins from the more experienced of his two quarterbacks.

Morton seized the opportunity, leading the Cowboys to a 49–37 shootout victory. With the late-arriving Thomas still waiting to be cleared from the "retired" list by the NFL front office, Hill and Garrison demonstrated that the Dallas running game was in fine shape without him. Calvin ran for 84 yards and four touchdowns, and Garrison rushed for 78. When they weren't running through the dazed Bills defense, Morton was enjoying an outstanding game passing. En route to completing 10-of-14 for 221 yards, he connected with Hayes for a 76-yard touchdown and a 19-yard score to Reggie Rucker.

While Buffalo quarterback Dennis Shaw constantly confused the Cowboys secondary, throwing four touchdown passes during the offensive free-for-all, celebrated Bills running back O.J. Simpson could gain but 25 yards on 14 carries.

A week later it was Staubach's turn. On his fourth passing attempt, he was intercepted. To complicate matters, he lay unconscious immediately afterward. Just as he released the ball, Eagles defensive end Mel Tom had reached him, spun him around, and delivered a malicious elbow to the side of his head. The play would eventually cost Tom a $1,000 fine levied by the league office. It also cost Staubach a first chance to prove himself in a starting role.

Morton came on to direct an easy 42–7 victory and after the first two weeks of the new season was the No. 1–ranked quarterback in the NFL.

Though Tom's blindside blow had denied Roger a legitimate opportunity against the Eagles, Landry stubbornly kept to his alternating plan and announced that Craig would quarterback against Washington. One of the preseason selections to contend for the division title, the veteran Redskins would, the coach anticipated, be a far more formidable foe and privately felt Morton's experience would be needed.

Experience was an ingredient George Allen, who had moved from Los Angeles to coach Washington, obsessively valued above all else. Whenever the opportunity presented itself, he collected the aging cast-offs of other teams in the belief that he could summon one more good season from them. Ignoring the concept of eventually developing young players into winners, his rallying cry was, "The future is now," and his team prided itself on being called The Over-the-Hill Gang.

Allen, who had never attempted to hide his disdain for the Cowboys, delighted as his team built a 17–9 advantage by the end of the third quarter. When Landry substituted Staubach for the ineffective Morton, things didn't get much better. Roger managed to direct a late Dallas touchdown drive, but by then the outcome was obvious. The Redskins won 20–16, and new volume was added to the Cowboys' quarterback controversy.

Playing before a *Monday Night Football* audience in the Cotton Bowl the following week, Dallas started slowly, playing the role of its own worst enemy. After once reaching the Giants' 4-yard line, Roger fumbled the ball away. Hill also committed a costly fumble and passes were either off-target or dropped. Despite getting into scoring range on four occasions, there was little rhythm to the offense. Still, Staubach's touchdown throw to Billy Truax just before halftime put the Cowboys into a 13–6 lead.

And in the dressing room, Landry told the team that Morton would start the second half.

Morton wasn't the only new face in the Cowboys backfield as the third quarter began. Thomas replaced Garrison at fullback and looked like anything but a player who hadn't spent a minute in training camp preparing for the moment. He averaged 6.7 yards on his nine carries and provided devastating blocks for Hill. When Calvin left with a knee injury, Thomas remained at fullback with Dan Reeves filling in at Hill's spot for the remainder of the game. In the press box, however, the buzz about Thomas soon becoming the team's running back had already begun.

Meanwhile, Morton and Hayes combined on a 48-yard touchdown that gave the Cowboys a 20–13 victory.

When reporters approached him with questions about Landry replacing him in the second half, Staubach's answer was one he'd never before given to a member of the press. "No comment," he said. For the first time since joining the Cowboys, he felt he'd been treated unfairly.

Across the room, Landry's explanation to reporters was simple. "I just felt we should have been ahead by more than 13–6 at the half," he said.

The dressing room had all but cleared when the coach approached Roger. Staubach was already shaking his head as Landry walked toward him. "Coach," he said, "don't say anything. What you did to me out there wasn't called for. You'll never understand me."

Later, in his *First Down, Lifetime to Go*, Staubach remembered his feelings. "I thought I deserved a chance to go all the way. I felt my play had picked up near the end of the first half, and I could have come back strong. I was very confused and discouraged. I didn't even know if I was going to practice that next week. I was thinking how Coach Landry didn't believe in me and was just waiting to get Craig back in there."

Which is exactly where Morton was the following Sunday as the Cowboys hosted the New Orleans Saints. It was, after all, his turn to start. This time, however, he would be the one pulled from the game after an unproductive first half. With Dallas trailing 17–0, Staubach came on to throw touchdown passes to Gloster Richardson and Bob Hayes. Still, the Cowboys lost 24–14, and at 3–2 for the season, were fast losing ground in the division race to the Redskins.

As the Cowboys prepared to host the New England Patriots, at least one long-standing feud—this one between the team's owner and the city of Dallas—had finally come to an end. For several years, Clint Murchison had argued that the Cotton Bowl, despite its long and colorful history, had become outdated, downtrodden, and unwelcoming to fans. He urged the city fathers to consider building a new stadium at a location near the downtown area. After his urgings continued to fall on deaf ears, he purchased land in the nearby suburb of Irving and ordered construction of a facility that would be the envy of all others in the NFL.

The grand opening of state-of-the-art Texas Stadium, a $25 million facility complete with a synthetic turf field, luxury boxes, and an unusual hole in its roof that allowed the unique fan experience of sitting indoors while watching a game being played outdoors, was full-bore Texas. Bands played, balloons were released, and joining the celebrities in the sellout crowd were former U.S. President Lyndon Johnson and wife Lady Bird.

The Cowboys responded with a 44–21 victory that not only breathed a new sense of optimism into the team but provided Staubach his first giant step toward his goal. Twice he connected with Hayes for long touchdowns, and ran for one himself. By day's end, he had completed 13-of-21 passes for 197 yards.

In the dressing room afterward, President Johnson shook his hand. "Son," he said, "you sure know how to break in a new stadium."

Any euphoria that Staubach might have felt in the aftermath of his performance against the Patriots disappeared during a team meeting the following week. Landry praised the performances of both quarterbacks, then stunned everyone in the room by announcing that against the Chicago Bears the following Sunday, they would alternate on each offensive play. No longer would the tight ends serve as in-and-out play messengers. Landry would give the play directly to whichever quarterback was standing next him on the sidelines. While he was on the field, carrying out the play, the other quarterback would await Landry's orders. It was a system the Cowboys coach had unsuccessfully attempted with early days quarterbacks Eddie LeBaron and Meredith. It hadn't worked then. And there were few hearing the news who believed it would now.

Morton and Staubach looked at each other in disbelief. While Landry explained that the shuttle system would allow the opportunity for him and the quarterback to discuss down-and-distance situations, defensive alignments, and the proper play to be called, neither player believed it could work. No productive rhythm, they felt, was possible unless a player could get into the flow of a game. Talking over the matter following the meeting, both admitted their disappointment in the plan, then resigned themselves to try and make it work.

It didn't. Despite the fact the Cowboys generated 481 yards of total offense, the Bears won 23–19. By the end of the game, it appeared that even Landry had judged the experiment a failure. In the final minutes, with a chance to still win, he had deserted the shuttle and left Morton on the field in a failed attempt to rally the offense.

To Staubach, those final minutes in Soldier Field signaled more than the end of the short-lived shuttle system. It indicated to him that Landry felt the Cowboys' best chance of winning through the remainder of the season was with Morton quarterbacking.

With the season half over, a confused and despondent Dallas team trailed division leader Washington by two games. And things would get worse. Tackle Ralph Neely, taking advantage of a postgame day off, had broken his leg during a dirt bike accident and would be lost for the remainder of the year. To fill his spot, the Cowboys persuaded 31-year-old Tony Liscio out of retirement.

It was a distraught and discouraged team that looked ahead to its game against the St. Louis Cardinals.

Staubach received an out-of-the-blue phone call that proved even more important than the one he'd received as a rookie-to-be, alerting him to Meredith's surprising decision to retire.

There had been nothing about that Tuesday's practice to indicate that the course of Roger's life was about to take a dramatic turn. Morton had worked with the first team, and Staubach had returned home convinced that his playing time in the upcoming game against the Cardinals would be, at best, limited.

Until Landry called. "Roger," the coach said, "I've made a decision. I've decided you're going to be the starting quarterback for the rest of the season."

For a moment Staubach was too stunned to speak. Then he replied, "Coach, I really appreciate that. I won't let you down."

From that brief conversation, a new era of Dallas Cowboys football was born.

The same critics who had railed against Landry's earlier indecisiveness now questioned whether his plan to make Staubach his starter signaled a give-up attitude toward the remainder of the season. "There's no doubt that our backs are to the wall," the coach admitted. "If we lose in St. Louis, our season will be finished as far as any championship hope is concerned."

The Cardinals and Cowboys were tied 13–13 late in the fourth quarter when Dallas' new quarterback previewed the unique energy he had promised to deliver to the team. Deep in his own end of the field and facing a third-down situation, he connected with Alworth to keep the drive alive. Then he threw to Truax for a big gain. He scrambled for 15. And with less than two minutes remaining, former Austrian soccer player Toni Fritsch came into his first-ever pro football game to make the difference. Called up from the team's practice squad to replace Mike Clark, who had missed on three field-goal attempts against Chicago, Fritsch kicked a 27-yarder that was the game-winner.

The following week, Staubach completed 14-of-28 passes for 176 yards and ran for 90 in a relatively easy 20–7 win over Philadelphia to set up a showdown match-up with the Redskins. Dallas, with its 6–3 record, would go into the game trailing Washington 6–2–1 by a half game in the NFC East race. The winner would take sole possession of the division lead.

The Cowboys defense responded with its finest game of the year, holding the fading Redskins scoreless. When Alworth was covered on a deep route that Landry had called in the first quarter, Staubach managed to elude the grasp of Washington defender Diron Talbert and started running. His 29-yard touchdown and two later field goals by Clark, back in his role as kicker after Fritch had suffered a hamstring pull in practice, were all Dallas needed.

Afterward, Washington coach Allen expressed his disappointment in the loss. "The only difference in the two teams," he observed, "was Staubach."

For the remainder of the season, the tiring Over-the-Hill Gang would not be a factor. The once-struggling Cowboys, meanwhile, were gaining momentum.

On Thanksgiving Day, they defeated the Rams 28–21 despite a remarkable passing day by Los Angeles quarterback Roman Gabriel. Avoiding relentless pressure from the Cowboys rush, he completed 20-of-35 attempts, one a 41-yarder to former Cowboy Lance Rentzel that set up a touchdown. Staubach, however, matched Gabriel's long-ball efforts with a 51-yard scoring throw to Hayes, then a 21-yarder to Alworth. Dallas' running game, featuring Thomas and Garrison, did the rest. The final score was not a proper indication of the manner in which the Cowboys offense had dominated.

In the final three games of the season, Dallas scored 52 points against the New York Jets, 42 against the Giants, and 31 in their win over the

Cardinals to end the year with seven straight victories and the NFC title. During that stretch, Staubach threw nine touchdown passes.

As the team looked ahead to its return to the playoffs, the awards began to flow. Tackle Rayfield Wright and guard John Niland were named to several All-Pro teams, as were defensive standouts Lilly and Mel Renfro. Though he would not be recognized on any All-Pro lists, Staubach was named the winner of the Maxwell Club's Bert Bell Award, given annually to the NFL's most outstanding player. And he would be joining teammates selected to play in the Pro Bowl. He had ended the season with the highest ranking of any quarterback in the league and had set a new club record by completing 59.7 percent of his passes. Interceptions had become a rarity.

More importantly, he had won the confidence of the team he was now leading.

The individual honors bestowed on the players were a reflection of the impressive achievements of the team. Over the course of the 14-game season, Dallas' offense had scored 406 points, more than any other in the NFL, led the league in total yards gained (5,035), and had scored more rushing touchdowns than all others. The passing game had produced 22 touchdowns, tops in the NFC. Defensively, the Cowboys had given up only 1,144 yards rushing and had caused a league-high 40 fumbles, 25 of which they had recovered.

As they traveled to Bloomington, Minnesota, for the Christmas Day division championship game against the Vikings, there was a differ-ent attitude. Businesslike, focused, and quietly sure of themselves, the Cowboys had evolved into a team that simply refused to entertain any doubts that they were the best in the NFL. And, at long last, the time had come to prove it.

The process began on a snow-banked, 25-degree day in Metropolitan Stadium.

Minnesota came into the game with the same won-lost record the Cowboys had posted, and their defense was considered by many to be the best in the league, having allowed opponents an average of just 10 points per game. Analysts were hard-pressed to find an edge for either team. The home-field advantage might benefit the Vikings, but only slightly. Personnel-wise, the match-ups were pretty much a wash, except at one position. Vikings coach Bud Grant had, like Landry, spent the early part of the season attempting to choose a starting quarterback. At various points, he had used three—Gary Cuozzo, Norm Snead, and finally Bob Lee. Lee would be the starter against the Cowboys, directing an offense with big-play promise despite having ranked eighteenth in the final league standings. The majority of the sportswriters previewing the game felt Staubach, with his arsenal of pounding backs and long ball receivers, gave Dallas an edge.

The general consensus was that for the Vikings to win, its famed Purple People Eaters defense would have to rule the day.

Instead, it was Dallas' Doomsday Defense that stepped up. On the Vikings' first possession, Larry Cole ran down running back Dave Osborn, forcing a fumble that was recovered by Jethro Pugh. Staubach quickly completed an 18-yard pass to Hayes to set up the day's first points, a 26-yard Mike Clark field goal.

Later, after Minnesota had tied the score, Lee attempted to avoid a Dallas blitz and lobbed a short safety-valve pass in the direction of Osborn. Linebacker Howley intercepted and returned the ball 26 yards to the Vikings' 37. Clark then kicked a 44-yard field goal that gave Dallas a 6–3 halftime lead.

In a game that Landry had predicted would necessitate great patience from his offense, the Cowboys had hardly been flashy, posting only three first downs during the first half. But they had managed to score each time their defense had provided them an opportunity.

The same would be the case as the third quarter got underway. Safety Cliff Harris intercepted a Lee pass and returned it to the Minnesota 13-yard line. On the next play, Thomas followed a thundering block on the middle linebacker by Dave Manders to score Dallas' first touchdown.

It was a Charlie Waters punt return that put the Cowboys into position for its final score of the afternoon. The exhausted Vikings defense chased a scrambling Staubach as he waited for a receiver to get open. Finally, Hayes got a step on his defender, and Roger threw to him for a touchdown.

The Vikings managed a safety midway through the final period, then a meaningless touchdown with just two minutes left to narrow the final margin to 20–12.

In the visiting dressing room, the Cowboys took an almost muted approach to the victory. The celebration was brief. The day's work had been done; another roadblock had been cleared, and it was time to get back home and prepare for what lay ahead. Instead of dwelling on the win over the Vikings, they talked of the next week's likely NFC Championship game foe, San Francisco.

The primary challenge it posed, they knew, would be more difficult—stop 49ers quarterback John Brodie.

On the West Coast, the San Francisco defense was voicing a similar concern. To have a chance to win, it would have to contain the elusive Staubach.

An interesting subplot played out in the Cowboys-49ers meeting in Texas Stadium. San Francisco coach Dick Nolan and Landry were defensive teammates with the New York Giants during their playing days, and the two had almost identical philosophies. Nolan, in fact, had been the only other coach in the league who had adopted Landry's controversial and often perplexing Flex defense.

The Cowboys, however, had been playing it much longer and were verging on perfection.

Early in the second quarter, Brodie attempted a screen pass from his own 14-yard line and was intercepted by George Andrie who returned it to the two. From there, Hill scored. By halftime, the 49ers had managed only one first down. The difference was the unrelenting Dallas rush that repeatedly caused Brodie to throw quickly and off-target. In the third quarter, however, he finally managed a long completion to tight end Ted Kwalick that set up a 28-yard San Francisco field goal.

With the defense having done its job, it was time for the Dallas offense to step up. A 7–3 lead against a quarterback of Brodie's status was hardly a guarantee of victory.

Early in the final quarter, Staubach and the Cowboys launched an 80-yard, seven-minute drive that showcased their myriad—and often unpredictable—talents. Setting up to pass in his own end of the field, Roger could find no open receiver and began to scramble, first to his left, then his right. Finally, he made a short throw to running back Reeves in the flat that picked up 17 yards. Garrison, subbing for an injured Hill, repeatedly ran for short gains that kept the drive alive. Staubach threw to tight end Ditka for yet another first down. Then, with nine minutes remaining in the game, Thomas, despite having lined up in the wrong spot in the backfield, took a pitchout and swept around right end for the touchdown that provided Dallas with breathing room and a ticket to another Super Bowl.

It had hardly been a thrill-a-minute game, but the win was decisive.

Afterward, Roger judged the 14–3 victory one of the most satisfying of his newborn career. Throughout the week, 49ers defensive players had responded to questions about his penchant to scramble, saying they hoped he would try. Their inference was clear—they were daring him to do the impossible.

During the afternoon, he had run the ball eight times for 55 yards.

Asked to comment on his quarterback's performance, a resigned Landry smiled as he shrugged. "He'll keep running until he keeps getting hit," he said. "Then he'll slow down. The more he learns, the less he'll run."

The city of New Orleans danced to a Mardi Gras beat as it prepared to host Super Bowl VI. The Dallas Cowboys and the Miami Dolphins were coming to town along with 80,000 fans who would visit the city's historic jazz joints, feast on red beans and rice and boiled crawfish, and dance along Bourbon Street before finally jamming into Tulane Stadium.

The NFL's championship game had grown into a full-blown celebration. Though the telecast of the previous year's Super Bowl, matching

Dallas and Baltimore, had ranked as the most watched sports event in history, that record was certain to be eclipsed.

For Staubach, it was an exciting new world. A year earlier he had been only a bystander as Dallas played for the NFL championship. Now he was preparing to perform on center stage. The Cowboys were *his* team, its soon-to-be-determined destiny was in his hands.

Comfortable and confident, he welcomed the final challenge of the season. So did his teammates.

And in the days leading up to the game, Tom Landry set about to make certain Staubach was ready.

The preparation for the game was unlike anything Roger had ever experienced. He had come to expect the Saturday night phone calls from Landry before home games. At a specifically designated time, the phone would ring in the Staubach home, and the coach and quarterback would discuss the game plan. No salutations, no small talk. As soon as Roger would answer, the game plan print-out in front of him, Landry would begin the discussion. On road trips, the conversation was routinely held in Landry's hotel suite.

In Miami, as the two met, attention to the smallest detail was undertaken. Nightly, Roger would arrive at Landry's room and for hours they would discuss which plays would work, when best to call them, and myriad situations that might arise during the course of the anticipated game. It was clear that Landry was determined that his team win. And the best way to ensure that was to be absolutely certain that his quarterback was well prepared.

"I don't think we'd ever been as prepared for a game as we were that one," Staubach told Associated Press reporter Denne Freeman. "Every night, after practices and team meetings, I'd go to his room and we'd watch film and go over and over everything."

Nearby, Alicia Landry would read as her husband and Staubach planned for the game. Finally, one night after hearing the same questions asked and the same answers given, she approached the two men and made a suggestion Roger was delighted to hear.

"Tommy," she said, "why don't you let Roger go back to his room and get some sleep?"

The only unhappy person in New Orleans, it seemed, was Dallas' enigmatic running back Duane Thomas.

Throughout the year, his behavior had been a constant irritant, dividing team members and coaches into two camps. There were those who viewed his sulking manner and refusal to adhere to the most simple of team rules as childish and boorish. Many of the players wondered why Landry, a man whose rules had always been chiseled in stone, would tolerate such open defiance. It seemed to most that two sets of rules were in place—one set for Duane, another for the rest of the squad. And while the feeling was that Thomas was a valuable and talented part of the team on Sundays, most believed that Landry would have summarily dismissed any other player who demonstrated such rebellion.

Despite the fact he had ended the regular season as the team's leading rusher, Thomas was not a young man who bred harmony among his co-workers.

During one practice session, a winded Garrison looked to Duane and pointed out that it was his turn in the rotation. When Thomas ignored him, Walt spoke out. "What the hell's wrong with Thomas?" he asked. Staubach, attempting to calm things, urged Duane to join the huddle. "You," Duane shot back, "just shut up."

Landry settled the issue by telling Garrison to go ahead and run the play.

Then, as the team began its preparations for the Super Bowl, Duane skipped practice without explanation, giving rise to rumors that he was planning to boycott the game.

The following day, however, he showed up at the practice field on time, spent a half hour in Landry's office, and silently went to the practice field. When one of the assistant coaches asked how the conversation had gone, Landry replied with a puzzled look. "I don't really know. I talked, but he didn't have much to say."

"Is he going to play?"

"He's here and ready to practice. I assume he's going to play."

While many of the veterans were perplexed and put off by the manner in which Landry had dealt with Thomas, others on the team viewed the coach's actions more charitably. Though Landry had not and would not admit it, it was his way of attempting to extend a helping hand to a young man he believed to be woefully troubled and seriously ill-advised.

Landry wanted to be Thomas' savior. Meanwhile, a growing number of teammates wanted to punch the ill-tempered running back in the mouth. All, however, hoped he would play the game of his life against the Dolphins.

Miami had made its way to the Super Bowl by first defeating Kansas City 27–24 in an exhausting overtime that had lasted 22 minutes and 40 seconds. Then, despite being underdogs to the defending champions, they had eliminated an injury-depleted Baltimore 21–0.

Despite the Dolphins' impressive victory in the AFC championship game, the fact that their quarterback Bob Griese had led the conference in passing and that their running backs Larry Csonka and Jim Kiick provided the ground game a devastating one-two punch, the odds-makers declared the Cowboys the favorite.

The difference, the experts agreed, would be the Dallas defense. And Doomsday immediately set out to prove them right.

Six minutes into the game, Howley recovered a Csonka fumble. Runs by Garrison picked up 18 yards, and a Staubach-to-Hayes pass advanced the ball another 18 before the drive stalled at the Dolphins' 2-yard line. Clark came on to kick a chip-shot field goal.

In the second quarter the Cowboys running game took control as the offensive line provided gaping holes for Garrison and Thomas. After the ground game had advanced to the Miami 7-yard line, onlookers fully expected Dallas to continue to pound its way into the end zone. Instead, Staubach sent Alworth on a sideline route and threw for the day's first touchdown.

Though the Dolphins' Garo Yepremian would kick a 31-yard field goal just before halftime, the Cowboys were in control of the game.

Things would get only more one-sided in the second half as the Miami offense came to a standstill, failing to make a single first down during the third quarter. The Cowboys, meanwhile, engineered long touchdown drives in the second half. Thomas scored from three yards out in the third, then, following a Howley interception, which the agile linebacker returned to the nine, Staubach threw a touchdown pass to tight end Ditka in the fourth.

If the game had a signature play, it had come on Miami's third possession of the day. Attempting to avoid the Cowboys rush, Griese had frantically scrambled as his receivers were covered. He ran right to avoid a pursuing Larry Cole, then left to get away from Bob Lilly, losing ground with every turn. Finally, the chase ended when Lilly tackled the Dolphins quarterback for a 29-yard loss that brought a thundering cheer from the crowd. The play was the statement the Dallas defense had come to make.

The 24–3 Dallas victory was surgical. Defensively, it dominated. Offensively, it had enjoyed success up the middle with sweeps and even a Bob Hayes end-around. Thomas was the leading rusher with 95 yards on 19 carries. Staubach completed 12-of-19 passes for 119 yards.

As the final seconds ticked away, Rayfield Wright and Mike Ditka lifted a smiling Landry onto their shoulders for a long-awaited victory ride.

Unlike the button-down atmosphere that followed the NFC title victory, bedlam ruled in the Cowboys postgame dressing room. Lilly, his longtime goal finally achieved, happily puffed away on a cigar. Landry received a phone call from the White House as President Richard Nixon offered his congratulations. Owner Murchison added his touch of humor as he explained to surrounding reporters that the win had been "the successful end to our 12-year plan." Schramm, relishing the moment while already looking ahead, vowed that the Dallas victory was "just the beginning." Soon both Schramm and Murchison were hauled away by celebrating players and thrown into the shower.

One by one, players elbowed their way through the masses to shake Staubach's hand and congratulate him on his having been named the game's Most Valuable Player.

In his *First Down, Lifetime to Go*, Roger remembered the moment. "Like most of the time, the quarterback gets the spoils or takes the blame.

This isn't right, but it happens. I'd done a good job, but we'd set a Super Bowl rushing record with 252 net yards. Duane or Walt could have won the award. I was just one of many who could have received it... Renfro, Lilly, Howley, and others. I was extremely proud of it, but I knew a lot of other people deserved it, too."

The following day, Roger, Marianne, and his mother attended a luncheon at which the MVP award was officially announced. The prize would be an automobile of his choice.

Staubach, the no-nonsense father of three, said he'd like to have a station wagon.

Following the presentation ceremony, *New York Times* columnist Dave Anderson, looking for some final story angle that hadn't been addressed, spoke with Roger about his faith, at one point in the interview asking what he expected heaven to be like. "From what I understand," the smiling quarterback answered, "every pass is a touchdown up there."

The Pulitzer Prize–winning Anderson returned the smile. "But," he said, "if you're a defensive back, every pass wouldn't be a touchdown."

"Oh," Staubach replied, "they don't have any defensive backs up there."

The happy Dallas Cowboys had stepped from beneath the cloud that had so long hung over their heads, finally putting the assertions that they couldn't win the Big One to rest. Next Year's Champions had become Super Bowl winners.

And they had a new leader whose presence promised future days of success and sunshine.

CHAPTER 10

"Landry thought he'd died and gone to Heaven. He felt that when you've got a guy as dedicated as Roger, it was very easy to get the other players to go that extra mile."

Walt Garrison

For professional football's newest celebrity, the weeks following the Cowboys' victory sped by in whirlwind fashion. No sooner had he returned from his first appearance in the Pro Bowl—a less-than-memorable occasion during which he completed only one of six passes and threw two interceptions—the calls came in a steady stream. Manufacturers wanted his endorsement, banquet planners from coast to coast stood ready to pay him handsomely to serve as a guest speaker, politicians wondered if he might drop in on their fund-raisers and put in a good word, and organizations with awards ready to be handed out wanted to know when he could fit one more presentation into his schedule. Charity groups came out of the woodwork. So did reporters requesting interviews.

Staubach, with neither a business agent nor membership in any speakers' bureau, was overwhelmed. And he was having a difficult time saying no to anyone who wanted a piece of his time. Finally one morning he walked into the Cowboys offices, carrying with him a box filled with letters and phone messages he'd not yet found time to answer. "I need help," he told team vice president Al Ward.

A secretary was hired, her lone assignment to keep up with his correspondence and help manage his off-season schedule. The primary assistance Roger asked of her was that she slow the pace of his travels by selectively determining which speaking engagements or appearances to accept. He also explained a rule that he wanted her to make sure he adhered to: For every paid appearance he made, he would do a free one for charity.

His other concern was that he not allow the traveling to spill into the time he planned to set aside for pre-training camp workouts. "I knew after becoming the starting quarterback and winning some awards," he said, "that I would need to work even harder in the off-season to prove that I deserved to be in the position I was in."

By the time the Cowboys reported to Thousand Oaks to begin preparation for the new season, Landry had issued an edict that met with wholesale approval from his players and assistant coaches. Aware that the manner in which he had dealt with Duane Thomas' disruptive behavior over the course of the previous year had met with general disapproval, he said that everyone on the team would be treated equally and each man was expected to abide by the same rules.

Initially, it seemed that even Thomas had gotten the message.

During the off-season he had been a regular at the Cowboys practice facility, enthusiastically participating in informal workouts. There would be days when he was even friendly with those around him. And, he confided to Staubach, he had already established personal goals for the upcoming season. On several occasions, Roger invited him to stop by the house and have dinner with him and Marianne. Duane would accept the invitations then at the last minute phone to say he wouldn't be able to make it. Still, Staubach felt Thomas was making progress.

That all changed once the team reported for training camp. Again surly and distant, Thomas didn't even join his teammates for meals. Instead, he would sign in at the Cal Lutheran cafeteria as required, get a few pieces of fruit, and retreat to his dorm room to eat alone.

By the time the team traveled to Chicago to participate in the annual College All-Stars charity game, Thomas was again pushing the envelope, barely adhering to Landry's rules. On several occasions, teammates would stop by his dorm room in the evenings in hopes of determining what the problem might be. Duane had nothing to say.

On one occasion, Roger sat with Thomas, attempting to initiate a conversation. Duane was non-responsive. Finally, Roger asked if he would prefer that he leave. "No," Thomas replied, "I like hearing you talk."

Then, with no explanation, the troubled running back skipped a team meeting and an afternoon practice, testing Landry's rules and dwindling patience.

The coach went to Thomas' room and for over an hour talked of the importance of making a genuine effort to be part of the team, of working with people concerned for his welfare instead of against them, of adhering to the rules all were expected to follow.

Duane's response was light years shy of satisfactory. He wasn't paid to sit in meetings, he said. He was paid only to play on Sundays. And he had no intention of following rules he believed to be insulting to an adult.

When it became obvious he was getting nowhere, Landry finally left and sought out Tex Schramm. "That's it," he told the general manager. "Trade him."

Thomas' career as a Dallas Cowboy, once so promising, was over. Traded to San Diego for wide receiver Billy Parks and running back Mike Montgomery, he was active with the Chargers for only one game—a meeting with the Cowboys, ironically, in which he didn't play—and was soon released again.

In the Dallas camp, meanwhile, a sigh of relief swept through the organization. Though none had doubted Thomas' unique ability, neither did they view him as irreplaceable. Calvin Hill, injury-free and running like he did during his Rookie of the Year season, rejoined Garrison in the Dallas backfield. And there was another promising rookie on the way. University of Houston fullback Robert Newhouse, who had scored the College All-Stars' only touchdown earlier at Chicago's Soldier Field, had been impressive in the twice-daily practice sessions.

The Cowboys could live without Duane Thomas.

Soon, however, they had to question how they would fare without their starting quarterback.

In the off-season, Craig Morton had met with Landry to determine whether he would be allowed a chance to again compete for the starting position. The coach praised Morton's ability and pointed out his value to the team but made it clear that his decision that Staubach would, barring injury, be the starter was final.

Some had felt the idea of languishing in a backup role would cause Morton to immediately ask that he be traded or possibly choose to retire. Fortunately for the Cowboys, he accepted Landry's decision and remained in Dallas.

During the second preseason game in a sold-out Los Angeles Coliseum, the Rams and Cowboys were tied 3–3 when cornerback Herb Adderley intercepted a pass deep in Los Angeles' end of the field. Shortly thereafter, facing a third-and-9 situation at the Rams' 12-yard line, Staubach faded to pass but saw that all his receivers were tightly covered. Ducking under one onrushing defender, he began running to his left in an attempt to pick up the first down. As he neared the sideline, Rams middle linebacker Marlin McKeever raced toward him. Instead of stepping out of bounds and avoiding the tackle, Staubach ducked his shoulder and drove into the defender, hoping his momentum would carry him into the end zone.

McKeever stopped him cold. And immediately Roger felt a burning pain in his right shoulder. Even as he was being helped to the Cowboys bench, he knew the injury was serious.

The diagnosis of team doctors soon confirmed his fears. The shoulder had been severely separated, and immediate surgery would be necessary. In all likelihood, Staubach was told, his season was over.

Landry sat with Marianne throughout the three-hour operation, then joined her in a discussion with doctors. All, they were told, had gone well. Once fully mended, Roger would be able to resume his career.

Asked by members of the media to evaluate Staubach's future, Landry said, "I have no doubt that Roger will come back. The same competitive spirit that made him go after that touchdown will make him come back." The minimum waiting time, doctors said, would be eight to 12 weeks.

For Staubach, the inactivity was agonizing.

"I stayed away from the practice field," he wrote in *First Down, Lifetime to Go,* "not wanting to hang around and just talk. Gradually, I realized that you're paid to be a football player and that's it. If you can't play, you're of no value. The coaches had their jobs to do, so they never called. I didn't hear from many of the players, either. I began to feel sorry for myself. I read a lot of books, watched television, and got grouchy."

It was four weeks before the doctors removed the pin from his shoulder and the painful but welcomed rehabilitation process began. With hard work and a little luck, Roger began to feel he might be able to play again before the season ended.

Teammates, meanwhile, had warmly welcomed Morton back into the fold. The inactivity during the final half of the 1971 campaign and a rigorous off-season of preparation allowed him to return in better physical condition than he'd enjoyed in years. And the opportunity to be back in the starting lineup, even if had come in an emergency situation, revitalized his enthusiasm.

In its season opener, Dallas had little trouble beating Philadelphia 28–6. It was not, however, the Eagles that worried the Cowboys. Once again, the Washington Redskins, still aging yet still winning, would be the team to beat for the NFC East championship.

By the time the Cowboys had improved their season record to 5–2 at mid-season, the Redskins were 6–1. And one of those victories had been a 24–20 decision over Dallas.

The consistency the Cowboys had demonstrated through the second half of the '71 season was no longer in evidence. The defense wasn't dominating and, with the exception of Hill, who was well on his way to becoming the first back in Dallas history to gain 1,000 yards in a season, the offense was too often hit and miss. Week after week, Landry experimented

The Navy backfield in Dallas on December 27, 1963, as they opened drills for their Cotton Bowl game with Texas January 1, 1964. Left to right: quarterback Roger Staubach; halfback Ed Orr; fullback Pat Donnelly, and halfback John Sai. (AP Photo/Ferd Kaufman)

Prior to receiving the award formally at a luncheon, Navy quarterback Roger Staubach posed with the Heisman trophy in New York on December 11, 1963. (AP Photo/Jacob Harris, File)

Head coach Tom Landry confers with his quarterback, Roger Staubach (No. 12), during the waning moments of NFC Championship Game against the San Francisco 49ers in Dallas, Texas, on January 3, 1972. The Cowboys won 14–3. (AP Photo)

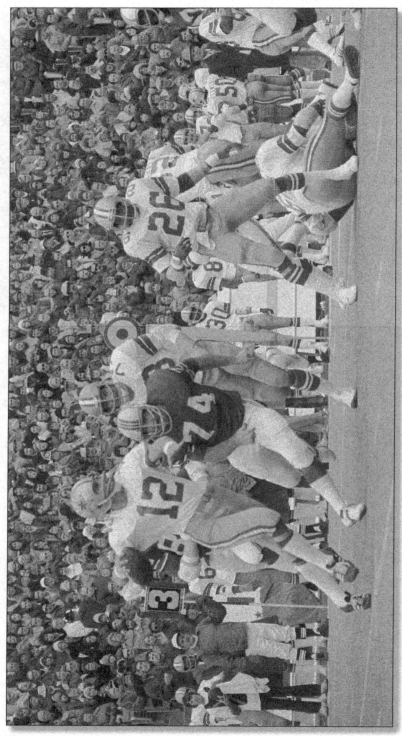

Roger Staubach (No. 12) looks for a pass receiver in the second quarter of the game against the New England Patriots at Schaefer Stadium in Foxboro, Massachusetts, on November 17, 1975. Closing in is Craig Hanneman (No. 74) of the Patriots. Staubach connected for three touchdown passes to give the Cowboys a 34–31 victory. (AP Photo)

Quarterback Roger Staubach looks to pass in the 37–7 win over the Los Angeles Rams in the 1975 NFC Championship Game played on January 4, 1976, at Los Angeles Memorial Coliseum. (AP Photo/NFL Photos)

Roger Staubach prepares to pass against the Pittsburgh Steelers in the first half of Super Bowl X at the Orange Bowl in Miami, Florida, on January 18, 1976. (AP Photo)

Roger Staubach calls out the signals at the line of scrimmage in Super Bowl XII against the Denver Broncos in New Orleans, Louisiana, on January 15, 1978. The Cowboys won 27–10. (AP Photo)

NFL Hall of Fame and Dallas Cowboys Ring of Honor member Roger Staubach before a halftime ceremony during the game against the New York Giants on September 20, 2009, in Arlington, Texas. (AP Photo/Donna McWilliam)

with a new set of receivers, choosing from Alworth, Hayes, Ron Sellers, and Billy Parks, but no combination seemed to deliver the passing attack he hoped for. The usually explosive Hayes, suddenly baffled by the new defensive alignments he was facing, had not scored a single touchdown.

And for all his renewed efforts, Morton was again hearing the boos. An impatient press corps wasn't too happy with him, either.

The volume of criticism went up another notch on Thanksgiving Day when the 49ers thoroughly embarrassed the Cowboys 31–10. Afterward, a furious Landry labeled his team's performance "pitiful."

With Washington showing no signs of fading as most had expected, the Cowboys' chance of defending their division title was fast disappearing.

Though he had been reactivated the week before the San Francisco debacle, Staubach could do little but watch. While able to throw, he did so with great pain in his shoulder. Too, his conditioning had suffered considerably during the lengthy layoff. While he insisted to the press that he had returned to "somewhere near 90 percent" effectiveness, it was an overly optimistic evaluation.

Dallas rebounded from the loss to the 49ers with a promising 27–6 win over St. Louis, then the team began preparing for a crucial rematch with the Redskins in Texas Stadium. In what had become a familiar routine in each of the team's victories during the course of the year, Dallas jumped out to a 28–3 halftime lead, then desperately hung on in the waning stages to win 34–24.

However, the roller-coaster trend continued a week later when any momentum that might have been gained in the victory over the Redskins was lost in a 23–3 defeat at the hands of the Giants. After Morton was ineffective in the first half, a frustrated Landry replaced him with Staubach for the remainder of the game. Roger, neither agile nor throwing sharply, wasn't much of an improvement as New York easily won 23–3.

The Cowboys, but a faint reminder of the team that had mightily stormed its way to a Super Bowl championship a year earlier, had lost the NFC East for the first time since 1965. Though their record was 10–4, they had finished a game behind Washington.

A wildcard entry in the playoffs, the Cowboys would have to travel west and face the same San Francisco team that had humiliated them four weeks earlier. The 49ers would be heavy favorites to mercifully end the up-and-down Dallas season.

San Francisco's Vic Washington ran back the opening kickoff 97 yards for a touchdown. After Fritsch got Dallas on the board with a field goal, Larry Schreiber scored on two short runs to put San Francisco ahead 21–3 in the second quarter.

It appeared that the almost certain end to Dallas' season wasn't going to be pretty. Though Morton briefly rallied the team to narrow the score to 21–13, a fumble, this one by Hill at his own 1-yard line, provided the 49ers another score by Schreiber.

As a dismal third quarter was coming to an end, Landry told Staubach to warm up. He entered the game with 1:53 remaining in the period.

Early in the fourth, Hill broke for a 48-yard run that set up a Cowboys field goal. Then, as 49ers quarterback John Brodie seemed to suddenly grow conservative, the Dallas defense stepped up.

With less than two minutes remaining in the game and San Francisco leading 28–16, fans began making their way out of Candlestick Park. Sportswriters left their places in the press box in anticipation of elevator rides down to the dressing rooms for postgame interviews.

As they did so, Staubach was avoiding an all-out rush from the 49ers and hit on three straight passes to swiftly move the Cowboys to the 49ers' 20-yard line. Parks then broke into the clear on a post pattern, and Staubach threw to him for a touchdown with 1:10 remaining in the game.

Everyone in the stadium knew that the Cowboys' lone chance at victory would be to get the ball back immediately.

Toni Fritsch's onside kick bounced in the direction of a San Francisco receiver, but he was hit by a teammate just as he tried to make the catch. Mel Renfro fell on the ball to give Dallas possession at midfield with 1:03 to play.

On first down, Staubach dropped into the pocket to pass but immediately saw that the 49ers rush had left the entire middle of the field open. Running for the first time since his preseason collision with Marlin McKeever, he advanced the ball inside the 49ers' 20.

Billy Parks then caught an out pattern at the 10 and quickly stepped out of bounds to stop the clock. After hearing another play called that would have Parks as the primary receiver, tight end Ron Sellers told his quarterback, "Look for me. They're not covering me over the middle."

Throwing quickly to avoid another all-out San Francisco blitz, Roger spiraled the ball into the arms of the open Sellers in the end zone with only 58 seconds left in the game.

In one of the most miraculous beat-the-clock displays in NFL history, Dallas had come back to win 30–28.

On the sidelines, Larry Cole did child-like cartwheels onto the playing field. Players hugged, slapped each other on the back, and lifted their arms in victory. Morton raced onto the field to congratulate Staubach. At midfield, longtime friends Landry and Nolan met. "I can't believe what just happened," the 49ers coach said. "This," replied Landry, "is the greatest comeback we've ever had."

With two touchdowns in a span of just 38 seconds, the Cowboys had earned their way back to the conference championship game. And for the third time in the season, they would face the Washington Redskins, winners over Green Bay in the other first round game.

And Landry had another tough decision to make.

Morton had started and played through 15 games during the season, while Staubach had been on the field just more than 13 minutes the previous Sunday. On the surface, the choice of starting quarterback for the NFC title game seemed simple. Yet as preparation for the trip to the nation's capitol began, Landry called Morton and Staubach into his office following the Thursday practice.

Author Bob St. John recounted the coach's words in his book, *The Landry Legend*:

"Craig, you've performed well all year and put us in the playoffs. But I've decided to go with Roger, which is certainly no reflection on you. The primary reason is that Roger brought us into this game. I saw us put things together in those last few minutes of the 49ers game like I haven't seen all season. I believe we have momentum going now. If what I saw was right, then Roger will continue this trend against the Redskins."

Morton was understandably crestfallen. Staubach, who was battling a case of the flu and hadn't practiced all week, was stunned. And hindsight would not treat Landry's choice kindly.

Players, particularly members of the offensive line, were not pleased with Landry's decision. Over the course of the demanding season, they had become comfortable with Morton at quarterback. Hadn't he always enjoyed success against the Redskins, leading them to 54 points against them in the previous two meetings? Staubach, they knew, was a player of remarkable talent, but his San Francisco miracle aside, Roger had not seen enough playing time to have fully regained his old form.

The clinical no-nonsense Landry, they feared, had allowed himself to be caught up in the emotional aftereffect of the previous week's comeback win.

The game plan George Allen and his staff had devised for the New Year's Eve meeting was simple—stop the running game that had been Dallas' primary weapon throughout the season. And the Redskins carried it out with a vengeance. Hill, who had run for 125 yards against the 49ers, was swarmed every time he touched the ball, ending the day with only 22 yards. Running mate Garrison's numbers were even more dismal as he contributed just 15.

And Staubach, repeatedly hurried and frustrated by the Washington defense, showed none of the magic he'd performed just a week earlier.

The Redskins' 26–3 victory was the most one-sided defeat an Allen-coached team had ever dealt the Cowboys.

Afterward, Landry found himself in an unfamiliar position of defending himself. Why, reporters wanted to know, had he not given Morton a chance to rally the team when it had become obvious that Staubach was rusty and non-productive?

"If we had been in a different situation, moving the ball but having breaks go against us, I would have put Morton in," he said. "But we just weren't moving the ball. No, Roger didn't have a good game, but under similar circumstances, I'd go with him again."

As unsatisfactory as the explanation might have been, it seemed to make one thing clear—Roger Staubach was Landry's quarterback.

Or so some thought.

CHAPTER 11

"I saw how he dealt with teammates, coaches, the media, and I said, 'I'm going to follow that guy.' Roger has a big back. He can carry a lot of people. He's that kind of person."

Drew Pearson

In matters of money, professional football has few secrets. On the banquet circuit, while socializing at the Pro Bowl and waiting to tee off in celebrity golf tournaments, players have historically traded information on who is making how much. Years before the NFL Players Association would make a decision that all information on salaries should be shared, it wasn't at all difficult to find out the amount of others' paychecks. In Dallas, there had been a long-held belief among the players that they were working for one of the lowest-paying organizations in the league.

As the Cowboys looked ahead to the 1973 season, they began openly voicing their demands for better pay. And the media was having a field day with the unrest. Bob Lilly and Lee Roy Jordan, players who had for so long been major contributors to the defense, were unhappy and threatening retirement. So was center Dave Manders. Morton, still peeved over being benched for the final game of '72, was considering not reporting to training camp until his contract was revised. Chuck Howley, Mike Ditka, Lance Alworth, Herb Adderley, and George Andrie had announced their intentions to retire.

The demise of the proud and successful franchise, it seemed, had finally begun.

It was but one of many concerns Roger was dealing with. His mother had been diagnosed with terminal cancer, and doctors had confided to Staubach that it was unlikely she would live more than another year. Since the death of her husband in the spring prior to Roger's second season with the Cowboys, Betty Staubach had lived alone in Silverton, strong, energetic, and self-reliant until the cancer struck. So they might be able to care for her during the anticipated decline, Roger and Marianne had persuaded her to come live with them in Dallas.

Professionally, his shoulder still pained him as he worked through the off-season months. The team's receiving corps had undergone a radical turnover with Alworth and Ditka retiring and Ron Sellers traded to Miami. And it was no secret that Bob Hayes had again fallen from favor and was in danger of losing his job to a highly drafted rookie named Golden Richards.

Meanwhile, Landry had again told the press that the quarterback job was up for grabs and that he would make a determination based on performances during the preseason.

By the time the team got to California, things had only worsened. When Manders failed to report, saying that he'd decided to retire, Roger learned that the Cowboys had refused to improve the center's contract by only the few thousand dollars that Manders had requested. Staubach went to Schramm, urging that he meet Manders' modest demands and get him to camp. The hard-bargaining general manager pointed out that salary guidelines were in place and would not, under any circumstances, be revised. "Overall," Schramm argued, "the Cowboys are well paid. We don't have a lot of guys being paid extremely high salaries, but on an average, they're paid as well as anybody in the league."

If Manders chose to retire, Schramm said, newcomer John Fitzgerald would move into his job and perform quite well.

Schramm's attitude would be less cavalier when the team's most beloved player broke from the ranks. Reluctantly, Bob Lilly had boarded a flight from Dallas to Los Angeles to report to a training camp he felt was in upheaval. During the flight, he found himself becoming increasingly angry over management's stubborn, almost arrogant refusal to share the wealth among players who had for so long been vital participants in the team's success. When the plane landed at Los Angeles International, where a Cal Lutheran student waited to drive him to Thousand Oaks, Lilly told the surprised youngster that he wouldn't need a ride after all. Instead, the most celebrated player in the history of the Cowboys immediately booked a return flight to Dallas.

Word that Lilly wasn't reporting spread quickly. Staubach and Jordan phoned him, urging that he reconsider and report and that his talent was badly needed as was the calming effect he could have on others. They had no luck changing their teammate's mind.

In an unprecedented move, Schramm was soon en route to Dallas to talk with the All-Pro defender. The "guidelines" the tough negotiating general manager had so often referenced apparently did have some wiggle room. Someone like Dave Manders, it became clear, might be expendable. An icon like Lilly wasn't.

Shortly, Lilly signed a new contract and reported to camp. Begrudgingly, Schramm also reached a new agreement with Jordan.

Then Morton, still unhappy with his contract, the notion of having to again compete for the starting job, and generally fed up with the negative atmosphere that hung over the team, briefly walked out.

The Dallas Cowboys were not happy campers.

While Staubach's power of persuasion in the Manders and Lilly matters made no impact, he enjoyed a small victory earlier in the summer—one that would greatly figure into the team's future.

During off-season workouts, a relatively unknown free agent named Drew Pearson had impressed him. The University of Tulsa quarterback-turned-receiver had moved to Dallas in May in hopes of improving his chances of earning a spot on the team. Though small and far from the fastest among those running routes for the quarterbacks, it was Pearson who caught Staubach's attention. Not only did he run precise routs, but he caught anything thrown near him. Also, long after others had showered and left, Pearson remained to continue working with Roger.

He would have stayed even longer had it not been for the fact he had to report to an evening job loading trucks for a Dallas freight company. When Staubach noticed that the demanding routine was beginning to take a toll on the determined youngster, he went in search of a solution.

Explaining to player personnel director Gil Brandt that he badly needed a practice receiver willing to work long hours and praising Pearson's work ethic, Staubach asked if the Cowboys might find a way to help the free agent with his living expenses.

Acting on Staubach's endorsement, Brandt told the surprised Pearson that he had earned a bonus for the hard work he'd been putting in. The young receiver, who had received only $250 for initially signing with the Cowboys, was suddenly to earn $500 to serve as Staubach's personal passing partner for the month leading up to training camp.

Soon, a unique bond had been forged.

Morton, having finally reached a new agreement with Schramm, returned to the team the week before the preseason schedule was to get underway. And the quarterback derby was back on. Each was allowed to call his own plays, and the competition took on the look of a well-played tennis match. By the time only two exhibition games remained, neither appeared to have a decisive edge. Sharing time against the Kansas City Chiefs, Roger completed seven of nine passes, while Morton connected on 5-of-10 but had two interceptions. Against Miami, Craig entered the second half with the Cowboys trailing and led the team to a come-from-behind victory.

While Staubach held a slim statistical edge during the course of the preseason—42 completions for 671 yards and five touchdowns to Morton's 35 for 399 and three touchdowns—members of the media were erroneously reporting that Craig's performance against the Dolphins had finally won him the job.

If that proved to be the case, Staubach had privately decided, the time had come to ask that he be traded.

As the team returned to Dallas to begin preparations for the regular season, Landry phoned and summoned him to the practice facility. As he drove to the meeting, Roger contemplated his options. His ill mother had begun to feel comfortable with the move to Dallas, thus staying with the Cowboys for another year, even if it meant playing little, might be the best thing to do. On the other hand, if he chose to accept a back-up role, it might well doom his chances to ever fulfill his goal of becoming a starting quarterback. Time, he knew, was not in his favor.

Already he had surveyed the NFL marketplace and taken note of the fact Atlanta was not satisfied with its quarterback situation. Perhaps a move to the Falcons, he thought, would provide him the opportunity he so badly wanted.

In his autobiography, Staubach later recalled the meeting that would determine the future of his pro football life:

"Coach Landry and I talked for an hour. He went over my positive points and my negative points. He asked me how I felt about the situation. 'Coach, I've given this all a lot of thought,' I told him. 'I think you need to make a decision and stick by it. If you aren't going to start me, I want to be traded. If I have any choice in the matter, I'd prefer you trade me to Atlanta.'

"It was difficult to read him as we talked. Sometimes I felt he wasn't sure."

Finally, the coach voiced his decision. "You will be the starter," he said.

That evening, Landry called Morton to his home to advise him of his choice.

And with that, the long-standing quarterback controversy in Dallas came to an end.

Though the Cowboys won their first three games of the new season, defeating Chicago, New Orleans and St. Louis, Staubach displayed only flashes of the take-charge sharpness he'd showed two year earlier in the team's Super Bowl drive. Occasionally, he even found himself the target of the boos once directed at Meredith, then Morton. Clearly, not every Cowboys fan was happy with Landry's decision.

In Dallas' win over the Saints, Roger had settled into a comfortable rhythm, leading the team to a 26–3 lead. Then in the late stages of the third quarter, he was knocked unconscious and Morton came on to play well, improving the margin of victory to 40–3.

Still, a week later Roger was again the starter, his confidence renewed by an outstanding performance as the offense scored 45 points against the St. Louis Cardinals.

The real test, he knew, would come the following week against the Washington Redskins.

Things did not go well. After he had thrown to Otto Stowe, who had come to the team from Miami as part of the Sellers trade, for a first-quarter touchdown, the Redskins defense shut out the Cowboys for the remainder of the half. And it was delivering a severe beating to Staubach.

In the third quarter, with Dallas still leading, Roger developed spasms in his leg. Then he misread a defensive key on a critical third down and was sacked. For Landry, it was the signal he needed to put the more experienced Morton into the game.

The Redskins came back to win 14–7 as an angry Staubach looked on.

In the postgame news conference, Landry explained to reporters that he'd decided to use Morton because of Roger's "leg injury." When reporters came to him, Staubach set the record straight. Landry, he said, had benched him because he'd made mistakes, not because of a simple charley horse that could have been quickly massaged away.

The effect of the Washington defeat lingered, and Dallas lost two of its next three games. Rams quarterback John Hadl stunned the Cowboys secondary with four touchdown passes to wide receiver Harold Jackson. Then Philadelphia, coming into the game with only one win, defeated Dallas 30–16. By mid-season, Dallas was 4–3 and again trailing the Redskins in the race for the NFC East title. Though Staubach felt his play-calling and execution was improving with each game, the team still lacked consistency.

Part of the problem was a seemingly endless sequence of injuries, particularly to the Cowboys receivers, early in the season. Otto Stowe had suffered a fractured ankle and missed the first month. Mike Montgomery filled in for him but was soon sidelined with a pulled groin muscle. Tight end Billy Joe DuPree had a badly sprained foot, and Jean Fugett was experiencing hamstring problems. And Billy Truax had developed ulcers that sent him to the sidelines.

Soon Landry had looked up to find that one of the few receivers still available to him was rookie free agent Drew Pearson. In his first start, he caught seven passes for 71 yards. The person least surprised by the performance was Staubach.

The emergence of a rookie receiver and the fact others had become healthy added renewed promise to the Cowboys offense, but Landry still hadn't seen the progress he'd hoped for. It was time to try something new. This time, however, it would not involve personnel.

The week after the Cowboys had lost to Miami, Landry again summoned his quarterback to a meeting.

One of the few people in the organization who was aware that the health of Staubach's mother had grown steadily worse as the season progressed, Landry explained that he had been searching for a way to relieve some of the pressure he knew Roger was dealing with. "Your play-calling has been good," the coach said, "but we haven't won the close games and we seem to be missing on some big plays."

In an attempt to solve the problem, Landry explained that he would assume the play-calling, using tight ends DuPree and Fugett as messengers.

Roger wasn't happy with the plan, viewing it as a criticism of his ability to lead the team. Yet in the final three weeks of the season, even Marianne recognized that much of her husband's stress seemed to disappear.

Against Denver, he completed 14-of-18 passes, two for touchdowns to his new messenger Fugett, in a 22–10 win that set up a rematch with the Redskins.

Washington, a team determined to return to the Super Bowl where it had lost to the Dolphins the previous January, had a one-game lead over the Cowboys when they arrived at Texas Stadium. With a victory, the Redskins could clinch the NFC East title.

Even before kickoff, members of the media were calculating the importance of the game, attempting to de-code the NFL's complicated tie-breaker rules in the event Dallas won and the two teams wound up with identical won-lost records. Simply put, for the Cowboys to advance past Washington and into the division lead, they would have to win the game by a wider margin than the Redskins had in their previous meeting. Not only did Dallas need to win, it had to do so by a margin of more than seven points.

In an effort to provide his quarterback easier escape from the Redskins' defense as he attempted to throw, Landry had devised a game plan that called for less from-the-pocket passing and more play-action and roll-outs. On the move, he felt, Roger would be a far more difficult target for Washington's rush.

The Cowboys responded with their most outstanding performance since their Super Bowl victory. While an inspired defense held the struggling Redskins to only a single late-in-the-game touchdown, Dallas' offense dominated. Staubach directed two 70-yard scoring drives, one ending with him running in from the five. For the day, Roger completed 16-of-25 passes for 223 yards.

Punctuating the dominant 27–7 victory was the fact Dallas had the ball at the Redskins' 2-yard line with a minute remaining to play. Rather than attempt to add to the score, the Cowboys opted to let time run out.

Staubach's celebration of the victory was short-lived, however. Four days following the game, his mother passed away. On Friday he and his family traveled to Cincinnati where Roger delivered the eulogy at the Saturday afternoon funeral.

On Sunday he was in St. Louis, ready to play in the regular season's final game against the Cardinals.

It would be an afternoon when Gil Brandt's $500 bonus payment to Drew Pearson paid off handsomely. The rookie receiver caught five

Staubach passes for 140 yards and two touchdowns as the Cowboys posted a 30–3 victory.

"Considering what he's been through this week," Landry observed afterward, "the game he played was remarkable." It was Craig Morton's idea that Roger be awarded the game ball for his performance.

Despite the frustrations and unrest that had earlier threatened the team's chances, the Cowboys had put differences aside and reclaimed their NFC East title with a 10–4 record. Suddenly, the pluses far outweighed the minuses. Staubach, who had thrown for more than 200 yards in six games and accounted for 23 touchdowns, ended the season as the NFL's highest ranked passer. Hill, despite constant knee problems, had broken his own club rushing record, gaining 1,142 yards. When Garrison was sidelined by an injury, newcomer Robert Newhouse had stepped in to play well at fullback. Rookie receivers Pearson and DuPree had become vital parts of the offense. When problems developed at center, Dave Manders agreed to come out of retirement. And the defense, led by All-Pro selections Jordan and Renfro, had regained its form.

And along the way, a subtle change had taken place on the Cowboys sideline. Landry was becoming increasingly confident in his quarterback. Roger, meanwhile, was learning how to deal with the idea of the coach calling plays. That new understanding would be obvious as the team met Los Angeles in the opening round of the playoffs.

The Rams, the highest-scoring team in the NFL, were judged by many as a legitimate Super Bowl contender. Experts had only to look back to the October victory they had scored over the Cowboys before making the Rams the favorite to do it again.

It would, however, be a much different Dallas team that the Rams faced in Texas Stadium just two days before Christmas.

The first two times the Rams had the ball, they turned it over deep in their own end of the field. Jordan intercepted John Hadl to set up a three-yard touchdown run by Hill, then on Los Angeles' next possession, defensive end Pat Toomay knocked the ball loose from running back Lawrence McCutcheon and Renfro recovered at the 35. Three plays later, Staubach threw to Pearson for Dallas' second touchdown. By early in the second quarter, the Cowboys had added a field goal and led 17–0.

As the teams entered the fourth quarter, however, Los Angeles had narrowed the score to 17–9. Not only had the game's momentum dramatically changed, but the Cowboys were suddenly without the services of running back Hill. On an attempt to run wide, he had fumbled and a pile-up involving Hill, Neely, and Rams defender Fred Dryer fought for the ball. Dryer recovered at the Cowboys' 17, setting the stage for a score that narrowed Dallas' margin to 17–16 with 10:28 remaining.

Hill, having suffered a separated elbow while attempting to recover the fumble, was lost for the remainder of the game.

Following the kickoff, the Cowboys had stalled at their own 17-yard line and were facing a third-and-14 situation when Landry sent in a play that called for Bob Hayes to run a deep sideline pattern while Pearson was to run a turn-in route. Hayes, per Landry's instructions, was to be the primary receiver.

But before leaving the huddle, Staubach instructed Drew to forget the turn-in. "Run a deep post," Roger said.

Angling across the middle, Pearson briefly broke open between two Rams defenders, and Roger arched a perfectly thrown pass in his direction. Making the catch at midfield as the pursuing Los Angeles defenders collided, Drew raced toward the end zone to complete an 83-yard scoring play.

On the jubilant Dallas sidelines, Landry made no mention of the fact the play he'd called had been changed. Instead, he congratulated his quarterback on a job well done. It wasn't the first time Roger had deviated from Landry's instructions during the course of the season. Carefully picking his spots, he had learned how to "play" his coach.

Dallas later added another field goal to win 27–16 and head into the NFC championship game for the sixth time in an eight-year span.

With both Hill and Garrison injured, Dallas would be facing the Minnesota Vikings without a weapon that had served it so well all season. The ground game would fall onto the shoulders of rookie full-back Newhouse, a capable runner but hardly the breakaway threat Hill had been all year.

Adding to the disappointment was the fact that despite losing to the Vikings the week before, the Redskins had enjoyed considerable success running the ball.

Thus the Cowboys offense would rise or fall on the arm of Staubach. And it fell with a resounding thud as he played what he would judge "my worst game as a pro."

Though it dominated the early stages of the game, Minnesota held only a 10–0 halftime lead. Then a 63-yard punt return for a third-quarter touchdown by rookie Golden Richards gave the Cowboys brief hope of a comeback. But Vikings quarterback Fran Tarkenton quickly responded with a 53-yard touchdown pass and defensive back Bobby Bryant returned an interception for a 63-yard score as the visitors went on to a 27–10 victory.

Unable to establish any semblance of a running game, Dallas had tried to rebound through the air without success as Staubach completed the game with four interceptions, including Bryant's for Minnesota's final touchdown.

Afterward, Landry admitted the obvious, "Roger wasn't as sharp as usual." Then, however, he looked to the bright side. "I think overall that he had an outstanding season, which is even more impressive when you consider the mental strain he was under. He's still young and will do nothing but improve each year. Right now, he already ranks with the best quarterbacks in the game, but we feel his potential has not yet been reached."

He then made an uncharacteristically bold prediction. "We'll be back a lot stronger next season," Landry promised.

It wasn't to be.

CHAPTER 12

"I don't know if leadership can be traced to a social or environmental background or what. It's a difficult thing to define. All I know is Roger had all the rare qualities necessary to be a great leader."

Tex Schramm

L ong after his days as Cowboys president and general manager had ended, Tex Schramm still delighted in telling the story of a time when he negotiated the renewal of Staubach's contract. While the concept of full-time sports agents had yet to become commonplace, most of the players hired local attorneys to deal with management. Roger, however, felt more comfortable visiting Schramm personally and working out matters one-on-one.

When his initial three-year agreement ended, he had scheduled a meeting with Tex at the Cowboys' offices. Arriving well ahead of time, Roger sat outside Schramm's office as a secretary explained he was on an important long-distance call and would be with him just as soon as it was completed.

In time, Staubach tired of waiting. Walking down the hallway, he located a window that opened onto the 2-foot wide ledge that circled the eleventh floor of the North Central Expressway building.

Minutes later, the phone still cradled to his ear, Schramm turned to look out of his floor-to-ceiling window onto the Dallas landscape. As he did, a figure suddenly moved into view. Two hundred feet above ground level, a grinning Staubach stood, waving his arms in a mock hey-let-me-in gesture. Schramm did a double-take, then quickly explained to his caller that he would have to get back to him later. "I've got to go," he said. "You won't believe this, but my quarterback is standing on the ledge outside my office," he said.

Staubach was still laughing over his successful prank as he was ushered into the Schramm's office. In short order, a new contract agreement was reached.

For other players, such negotiations were neither funny nor pleasant.

Disillusionment with the Cowboys' pay scale had continued to escalate prior to the 1974 season and was compounded by the announcement that yet another new professional football league was preparing to open for business. The World Football League, a brainchild of entrepreneur Gary Davidson—whose American Basketball Association was in a heated battle with the established NBA, and his World Hockey Association was competing for fans of the NHL—had taken on the pro football establishment.

The new league's plan was to immediately conduct raids on NFL teams, luring high-profile players to the WFL with large signing bonuses and promises of celestial salaries.

Dallas was a prime target. Though none would be free to join the new league until their current contracts expired, Craig Morton, resigned to the fact his career with the Cowboys had reached a dead end, signed to play for the Houston Texans in 1975. Calvin Hill and Mike Montgomery also signed lucrative agreements to join the new league once their contracts with Dallas expired. Soon a chain reaction was underway as they were joined by Otto Stowe, D.D. Lewis, Jethro Pugh, Rayfield Wright, and Pat Toomay. Additionally, Danny White, an All-American quarterback and punter from Arizona State who had been picked high in the draft by the Cowboys, opted to begin his professional career with the Memphis Southmen of the WFL.

Suddenly the Cowboys roster was filled with lame-duck players threatening to stick around only until their contracts expired. Landry, who had

maintained a policy of not getting involved in player-management negotiations, finally spoke out, saying that he feared the lure of WFL dollar
signs was creating an impossible situation for NFL teams. "As a team
sport, we must have a joint effort for any championship drive," he told
writer Bob St. John. "There can be no doubts about any player putting
out everything he has. Every player must be rewarded if we win or suffer
if we lose. I just don't believe the players who have signed these future
contracts will suffer since they'll ultimately be rewarded regardless."

And, as if the problems created by the World League weren't enough,
the NFL Players Association was urging its members to boycott the
upcoming training camps unless management agreed to its demand for
free agency. The players' union, headed by an outspoken leader named
Ed Garvey, was insisting that players be given the freedom to negotiate
with any team of their choosing once their contracts had expired. NFL
management, including Tex Schramm, dug in to fight.

As time for training camp neared, the revolt Garvey was encouraging had begun to get ugly, pitting players against management, veterans
against younger team members, even blacks against whites. The logo and
slogan that the NFLPA had adopted was a raised fist reaching out over
the words "No Freedom, No Football." To many, it brought back to mind
the racially toxic atmosphere of the '60s.

Veterans were urged to picket rather than report to camp. And those who
crossed the picket lines were publicly chastised by NFLPA management.

Several Cowboys players—Lilly, Jordan, Toomay, and Fitzgerald—
who didn't sympathize with Garvey's heavy-handed approach, refused
to support the strike and reported to camp on schedule, angering their
striking teammates.

For Staubach, the situation offered a dilemma. While comfortable with his own contract, he was eager to see his teammates better
compensated. Though far from being one of the league's highest-paid
quarterbacks, he knew that his name had often come up during others'
negotiations. Schramm's mantra was familiar to everyone on the team:
"I can't even think about paying you *that* much. If we did, we'd have to
raise Roger's salary."

In principal, Staubach supported the ideas of free agency, better medical coverage, and improved retirement benefits. From there, however, the list of demands had bordered on the absurd—no player curfew in training camp, shorter practices, and full salary payment to a player even if he was released during the preseason roster cut-down. And the manner in which the union had chosen to fight the battle was off-putting.

Eager to test an ankle on which he'd had off-season surgery and to begin preparation for the new season, Roger was among those who finally chose to report to camp. Ed Garvey's snide response angered Staubach. "I'd hate to have been at Pearl Harbor with him," the union leader told members of the press.

It was a foot-in-mouth comment that cost him favor with a number of Cowboys players who also arrived at camp.

Hill, among the most adamant union sympathizers, admitted that the Dallas strike effort was doomed to failure the minute Staubach crossed the picket line. And Garvey's comment hadn't helped matters.

The Pearl Harbor reference had not only been personally offensive to the Cowboys quarterback; it had convinced him that the strike was not only misguided but misled.

Wrote Peter Golenbock in *Cowboys Have Always Been My Heroes*, "[Staubach] accused Garvey of arrogance. 'He immediately made the owners mad, which doesn't seem like a good way to me to begin negotiations. It makes more sense if a person stands up for what he believes is right rather than go along with a man who had no more common sense than to make an analogy like that one about Pearl Harbor. I just think this man has done a lot of harm.'"

Lilly went Roger one better, calling Garvey "the Jimmy Hoffa of the players' union."

In time, the movement fell under its leader's own weight, and players went back to work with little to show for their efforts except the scars left by hard feelings.

Even as the full roster finally assembled in Thousand Oaks, there were faces missing. Six-time All-Pro linebacker Chuck Howley had retired, and wide receiver Billy Parks was traded to Houston. And soon the Cowboys would finally fulfill Craig Morton's wish. By mid-season, the frustrated quarterback would be traded to the New York Giants where, he was told, he would have an opportunity to be the team's starter.

The Cowboys entered the '74 season with false promise.

After defeating Atlanta 24–0 in the opener, they went into a tailspin, losing four straight and finding themselves in last place in the division standings. Landry's fears were being played out Sunday after Sunday. The off-season distractions had clearly taken their toll. His team, offensively and defensively, was playing as if it was stuck in second gear.

During a three-game stretch, Staubach threw nine interceptions. In a move that distressed some of the veteran players, Landry elevated Golden Richards to the starting flanker job, effectively signaling the end of Bob Hayes' colorful career as a Cowboy.

And suddenly there was a new challenger for the NFC East title. While preseason prognosticators had held to the tradition and predicted a Dallas-Washington battle for the championship, the St. Louis Cardinals had moved to the top of the standings. By the time they faced Dallas at mid-season, they had won seven in a row, including a 31–28 victory over the Cowboys in the fifth week of the season.

Briefly, the Texas Stadium crowd saw a glimmer of the team it had expected as Dallas defeated the Cardinals 17–14 when new kicker Efren Herrera, who had replaced the injured Fritsch, came on to kick a winning field goal with just four seconds left in the game.

Still, the dramatic victory was not enough to jump start the kind of late-season stretch run that had become a Cowboys trademark. By the time they visited RFK Stadium to face the Redskins, they were 5–4. As had been the case much of the season, Dallas' running attack was sporadic and too many of Staubach's passes were off-target. Meanwhile, Washington's first touchdown had come on a nine-yard run by new Redskins running back Duane Thomas, who was attempting to reestablish his career as the latest player in George Allen's ongoing reclamation project.

By halftime Washington led 28–0. Dallas, however, came back strong in the second half, narrowing the score to 28–21 on a Staubach-to-DuPree touchdown pass. Then, with time running out and facing fourth down at the Washington six, Roger threw to Pearson in the end zone. The ball caromed off the receiver's shoulder incomplete, and Washington fought off the Cowboys' comeback to preserve their victory.

Afterward, a jubilant Allen reminded reporters that every time Dallas and Washington played, it was like a championship game. "This," he said, "is one of the greatest rivalries in the history of the NFL."

In the visitors' dressing room, Landry's only thoughts were on the final pass that might have pulled his team into a tie. "The pass could have been better," he said, "but it was catchable."

Two weeks later, on a brisk Thanksgiving afternoon, the two old rivals met again. Dallas, with a 6–5 won-lost record, was faced with an almost impossible scenario if it hoped to save its season. To reclaim the division championship, it would not only have to defeat the Redskins but then win its final two games. And even that would not be enough. Washington, which had replaced St. Louis as the division leader, would have to lose its last two games. The math was hardly in the Cowboys' favor.

Redskins defensive tackle Diron Talbert had added fuel to the fire with what amounted to a subtle threat. Should Staubach be injured during one of his scrambles, he pointed out, Dallas had only an inexperienced rookie quarterback to replace him.

The first half was a battle of field goals as Washington built a 9–3 lead. Early in the third quarter, Redskins quarterback Billy Kilmer ended a drive with a nine-yard touchdown pass to Thomas, causing a mixture of boos and cheers from the sellout Texas Stadium crowd.

Soon thereafter, Talbert's prediction came true as Staubach was helped from the field after being knocked unconscious. As he slowly moved toward the sidelines, some of the fans in Texas Stadium began heading for the exits.

In his place came rookie Clint Longley, a free-spirited youngster who had earned the reputation of a strong-armed but often erratic passer during his collegiate days at little Abilene Christian College. He hadn't played a single down during the course of the season.

The Redskins, aware that the Cowboys rookie would attempt to pass his team back into contention despite limited knowledge of his receivers or experience with picking up keys, opted to go into a prevent defense for the remainder of the afternoon.

With just less than 10 minutes remaining in the game, Longley began moving the Cowboys on a drive that ended with a 35-yard touchdown pass to DuPree. Along the way, the baby-faced quarterback had made it clear he had taken charge of the Cowboys offense. When fullback Newhouse had felt he was taking too long to call a play and had urged Longley to hurry up, Longley responded with a glare and told the veteran to shut up.

By the time Garrison ran in from the Redskins' 1-yard line for a touchdown that put the Cowboys ahead, players on both sidelines were looking on in disbelief.

Washington, however, quickly regained the lead when Thomas scored on a 19-yard run. And by the time the Redskins lined up for a field-goal attempt minutes later, it looked as if the Cowboys were officially eliminated from any playoff hope.

However, rookie defensive end Ed "Too Tall" Jones, extended his 6'9" frame and blocked the attempt. But on its next possession, Dallas fumbled the ball away.

The Cowboys got their final chance with 1:45 left to play. With time fast ticking away, they had reached midfield when Landry sent in a desperation play that called for Drew Pearson to run a deep pattern over the middle. Once Longley relayed the play, however, Pearson told his quarterback that he would fake the route and instead go deep down the sideline. In anticipation, the Redskins had seven defensive backs on the field.

With only 35 seconds remaining, Longley's pass fell into Pearson's arms at the 4 and he went in for the touchdown as the crowd erupted. Herrera's extra point provided Dallas a 24–23 victory that would not only stand as the highlight of a lackluster season but one that would become part of the Cowboys' lore for years to come.

In the dressing room, Landry could only shake his head when asked about the game-winning touchdown. "There was no way," he said, "that we could complete that pass." Across the way, teammate Blaine Nye was calling Longley's performance "a triumph of the uncluttered mind."

Despite the brief excitement generated by the win over Washington, Landry's big-picture view of the fast-ending season was far from positive. It had gone much as he had feared. The disruptions produced by the World Football League and the NFL Players Association had taken their toll. The Cowboys had been out of kilter, distracted, and often lethargic for much of the year. And he felt his quarterback had over-compensated in an effort to set things right. The lack of success had clearly had a devastating effect on Staubach.

Thus the week following the Redskins game, he was summoned to Landry's home for the first time in his career as a Cowboy.

Roger recalled the meeting in his *Time Enough to Win*:

"Landry used that time to talk to me about the whole season. He had sensed my despondency. Things had been rocky. I was taking the brunt of the criticism, and a lot of it was justified. Overall, I was feeling terrible. But Tom said, 'The season hasn't been your fault. It's been the team, the way we started out by losing four close games, and all the things that happened to us in the off-season.'

"He sensed that I was trying to overcome the problems single-handedly. In his view, I was trying too hard."

Staubach admitted that his coach was right.

Whether cheered by Landry's words or simply feeling relief that the tumultuous season was nearing an end, he had one of his best games a week later against Cleveland. He threw for 230 yards and three touchdowns as the Cowboys scored a 41–17 victory. There was little cause for celebration, however, since Washington also won, ending any hope the Cowboys had of making the playoffs.

With a 27–23 loss to Oakland, Dallas ended its season 8–6, the poorest record the team had posted since the sixth year of the franchise's existence. Staubach, the league's leading passer just a year before, dropped to fourteenth place. There had been no 1,000-yard rushers, and Pearson was the lone player selected to any All-Pro team.

For weeks after the season ended, Staubach pondered the status of the team. He made a mental list of those who had been among his teammates when Dallas had won Super Bowl VI. Many were now gone and, if the rumors he was hearing were true, others would soon be.

If the Cowboys were to rebound any time in the near future, it would be accomplished with a new cast of players led by a quarterback who was suddenly beginning to feel very much like an old-timer.

CHAPTER 13

"Roger and Coach Landry were good for each other. Both were tremendously competitive. Both studied hard. Roger knew the assignment of every offensive player when most of us were having trouble just learning our own. And he never thought a game was over until the players were in the locker room and the crowd had gone home."

Preston Pearson

Tom Landry, ever the innovator, knew well that a dramatic change would be needed if he was to resurrect his team from the disappointing 1974 season. What he had in mind as he laid the groundwork for the new year was a plan that would, in time, revolutionize the manner in which the National Football League viewed its game.

Defenses, he realized, had begun to change, bringing in an extra back on obvious passing downs. They would rush only three linemen and, in the new scheme, were routinely stopping the third-down pass. As a result, offensive productivity was down, not only in Dallas, but throughout the league.

Landry had an idea—and the right quarterback—to provide opposing defenses something new to consider. What he had come up with was, in truth, nothing new. It had been hidden away in his encyclopedic playbook since the birth of the Cowboys in 1960. And he had originally borrowed the idea from a pioneer NFL coach who had introduced the extraordinary concept before the Dallas franchise even existed.

136

Landry would call it the Spread. The media would refer to it as the Shotgun. And Red Hickey, the former San Francisco 49ers coach who was credited with being its inventor, would call it long-overdue redemption.

Staubach, who had been sacked no less than 88 times during the past two seasons, viewed it as a Godsend.

"I've never understood," Landry explained, "why a quarterback has to take the ball from center, turn, and run back 10 yards on downs when everyone in the stadium knows he is going to throw a pass." By simply lining up for a direct snap from center at the spot from which he would throw, the quarterback would have more time to view the field while, in turn, offensive linemen would be required to hold their blocks a shorter length of time and defensive linemen would be faced with additional distance to travel before reaching the passer.

It was a scheme Landry had briefly considered during the early days of the Cowboys when Don Meredith was quarterbacking. But the poor quality of offensive linemen on the Dallas roster at the time doomed the plan. Repeatedly sacked as he waited for receivers to get open, Meredith quickly became uncomfortable with the formation and urged his coach to junk it.

"It will work," Landry told his players, "only if you have confidence in it."

Led by an enthusiastic Staubach, the Cowboys quickly embraced the idea. They were willing to try anything that would remove the bad taste of the previous season.

On one hand, it was the perfect time for experimenting since the Cowboys had been all but written off as yet another NFL team that had climbed to the heights only to quickly fall back into mediocrity as players aged, retired, and defected; on the other, it was a swing-for-the-fences gamble. After all, its originator Hickey, who had boldly installed the Shotgun in an effort to resurrect his floundering 49ers years earlier, wound up losing his job. His players simply never bought into the bizarre new offensive philosophy.

"Once they lost confidence in what we were trying to do," he later recalled, "it was over."

Jack Christiansen, who would inherit Hickey's job, immediately stored the Shotgun in mothballs and brought back the standard T-formation alignment, returning the NFL world to its traditional ways.

For his experiment to succeed, Landry knew his players would have to believe. And the individual he felt could make that happen was Staubach.

"If we make this work," Landry told him, "I think you could have your best year ever."

By the time training camp ended, the Shotgun had been installed and thoroughly rehearsed. It was not, however, the only big news. As the team's final roster was announced, a record number of rookies were included in the mix. In time the star-studded group would even be given a nickname—the Dirty Dozen.

At the head of the class were two first-round draft selections whose only thing in common was their incredible talent. Randy White was a quiet, all-business All-American and Outland Trophy–winning defensive lineman whose modesty belied his athletic accomplishments. Then there was linebacker Thomas Henderson, a mile-a-minute self-promoter from tiny Langston University in Oklahoma. He was Muhammad Ali in shoulder pads—handsome, gregarious and incredibly talented. "Call me Hollywood," he said to members of the new team he was joining.

Additionally the celebrated roster of rookies included linemen Herb Scott, Burton Lawless and Pat Donovan, defensive backs Randy Hughes and Rolly Woolsey, linebackers Bob Breunig and Mike Hegman, running back Scott Laidlaw, center Kyle Davis, and punter Mitch Hoopes.

Indicative of the richly talented class of newcomers that Gil Brandt and his scouting staff had assembled was the fact that six would immediately become starters for a coach who, historically, had never made any secret of his hesitancy to place first-year players into such pressurized situations.

Clearly, this was to be a learn-on-the-run group.

Then, just a week before the regular was to begin, the good fortune continued. The Pittsburgh Steelers, still irritated with running back

Preston Pearson over his having been one of the NFL Players Association members who organized a picket of the Steelers practice facility during the previous summer's strike, had placed the 30-year-old veteran on waivers. Landry had already determined that he needed an additional running back, and for the bargain-basement sum of a $100 filing fee he was able to claim one from the waiver wire.

It would, dollar for dollar, be the best investment in Cowboys history.

During the course of an eight-year NFL career, Pearson had performed well as a backup running back, receiver, and special teams player. And he brought with him a background of winning. He had been a member of the Baltimore Colts Super Bowl III team. Then, traded to Pittsburgh prior to the 1970 season, he had earned a championship ring while playing there. Tutored by two coaches Landry viewed as among the league's best—Don Shula in Baltimore and Chuck Noll in Pittsburgh—Pearson was a well-schooled, thinking man's player who Landry felt could provide leadership as well as a genuine threat the Cowboys had never enjoyed. Despite the impressive list of receivers who had played for the franchise, it had never had a consistent and reliable target among its running backs. If the Shotgun was to fire properly, such a player would be vital. And the former University of Illinois standout was perfectly suited for the job.

No one was more pleased with Pearson's arrival than Staubach. As he had a few years earlier with Drew Pearson, Roger had sensed something special in the ability and work ethic of his new teammate and thus following every practice, the two remained on the field for additional work on pass patterns. Roger was immediately impressed by the 30-year-old's speed, the crisp routes he ran, and the manner in which he caught the ball with his hands rather than attempting to cradle it into his chest. Aware that Pearson was living alone in a Dallas apartment while his family remained in Pittsburgh, Roger regularly invited him for Marianne's home-cooked dinners.

When Pearson had agreed to the Cowboys' offer, Landry's final preseason decision was made. Though left-handed rookie quarterback

Jim Zorn had been impressive throughout training camp, challenging Clint Longley for the back-up position, it was decided that Pearson's presence was more vital than keeping a third quarterback on the roster. Longley was more familiar with the Cowboys offensive system and, of course, there was the lingering promise built on that dramatic come-from-behind victory over the Redskins that he'd engineered as a rookie. Longley stayed. And Zorn was released and moved on to Seattle where, in time, he would become one of the league's finest quarterbacks.

As the season approached, Landry privately felt that if his team could get off to a fast start, perhaps winning in the opener against the Rams or the fast-improving St. Louis Cardinals in the second, some degree of momentum could be established. A 1–1 record after two weeks of facing playoff-caliber teams could point these new-look Cowboys in the right direction.

What he got was something even more promising. The reliable Dallas defense rose to the occasion in an 18–7 win over Los Angeles. While his gifted receiving corps was tightly covered much of the afternoon, Staubach kept the offensive alive by scrambling for more than 50 yards. A week later the passing game awoke as Dallas won over the Cardinals in overtime 37–31, with Staubach throwing for 307 yards and three touchdowns. Henderson, the rookie with more speed than any linebacker ever to play for the Cowboys, helped the cause with a 97-yard kickoff return for a touchdown.

Certainly there was no back-to-the-Super Bowl talk, but there *was* a strong hint in the air that something special might be brewing; perhaps the Cowboys were indeed not yet ready to fade into obscurity. They were fighting their way back with a wide-open, scratch-and-claw style long-time Cowboys followers had never before seen.

They won four straight before suffering a two-point loss to the Green Bay Packers.

A 30–24 loss to Washington went into overtime—and marked a dubious milestone in Staubach's career. Redskins safety Ken Houston intercepted a pass and was about to be tackled on the opposite side of the field from where the angered Roger watched. Out of the corner of his eye, he suddenly saw cornerback Pat Fischer charging toward him as if to throw an unnecessary block. Staubach put his hands out to deflect the blow, knocking Fischer to the ground. Roger also fell, landing atop Fischer, and an official threw a flag, charging Staubach with a personal foul. Fifteen yards. So much for the goody two-shoes image.

Along the way, Landry's revised offensive philosophy was coming into focus. Historically, the Cowboys' passing game had been a down-the-field attack that featured the wide receivers. Now added to the plan, particularly on long-yardage third downs, was matching Preston Pearson against linebackers as he came out of the backfield and ran routes to the sidelines or over the middle. With the now-well-known nickel defense not yet on any defensive coordinator's drawing board, Pearson's speed and sharp cuts were simply too much for those assigned to cover him.

And with this new threat, other Dallas receivers benefited—particularly Drew Pearson. An October game against the Philadelphia Eagles in Veterans Stadium served as a prime example.

Always a slugfest, the game saw the Eagles leading 17–10 with less than four minutes left to play. It was the kind of situation upon which Staubach thrived.

From his own 33, he connected on a screen pass to Newhouse that gained 18 yards and was supplemented by another 15 when an unnecessary roughness penalty was assessed Philadelphia defender Bill Bradley. Then, from the Eagles' 21, Staubach called a curl pattern for Drew Pearson. Seeing two Eagles defenders in his path, Pearson quickly altered his route, heading across the middle as a perfectly timed pass came his way. Moments later the score was tied.

After the defense stopped the Eagles, forcing a punt, only 35 seconds remained when the Cowboys offense took over at its own 40-yard line. In the next half-minute, the hurry-up Cowboys would manage to run no less than six plays as Roger sent receivers toward the sidelines for short gains.

Facing a second-and-10 with just seconds left, he went for broke. Drew Pearson took off on a deep sideline route, gaining a step against a double-covering Eagles defense. Reaching up between the defenders, Drew made the catch and immediately stepped out of bounds to stop the clock, leaving time for Toni Fritsch to kick the winning field goal.

The Staubach comeback magic had once again been played out.

By the time the Cowboys reached Week 11 of the season with a 7–3 record, the general consensus was that Tom Landry was having his best coaching season ever, that Staubach's game had elevated to a point where he was again completing 70 percent of his passes, and that the rookies had provided a new infusion of excitement. "This was a happy team," Staubach wrote in his autobiography. Those same pundits who had earlier predicted that the Cowboys would finish dead last in the NFC East were now cautiously suggesting that this team, which seemed to revel in the underdog role, might well make a return to the playoffs.

And there were those who were seeing the possibility of even greater things in the immediate future. In a players-only meeting held the week before the Cowboys were to face the New York Giants, it was veteran linebacker Lee Roy Jordan who stood before his teammates and delivered an emotional talk in which first mention was made of the possibility that the team could make a return visit to the Super Bowl.

Against the Giants, Dallas scored twice in the first quarter, one touchdown coming on a third-and-10 Staubach throw to Jean Fugett. Calling the play, Roger added a wrinkle that he felt might surprise the New York defense. The tight end was to race downfield and turn back to the quarterback as if in hopes of catching a pass that would pick up the first down. Quickly, however, he was to turn and continue downfield, hopefully catching his defender off guard. The play worked to perfection and resulted in a 54-yard scoring play. The hook-and-go surprise was so uncharacteristic of the Cowboys' style the Giants had come to expect of their arch rival that some New York defenders suggested in their post-game comments that the route looked as if Staubach had drawn it up on a whim, as if playing pass-touch out in the parking lot.

The obviously sarcastic reference was viewed by Dallas players as a nod to the inventive nature of their gifted quarterback.

The first quarter scores held up as the Cowboys managed a 14–3 victory during which the defense repeatedly tormented the Giants new quarterback Craig Morton. The man who had led Dallas into its first Super Bowl and still had numerous friends on the Cowboys team he was facing, was sacked four times and threw three interceptions.

Following a loss to the front-running St. Louis, Dallas closed out the regular season with wins over Washington and the New York Jets to finish 10–4, just a game behind the division champion Cardinals.

Even Landry admitted his surprise at the won-lost record his team would take into the playoffs as a wildcard entry.

The role of a wildcard in the NFL playoff bracket is, at best, that of a long shot. The pairing system matches it against a top-rated team and demands that its playoff season, however long it might stretch, be an endless road trip. No team had ever managed to take such a route all the way to the Super Bowl.

Traveling north to play the Minnesota Vikings the week after Christmas, Dallas was everyone's underdog as it prepared to go up against a team that had reached the Super Bowl the previous year and lost only twice over the course of its 14-game season. Its defense was outstanding, and its offense was directed by Fran Tarkenton, the league's No. 1–rated passer.

Still, the Cowboys doggedly stayed in the game, even taking a three-point lead early in the fourth quarter. Then, however, Tarkenton led the Vikings on a 70-yard scoring drive that lifted the hosts into a 14–10 lead with time fast ticking away.

With less than a minute remaining in the game, Dallas' offense was on its own 25-yard line. When veteran center John Fitzgerald was injured, rookie Kyle Davis came on and immediately made an errant snap that resulted in Staubach being sacked. The Cowboys found themselves facing an impossible fourth-and-16 situation.

So impressive had the Vikings defense been that wideout Drew Pearson, double covered throughout the day, had not made a single catch.

In the huddle, Drew Pearson frantically urged his quarterback to call his number. Instead of continuing to throw away from Minnesota's strongest coverage, he suggested, why not attack it? If Staubach would send the ball his way, he would find a way to beat the defenders.

Roger, moved by his teammate's determination and confident in his ability, told him to get ready.

Running as though he was on a deep post pattern, Pearson suddenly pulled up in front of defender Nate Wright and cut toward the sidelines. Staubach rifled the ball and connected for a 22-yard gain and a first down at mid-field.

With precious seconds clicking away, Roger again hoped to connect on a deep sideline pattern, but the Vikings had fallen back into a prevent formation and only Preston Pearson, cutting over the middle, was open. Despite having already made five receptions, he dropped the pass.

The incompletion left 26 seconds on the clock.

In the huddle, Staubach urged his line to give him time for a deep throw, then turned to Drew. "Remember in the Washington game how you made that move on an in route and then broke deep? Try that on Wright. I'll pump [safety] Paul Krause to hold him in the middle for a second."

From the Shotgun, Staubach stood his ground as his receiver faked to the inside, then raced down the sidelines. Launching the desperation pass, the quarterback was hit hard just a split second after releasing the ball. On his back, he could not see the result of his effort. Only when he became aware of the dead silence in the stadium did he sense that something spectacular might have occurred.

When Pearson came out of his break, Wright had been on his shoulder, running with him stride-for-stride. As the receiver turned to look for the ball, however, he realized that it had been slightly under-thrown, so he pulled up and reached behind Wright for it. It hit his hands but then slid down his side where Pearson managed to gain control of it, pressing it against his hip as he turned past the stumbling Wright and into the end zone.

From the stands, a shower of debris was thrown onto the field. A whiskey bottle hit one of the officials in the head, knocking him unconscious.

During postgame interviews Roger had off-handedly referred to the game-winning throw as a "Hail Mary pass." And in doing so, he assured the remarkable play its name and an enduring place in NFL history.

For the Vikings, with their explosive offense and highly publicized Purple People Eaters defense, the 17–14 season-ending defeat was devastating. And in the wake of the loss came a bitter footnote. The victorious Cowboys were en route back to Dallas when they learned that Fran Tarkenton's father, a Methodist minister in Atlanta, had died while the game was underway.

In Dallas, where gentle applause was normally reserved for anything that didn't generate millions of dollars or represent some giant step up the social ladder, the trappings of the city's self-proclaimed sophistication were discarded. When the team charter landed at Love Field, thousands of fans waited, hoisting quickly made signs and banners and chanting its admiration for the team's miraculous accomplishment. The name most often being called out as the plane taxied to a stop was that of Drew Pearson.

It was only fitting then that Landry broke tradition and called Drew to the front of the plane and allowed him to be the first out the doorway.

Clearly, it was Drew Pearson who Staubach had come to rely on for the big plays. The two had developed something of a sixth sense about each other, as if they had reached a point where they could read one another's thoughts.

Meanwhile, the other Pearson had quickly developed into one of the Cowboys' premier offensive weapons. After sharing the running back duties with Doug Dennison early in the season, he had become the starter in the fifth game. Teammates could not remember a player more dedicated to improvement and contribution. During team meetings he wrote down every word Landry spoke. Routinely, he was one of the first on the practice field and the last to leave.

His greatest impact was as a third-down receiver. "Coach Landry used me perfectly," Pearson would later write in his autobiography. "He let me do the things I did best, going against one-on-one situations." And the pro football world would take notice when the Cowboys, once again in the role of underdog, met Los Angeles in the NFC championship game.

Many of the experts judged the Rams defense superior to that of the celebrated Vikings. During the 12–2 season, it had allowed opponents only 135 points, second lowest in a 14-game schedule in league history. The forecast was for an easy Los Angeles victory, then a Super Bowl appearance against the AFC favorite, Pittsburgh.

What would transpire in the famed Los Angeles Coliseum was Dallas' finest performance in what some were beginning to call its Cinderella season.

The Flex defense was never better as it allowed the Rams offense a paltry 118 yards. The unrelenting front of Harvey Martin, Ed Jones, Randy White, and Jethro Pugh sacked quarterback Ron Jaworski five times and held LA running back Lawrence McCutcheon to just ten yards on 11 carries. Linebacker D.D. Lewis had two interceptions.

Meanwhile, Staubach and Preston Pearson put on a razor-sharp clinic. Three of the seven passes caught by Pearson were for touchdowns from distances of 18, 15, and 19 yards. The most remarkable of his receptions came just before halftime when Roger, feeling his targets were all covered, rifled the ball into an open spot in the end zone. A throw-away. However, Preston, with his body extended horizontally, stunned the 84,000 fans on hand by making the catch.

By halftime Dallas led 21–0 and was in complete control. The Cowboys would build a 34–0 lead before the Rams finally scored in the fourth quarter. For the day, Staubach completed 16-of-26 passes for 220 yards and a career-high four touchdowns, the three to Pearson and one to wide receiver Golden Richards. For good measure, he added 54 rushing yards.

Years later, as he reviewed his Cowboys career, Staubach would refer to the 37–7 playoff victory over the Rams as "the most perfect game we ever played."

And what that day of perfection yielded was historical. For the first time in NFL history, a wild card playoff team had advanced to the Super

Bowl. Too, while other franchises had made multiple trips to the championship game, Dallas had become the first "rebuilding" team, one with a large cast of new players, to return.

While the Cowboys had spent the year accomplishing the impossible, the defending champion Pittsburgh Steelers, 16–6 winners over the Vikings the previous year, had methodically done what most had expected. It was to no one's surprise that they were the clear favorite to win Super Bowl X. Quarterback Terry Bradshaw was quite capable of having the kind of hot-handed day St. Louis' Jim Hart had earlier enjoyed when the Cardinals defeated Dallas. Receivers Lynn Swann and John Stallworth were among the best in the league. Then there was powerful running back Franco Harris whose pounding assaults had worn down defensive lines all season. And the Pittsburgh defense, the Steel Curtain, was a collection of rare talent, from linemen Mean Joe Greene and L.C. Greenwood to linebackers Jack Lambert and Jack Ham to gifted cornerback Mel Blount.

Members of the media had little luck in their attempt to develop a Bradshaw vs. Staubach storyline in the days leading up to the game. Roger quickly dismissed the notion that the game was to be some kind of competition between the two quarterbacks. Deflecting the notion of a rivalry, he pointed out, "It's pretty hard to compete directly with each other when we're never both on the field at the same time."

Neither of the quarterbacks was asked about the genuine friendship that had developed between them. They had met on the sports banquet circuit following Bradshaw's rookie season and when in Dallas during the off-season, Terry and his wife would often have dinner with Roger and Marianne.

Staubach admired the unbending determination that Bradshaw, once the Steelers' first-round draft pick, had brought with him into the NFL. From little Louisiana Tech, making the transition to the professional game had been no easy task. "They expected so much of him," Roger said. "They brought him in and literally fed him to the wolves, immediately making him their starting quarterback. He had some really difficult times but stayed with it, kept improving. That experience, tough though it was, helped him to develop into a great player."

Flamboyant Las Vegas odds-maker Jimmy the Greek made no secret of his admiration of Bradshaw and the Steelers. He was, he admitted, being kind when he established Pittsburgh as a seven-point favorite.

Fans could only hope it would be that close. Too many previous Super Bowls had fallen woefully short of their pregame hype, becoming one-sided and sloppily played. This one, however, was destined to live up to its billing. Those who watched Dallas and Pittsburgh battle in Miami's Orange Bowl were treated to what would be overwhelmingly reviewed as the best game in the event's 10-year history.

It quickly became obvious that the Cowboys would not go quietly. "Our game plan was simple," Staubach said. "We were going to shoot the works. Instead of playing conservatively, we were going to take the chances necessary to make things happen."

As they had prepared for the game, Landry had repeatedly warned that the Steelers were a team that thrived on its brawling, bad boy image, intimidating its opponents with unnecessarily brutal hits, the occasional flying elbows and knees, slaps to the helmet, and taunting curses. It was no accident that they had been the NFL's most penalized team over the course of the season. The Cowboys coached warned his players not to retaliate, to walk away from such confrontations and let the Steelers suffer penalties.

Even Staubach questioned the pacifist approach. Preston Pearson, uniquely familiar with the style of play of his old teammates, even argued against it in one of the team meetings, but Landry stood firm. "We will," he said, "let them be the ones to make mistakes. We will not fight with them. If you do, you'll lose your poise and concentration. Don't descend to their level."

The shoot-the-works game plan was evident from the opening kickoff. As he had so often done while a member of the Steelers, Preston Pearson fielded the ball and took several strides upfield before suddenly handing off to Thomas Henderson who was racing across the field. The swift rookie went 48 yards down the sidelines before Steelers kicker Roy

Gerela managed to knock him out of bounds, suffering a cracked rib on the touchdown-saving tackle.

The Pittsburgh defense held, however, and forced a punt.

When Bradshaw was unable to get his offense moving, punter Bobby Walden bobbled the snap and Dallas recovered at the Steelers 29. On the Cowboys first play from scrimmage, Staubach connected with Drew Pearson breaking over the middle at the 15, continuing his magical season as he raced into the end zone for the only first-quarter touchdown the Steelers defense had allowed during the season.

Bradshaw quickly responded, driving the Steelers with a mixture of runs and passes that found weaknesses in the Dallas Flex. As the first quarter was winding down, he lofted a seven-yard touchdown pass to tight end Randy Grossman to tie the game.

Toni Fritsch's 36-yard field goal in the second quarter enabled the Cowboys to take a 10–7 lead into intermission.

And, even as the Steelers lived up to their street-fighter reputation, committing what several Cowboys players viewed as flagrant fouls—wide receiver Golden Richards had been kneed in the ribs in clear view of an official; Preston Pearson had suffered the same after-the-play-was-dead punishment—they had not received a single penalty in the first half.

The trend would continue. When the injured Gerela missed a field goal early in the second half, Cowboys rusher Cliff Harris tauntingly patted him on the helmet in a mock show of appreciation for the failed attempt. Steelers linebacker Lambert raced over and knocked Harris to the ground in clear view of the 80,000 spectators on hand. Referees quickly moved in to prevent any further confrontation but threw no flag.

There would be no further scoring until the fourth period when Reggie Harrison broke through to block a Cowboys punt from the goal line. The ball spiraled out the back of the end zone, giving the Steelers a safety that narrowed the Dallas lead to 10–9.

Ever so slightly, the momentum seemed to switch to the defending champions. On their next offensive series, they drove deep into the Cowboys end of the field and Gerela came on to kick a field goal that gave them the lead. Then, with just more than six minutes left to play, an errant Staubach throw aimed at Drew Pearson was intercepted by safety Mike Wagner who returned it to the Cowboys 7-yard line. Bradshaw sent the power-running Harris, who would need 27 carries to rush for his 82 yards for the day, at Dallas' begrudging defense with little success before Gerela was called on to kick another field goal, giving the Steelers a 15–10 advantage.

Despite their conservative nature, the Steelers were fully aware that theirs was not a comfortable lead against the tricky razzle-dazzle Dallas offense.

Facing a third-and-4 with just three minutes remaining, Bradshaw dropped back to pass as the Cowboys came at him with an all-out blitz. Linebacker D.D. Lewis was first to the quarterback, but Bradshaw ducked under his attempted tackle. Then a split second before Cliff Harris delivered a punishing blow that would knock the Steelers quarterback unconscious, he launched a pass in the direction of Lynn Swann. The all-out blitz had forced the Dallas secondary into one-on-one coverage, and Swann made the catch and raced away to a 64-yard touchdown. Gerela's missed extra-point conversion left Pittsburgh with a 21–10 advantage.

Staubach again brought the Cowboys back, needing only four plays to advance to the Steelers' 34-yard line. From there he connected with Percy Howard for a touchdown.

With 1:48 left in the game, Dallas had narrowed the margin to 21–17.

Though the Steelers were successful in covering the Cowboys' onside kick attempt at the Dallas 42, its offense failed to advance the ball. On fourth down, Steelers coach Chuck Noll opted not to risk a blocked punt and instead called for a fourth straight running play that he hoped would allow the final seconds of the game to tick away. Rocky Bleier was swarmed and tackled short of the first-down marker by the Dallas defense, which frantically called its final time out.

One minute and twenty-two seconds remained, and the stage seemed set for yet another dramatic Cowboys finish.

On this crisp and sunny January afternoon, however, the Cowboys ran out of miracles. After moving into Steelers territory, two hurried Staubach passes fell incomplete before his last attempt to again connect with Drew Pearson was intercepted in the end zone by Steelers safety Glen Edwards.

It had been a game in which individual statistics were blurred by the tenacious play of both defenses. Bradshaw had completed just nine passes, four of them to Swann, for 209 yards. Staubach connected on 15-of-24 for 204. Neither team's running game had achieved much.

Aside from the final score, the most glaring postgame number was a new Super Bowl record hidden far down the stat sheet. The Steelers had played the entire game without a single penalty.

There is a great irony in competitive athletes, regardless of its level, wherein winners are wildly celebrated and losers quickly forgotten. Sports offers little applause for the defeated, be it in the historic Olympic arena (Can you recall who finished *second* to Bob Hayes in the 100-meter dash in Tokyo?) or the Super Bowl. Cliché though it might be, in athletics the winner does take all.

Cowboys rookie Randy White perhaps best summed up the feeling of the Cowboys in a postgame interview. Asked if he felt any consolation in the fact the wild card Cowboys had made it to the championship game when none had expected them to, then played mightily against the defending champion Steelers, White pondered the question briefly before responding. "If so," he said, "I sure don't feel any now."

Bruised and exhausted, Staubach's mood was much the same. Disappointed that the hurry-up offense had not resulted in the hoped-for last-second touchdown, he issued the obligatory praise to the victorious Steelers. "But," he added, "there will be next season. We'll come back. We're still young and looking for better things."

CHAPTER 14

"No, we have no plays where Roger is supposed to run."

Tom Landry

s preparations for the 1976 season got underway, a subtle change was taking place on the Cowboys depth chart. While there was no question that Staubach was the undisputed leader of the celebrated Dallas offense, an off-season signing served as indication that Tom Landry had begun to lose faith in the stymied progress of backup quarterback Clint Longley.

Speculation was that Landry had begun to believe that he had erred when, a year earlier, he had chosen Longley over Jim Zorn for the No. 2 quarterback spot on the roster and was determined to remedy the mistake. It was time for Longley to show noteworthy strides as a serious student of the game and practitioner of the offense, or a change would be necessary.

Forcing the issue was the arrival of Danny White, who had been drafted by the Cowboys in 1974 but had chosen to spend two years playing in the short-lived World Football League. It immediately became obvious that White's quick-study familiarity with the Dallas offense was equal to, if not better than that of the carefree Longley. White's talent as a gifted punter also offered a big plus.

The luster of Longley's mad-bombing Thanksgiving Day triumph two years earlier had dimmed, and the NFL stock of the free-spirited Abilene Christian youngster had begun to drop. To some of his teammates, he seemed too content with being No. 2, too busy embracing his fun-loving image to continue to fit into any long-range plans. He might have served well as an emergency play-caller but not someone who could be depended on over the game-to-game long haul. While he never publicly acknowledged his concern, the last thing Tom Landry wanted was another free-wheeling quarterback bouncing through life in chase of rainbows.

And a free-wheeler Clint Longley was. "Football is fun, a big part of my life," he told reporters, "but there are other things."

Like picking and singing, hunting rattlesnakes, collecting antique firearms, and driving fast cars. He had reportedly received 18 speeding citations over the course of a single summer, earning a high of five on a round trip from Dallas to Abilene in the company of a pretty Dallas Cowboys Cheerleader.

He enjoyed playing his guitar and writing country and western songs. One night while visiting a Kansas City club to listen to a singer perform, Longley offered the entertainer $20 to let him come on stage and do a couple of numbers. Some said Clint could have made a name for himself in the music business if he'd chosen to focus on it.

Focus, alas, was one of the young Colorado native's greatest shortcomings. Life went off around him like a string of firecrackers.

In the backyard of his home, he had an old Civil War cannon he had spent some of his signing bonus on. Clint cleaned it up, got it in working order, and often amused guests by firing billiard balls from it into a nearby pasture.

He insisted to *Dallas Morning News* writer Bob St. John that he was the distant nephew of Old West legend Wild Bill Longley who had ridden with the infamous John Wesley Hardin and was said to have killed more than 30 men. "He didn't live long, though," Clint explained. "They hanged him for stealing horses."

And, of course, there was Longley the Prankster. He had been hunting rattlers since his collegiate days, occasionally returning to the Abilene Christian College athletic dorm with a metal trash can filled with the venomous reptiles and turning them loose in the hallways as his college buddies ran for safety.

That fun-loving Longley was nowhere to be found as he prepared for his third NFL season. In his place was a sullen, sulking young man. He'd apparently seen the handwriting on the wall.

Through the off-season, the dramatic change had become obvious. When quarterbacks and receivers met at the Forrest Lane practice field, Longley fell into a routine of timing his arrival to the departure of Staubach and newcomer White. He spoke with neither.

The dramatic change mystified Roger. Previously, his relationship with Longley had been good, friendly, one of willing mentor and eager student. Yet when Staubach confronted his teammate about his darkened attitude, Longley made it clear that he wanted nothing to do with him—or Danny White. "You guys do your thing, I'll do mine," he angrily replied.

His competitive juices had obviously begun flowing in a self-destructive direction.

Things had only gotten worse by the time the team arrived in Thousand Oaks for training camp. If anything, the chip on Longley's shoulder had grown in size.

Throughout the grinding routine of two-a-day practices and meetings, members of the media, ever in search of a new angle for the stories they would file back to Dallas, spent considerable time reporting on the battle for the back-up quarterback position. On a regular basis, they referenced White's accurate passes, quoted coaches and fellow players who praised his grasp of the Cowboys system, and lauded his booming punts.

It became increasingly apparent that only if Landry opted to return to a plan of having three quarterbacks on the roster would the Mad Bomber be around for another season with the Cowboys.

What the troubled Longley apparently refused to consider was that a three-quarterback situation for the '76 season was, in fact, likely. If White did make the team, which was a given, his punting talents would allow the Cowboys to utilize him in a dual role, thus freeing a valuable roster spot generally reserved for someone whose only function was to punt. That luxury would likely be accommodated by keeping a third quarterback.

Even as Longley brooded, Staubach viewed the battle between him and White for the No. 2 spot on the depth chart as a toss-up. He privately felt that Longley, with his strong arm, great potential, and the advantage of having been with the team for two seasons, had a promising NFL future.

None of which seemed to generate any optimism on the part of Longley. He was certain his status was slipping and resented it mightily. When not on the practice field, he kept to himself in his dormitory room. During evening meetings, he often appeared bored and disinterested. To a few teammates, he confided that he "had to get out of here." To Staubach, he said nothing.

En route back to camp following a preseason game against the Los Angeles Rams in which White had shown a clear edge in the battle of back-ups, Longley had confided to several teammates that he would not be with the Cowboys once the regular season got underway.

The waning days of training camp are always a mixed bag. Weary of the isolation from family and friends back home and exhausted mentally and physically from around-the-clock football, the ever-shortening fuses of players' tempers flair at the slightest agitation. In the boot-camp atmosphere, everyone is pushed to a ragged edge.

Staubach was no exception.

It was a Tuesday afternoon in the final week of camp, and the quarterbacks and receivers had remained on the field to fine-tune some new routes Landry had added to the playbook. When Drew Pearson dropped one of his passes, Longley shouted a string of curses in the direction of the All-Pro receiver, the same man whose key reception had helped make him an instant folk hero in his rookie campaign.

Staubach had had enough.

Earlier in camp Staubach had again tried to talk with Longley, to determine his teammate's problem, without any luck. Later, when he'd urged Longley to complete the after-workout laps that everyone else dutifully was running, Longley had sharply replied, "You're not my coach."

So Staubach had dismissed the idea of any further attempt at conversation. He'd decided that Longley's "you do your thing, I'll do mine" worked for him, as well. Until the cursing of Pearson.

In no uncertain terms, Roger made it clear that his patience with Longley's foul mood and angry attitude had run its course. "Keep it up," Staubach said, "and somebody's going to knock those Bugs Bunny teeth of yours in."

"You going to do it?" Longley shot back.

"Yeah, I'd love to."

And with that, two grown men suddenly turned schoolyard adversaries stormed toward the privacy of an adjacent baseball field.

Even before the physical confrontation would begin, Staubach was regretting the fact he'd allowed himself to be lured into the foolish game Longley was playing. He was 34 years old, the acknowledged leader of his team, yet here he was, marching off to participate in what amounted to a schoolyard tussle. What if he suffered some injury that would make all his training camp work a wasted effort? What if he were to injure a hand break a finger?

As the two tossed the helmets aside, Staubach had hoped that a wrestling match might settle the issue. Then, however, Longley unleashed a roundhouse swing, his fist grazing the left side of Roger's forehead.

Enraged, Staubach lunged at his adversary, wrestling him to the ground as assistant coach Dan Reeves, alerted to what was transpiring, raced toward the confrontation to break it up. As he pulled Staubach away, the two players glared at each other.

When Longley collected his helmet and turned to walk away, the still-angry Staubach said, "Clint, the next time I'm not going to let you up."

For several minutes Reeves and Staubach stood alone on the baseball field, the cool Pacific breeze helping return calm to what had been one of the most bizarre events in the quarterback's athletic life. The anger subsided, replaced by the embarrassing knowledge that he'd allowed himself to be drawn into the situation.

"I'm going to tell you one thing," Reeves finally said as they began to slowly walk toward the dressing room. "Don't turn your back on that guy again. I'd be careful."

Later that evening, as Landry conducted the nightly team meeting, he acknowledged that he'd been told of the incident. Calling the two quarterbacks aside, his reaction was brief and to the point. "It better not happen again," he said.

That, Staubach felt, was the end of it.

In the three days that followed the confrontation, Staubach and Longley avoided each other. Roger chose to try to put the incident aside, focusing on the final practices of training camp and the upcoming trip home to Dallas to family and preparation for the opening of the regular season.

On Friday, the last day of training camp, Longley received a summons to Landry's room in the Cal Lutheran dormitory. To this day no one knows the topic of discussion between the Cowboys coach and the player. Was the coach planning to break the news to Longley that he planned to begin efforts to trade him? Might he have reached patience's end and was simply going to release the troubled quarterback? Or was the meeting's purpose only to clear the air and offer encouragement by informing Longley that the Cowboys' plan for the new season was to keep three quarterbacks on the roster and to assure him that the No. 2 quarterback position was still up for grabs?

Since he opted not to report for the meeting, Longley would never know.

Staubach was in high spirits as he entered the Cal Lutheran dressing room to prepare for what he knew would be the final training camp practice of the summer. Even the sight of the sullen Longley, seated a short distance from his locker, failed to dim the euphoria that accompanied the knowledge that very soon the annual drudgery of the preseason was finally coming to an end.

He had just pulled on his shoulder pads and, with his head down, was adjusting the straps when he caught a glimpse of a blur on his left, accompanied by a hysterical scream. The charging Longley landed a dizzying, blindside punch to Staubach's face, knocking him to the floor and into a metal scale used by players for daily weigh-ins. Immediately the attacker was on Staubach's back, attempting to deliver additional blows when Lee Roy Jordan and Randy White hurried over and pulled him away.

Once separated, Longley managed to escape the grasp of the stunned players and members of the training staff who had restrained him and hurried out the door. Staubach, still dazed and with blood flowing from a cut above his eye, attempted to go after his attacker but was held back.

Convincing the enraged quarterback that immediate medical attention was more important than retribution, team trainer Don Cochran drove Staubach, still in his practice uniform, to the nearby hospital where six stitches were required to close the cut to his forehead.

Leaving the dormitory where members of the media were housed, *Dallas Times Herald* sportswriter Frank Luksa watched as Longley, dressed in his football pants and a T-shirt, silently hurried past him. His face was flushed and he seemed agitated, a state of affairs that caused no alarm to sound for the veteran reporter. Luksa, during the course of a celebrated career dating back to the origin of the Cowboys franchise, had become used to the flighty behavior of players during the dog days of training camp.

In short order, the young quarterback, having changed into jeans, reappeared, hurrying to the curb of a cul-de-sac rimmed by student housing and waving in the direction of visiting Dallas radio personality Allen Stone. Luksa was already making his way to the practice field by the time Longley stuffed his bags into the trunk of Stone's rental car and asked that he immediately take him to the Los Angeles airport.

And with that hasty departure, the Cowboys career of Clint Longley ended.

In the days that followed, it became obvious that his final attack on Staubach had not been borne of spur-of-the-moment rage but was carefully premeditated. Longley cashed his training camp paycheck and packed his bags before going to the dressing room to await Roger's arrival.

Seated with Charlie Waters at lunch earlier in the day, Longley mentioned that he had decided on a plan that would free him from the Cowboys and allow him to pursue his career elsewhere.

When Waters had asked what the plan was, Longley replied, "You'll see." With that, he got up from the table and left the dining room.

Was he so desperate to be gone from the Cowboys that he had indeed carefully planned his malicious exit? Since he has never discussed the bizarre sequence of events that played out in that troubling summer, it is impossible to say.

The end result, however, is well documented. Longley was traded to the San Diego Chargers where he stayed only one season before being released. The following year he played in six games for the Toronto Argonauts of the Canadian Football League. And with that, his once-promising football career was over.

As disquieting as the event was, its aftermath wasn't without a touch of humor. Almost immediately following the altercation, the phones in the makeshift office of the Cowboys public relations department on the Cal Lutheran campus began to ring. When a sports reporter at Dallas radio station KRLD reached public relations assistant Andy Anderson for details on the confrontation, he asked if Anderson could stay on the line for a short time until a scheduled local traffic report was completed. Unaware that his response was live and going out to a 50,000-watt audience, Anderson yelled back, "Hey, I don't have time to hold. I'm up to my ass in alligators out here."

As the team charter returned the team to Dallas, homesick players were greeted by their families. As Roger lifted young son Jeffrey into his arms, camera flashes began going off like a string of firecrackers. In truth, it wasn't the image of the warm family reunion the newspaper photographers hoped to capture. Instead, they wanted a photo of the bruised and stitched wound on Staubach's forehead for the following morning's edition.

Still, the Staubach-Longley feud, dramatic though it was, quickly faded into yesterday's news, overshadowed by anticipation of a new and promising season. The Cowboys, surprise visitors to the previous year's Super Bowl, their famed Dirty Dozen now seasoned, and their quarterback playing at the highest level of his pro career, were favored by many of the pundits to not only return to the championship game but this time win it.

In the early going of the '76 season, it looked as if they would live up to the predictions. With Staubach throwing the ball better than ever and the defense playing at a high level, the Cowboys handily defeated Philadelphia 27–7 in the season opener, then raced out to four more victories. Dallas fandom, giddy in its ever-growing anticipation, overlooked the fact that the Cowboys' running game, suddenly hobbled by injuries to Preston Pearson and Robert Newhouse, had become virtually non-productive. The Cowboys were living on the dominating effort of its defense and the big-play performance of Staubach and his gifted receivers. They edged the Baltimore Colts by three, won over the Seattle Seahawks 28–13, and Giants 24–14 before finally losing to the St. Louis Cardinals 21–17.

On paper, a 5–1 record in mid-October looked good. In reality, the team was struggling—at least when measured by the high standards it had set for itself.

In the second quarter of the game against the Chicago Bears, Staubach scored on a four-yard run. As he crossed the goal, he was met by Bears defensive back Virgil Livers who, attempting to knock the ball away, buried his helmet into the hand with which Staubach held the ball.

Even as the hand began to swell, the Cowboys quarterback continued to play through the remainder of the quarter, but X-rays taken in the locker room at halftime revealed a hairline fracture to the joint just above the little finger on his throwing hand.

The forgotten concern Staubach experienced back in sunny California as he and Clint Longley had squared off on that deserted baseball field had become a reality.

Danny White came on in the second half and threw two touchdown passes as the Cowboys scored a 31–21 victory.

A week later in Washington, Staubach returned determined to play despite the painful fracture. Late in the game, a Redskins defender stepped on the already damaged hand. And, despite the fact the Cowboys won the game 20–7, things would not be the same for the remainder of the season.

Compensating for the damage to the finger and his ability to grip the ball, Staubach unwittingly altered his throwing motion. Soon, he developed a constantly sore arm. Having completed 70 percent of his passes through the first eight games of the season, the percentage dropped to 50. Suddenly the Cowboys offense was struggling mightily Landry's famed Shotgun was all but silenced, the team managed a 9–3 win over the Giants, beat Buffalo 17–10, and lost by a touchdown to the Atlanta Falcons.

Despite an impressive won-lost record and a good shot at winning the NFC East title, the Cowboys were hardly a happy family. There was a steady grumble from members of the defense who felt the offense was simply not doing its part. While no one voiced such concerns directly to Staubach, he was keenly aware of the growing discontent. With the running game little more than a ghost—free agent signee Doug Dennison from little Kutztown State, who had previously been used only in short-yardage situations, would finish the season as the Cowboys' leading rusher with a paltry 542 yards on 153 carries—it was the passing game that had to drive the offense. And Roger knew he was throwing high, wide, and too often incomplete.

Against the Redskins in the final regular season game, he completed only 6-of-22 passes as Washington won easily 27–14.

Dallas completed its schedule with an 11–3 record, one win better than the previous season, was named the NFC East champion, and had six players, including Staubach, selected to play in the Pro Bowl.

Next stop—hosting the Los Angeles Rams in the divisional playoff.

It was an offensive disaster that brought a chorus of disdain from a disappointed hometown crowd. While the defense held the Rams to 14 points, the Dallas offense could only muster 12. With no running game to keep the hard-rushing LA defense honest, Staubach was forced to throw on virtually every down. Constantly pressured by the Rams, he completed only 15-of-37 passes and suffered three interceptions.

Privately, the disgruntled members of the defense bemoaned the team's desperate need for a reliable running back. As he would later write in his autobiography *Texas Thunder*, defensive end Harvey Martin summed up the attitude of the entire team: "One player...just one running back, and we'd have been the best damn team God ever gave breath to."

A harsh self-critic, Staubach viewed the second half of the 1976 season as a personal failure. Not only had the Cowboys ended the season with little more than an offensive whimper, he felt he had lost the confidence of his teammates. It had been his job to ignite the offense, to produce points, and he felt he had fallen far short of the mark. Sidelined running backs and sore throwing arms were, in his evaluation, poor excuses. His mood turned dark in the days immediately following the sudden end of the season. He made the decision to discuss matters with Landry.

The coach was surprised when Staubach voiced concerns that the team's confidence in him had slipped away. "Maybe," Roger volunteered, "it would be best if you traded me. I feel like I've let the team down. I don't know if I have them with me anymore."

Landry immediately dismissed the idea. He reminded his quarterback of the year-long problems with the running game. "And, considering your own injury, you played well." It was Staubach's supporting cast, the coach pointed out, that had come up short.

While the far-sighted Landry made no mention of it, a plan was already underway to remedy the problem.

If there is a downside to a year-to-year routine of winning in the NFL, it is the low spot afforded premier teams in the annual draft. General manager Schramm, Landry, and scouting director Brandt had, even before season's end, been contemplating ways to move up in the order so that a quality running back might be selected.

What they were able to come up with would change the history of the franchise.

Trading away four picks—a first-round and three second-round selections—to the expansion franchise Seattle Seahawks, the Cowboys suddenly advanced into a position to make the second pick on draft day.

Immediately after the downtrodden Tampa Bay Buccaneers made Southern Cal running back Ricky Bell the No. 1 pick of the day, the final piece of the Cowboys' plan fell into place. The wholesale draft-pick swap with the Seahawks had been contingent on Tampa Bay selecting the highly regarded Bell.

Bell, however, had not been the most coveted player on Dallas' well-thought-out want list.

When time came for the Cowboys to announce their selection, they called out the name of the University of Pittsburgh's running back Tony Dorsett—Heisman Trophy winner, three-time All-American, a speed-blessed young man who had become the first runner to gain more than 6,000 yards in a collegiate career.

The Cowboys' running-game problems were solved.

CHAPTER 15

"If you're lucky in life, you'll be put in the presence of someone who is exactly what you would like to be. Roger was and is one of my idols."

Thomas "Hollywood" Henderson

He was the franchise's first million-dollar player, and it was felt by many in the Cowboys organization that his arrival provided the magical last ingredient needed to assure a return to Super Bowl glory. Tony Dorsett was a running back unlike any who had ever worn a Dallas uniform. With his dazzling speed and unique ability to avoid tackles, he was the lone offensive weapon that had been missing during the previous season.

Followers of the team anxiously looked forward to the moment when the Cowboys would regularly break the huddle with not one but two Heisman Trophy winners in its backfield.

The wait would be longer than some expected.

Though aware of Dorsett's great potential, Landry was determined to bring him along slowly. The first stage of the 1977 season would call for him to watch and learn, getting considerable playing time but not as a regular.

Again healthy, Preston Pearson would enter his third Cowboys season as the starting running back, while Newhouse returned at full speed to his job at fullback. Staubach, his hand and throwing arm healed and his postseason funk long since passed, had viewed the landscape during training camp and privately felt the new year could welcome the best team Dallas had ever assembled.

Even with the retirement of middle linebacker Lee Roy Jordan, the defense, which had already proven itself to be among the best in the NFL, was only getting better. Bob Breunig moved from outside linebacker into Jordan's vacated spot, Thomas Henderson would fill Breunig's old position, and D.D. Lewis remained at the other linebacker spot. Randy White would settle into the weakside tackle position with veteran Jethro Pugh at the opposite tackle. At defensive ends, Harvey Martin and Ed Jones were nearing the peaks of their careers; as were the reliable one-two punch of safeties Cliff Harris and Charlie Waters. The lone new starter in the secondary was cornerback Aaron Kyle.

The offensive line remained solid despite the retirement of guard Blaine Nye. There was not only great talent among his receiving corps, but the draft had also produced additional depth. Rookie Tony Hill had not generated the media furor that accompanied Dorsett's arrival, but Staubach was excited about the potential of the young receiver from Stanford.

Most important, however, was the new offensive dimension offered by Dorsett's presence, promising to serve as the catalyst for something special.

That promise would get a severe test on opening day, however, as the Cowboys traveled to Minnesota to face the defending NFC champion Vikings.

Trailing 7–3 in the fourth quarter, Staubach put Dallas ahead with a seven-yard touchdown pass to Preston Pearson. But with just a minute and a half remaining in the game, a Fred Cox field goal lifted Minnesota into a 10–10 tie.

Butch Johnson then returned the kickoff 48 yards, and Staubach quickly passed the Cowboys to the Vikings' 15. With just six seconds remaining, Efren Herrera, who had not missed a field goal from inside the 30-yard line in three years, saw his attempt go wide.

Minnesota won the toss prior to overtime, but a Larry Cole sack of Tarkenton for a nine-yard loss had ended the Vikings' first drive, forcing a punt.

Staubach quickly connected twice with Drew Pearson, then threw to Golden Richards to move to the Minnesota 15. Carries by Preston Pearson and Newhouse advanced the ball to the 9.

On third down, Staubach sprinted to his left, looking for an open receiver. What he saw instead was a wide-open path to the end zone, and he ran in for the touchdown.

The early 16–10 victory was the most difficult Dallas would achieve as it stormed to a franchise-record eight straight wins by the first week in November.

Home and away, the Cowboys dispatched opponents—the Giants, Tampa Bay, Washington, St. Louis, Philadelphia, and Detroit—with remarkable precision. During the remarkable stretch, only the game against the Cardinals was even close.

Trailing 24–16 in the fourth quarter, Staubach, already leading the conference in virtually every passing category, responded with two fast-paced scoring drives. Dorsett completed one with a one-yard touchdown run. Roger threw for another, hitting Golden Richards with a 17-yard pass as Dallas scored a 30–24 come-from-behind victory.

Despite carrying the ball only 14 times, Dorsett ran for 141 yards, including a dazzling 77-yard touchdown run early in the game.

Then, just as championship talk was beginning to spread throughout Dallas, the Cowboys fortunes took an inexplicable turn. Facing the Cardinals for the second time, they were suddenly lethargic and error-prone. Still, they had led by a touchdown midway through the fourth quarter before Staubach suffered a sprained thumb on his throwing hand. For the remainder of the game, accurate passes were rare.

Jim Hart, meanwhile, connected on touchdown passes to wide receiver Mel Gray and tight end Jackie Smith to lift the Cardinals to a 24–17 win.

In an attempt to avert the same kind of tail-off his team had experienced the previous season, Landry announced during his weekly press conference that Dorsett, after having performed well in spot action, would replace Preston Pearson as the starting running back when the team traveled to Pittsburgh to play the Steelers.

Earlier, when Landry called him aside to make him aware of the move, the veteran Pearson made no effort to hide his bitter disappointment. While he had known that the job would ultimately be handed off to his replacement, he felt he'd played well enough through the first half of the season to keep it, at least for the remainder of Dorsett's rookie year. He didn't feel the celebrated young rookie had fairly won their week-to-week battle.

He also felt Landry's timing might have been better.

There was even a tinge of regret in Landry's voice when he discussed the move with *Dallas Morning News* columnist Sam Blair, "My timing wasn't the best because we were going to Pittsburgh, Preston's home, to play the Steelers. I know it hurt him not being introduced as a starter with family and friends sitting in the stands."

Publicly, Preston faced his demotion as a professional. "Tony and I are friends and teammates. He's a rookie, and I'll help him in any way I can. I want to help him and help this team."

Concluding his evaluation of the much-anticipated changing of the guard, Blair ended his column with a final reference to Pearson's handling of the situation: "The man has class."

While Tony's debut as a starter was impressive—he ran 17 times for 73 yards, including a 13-yard touchdown—the Steelers won 28–13, serving the Cowboys with a second straight defeat.

Still, an 8–2 record was hardly the end of the world, Landry insisted. A "new season" awaited. In team meetings, he referred to what lay ahead as the "playoff drive." Team members knew what he meant. Historically, Landry had believed that it was essential for any team hoping to do well in the playoffs to end its regular season on a high note. The Cowboys had four regular-season games remaining to accomplish the goal.

They won them all.

Facing the Redskins in RFK Stadium, Dallas viewed the game as a multipurpose task. Breaking out of its two-game losing streak was the primary goal. Second, a win would put additional distance between them and the only team in the division with a chance to challenge them for the NFC East title. Third, a victory would provide the Cowboys a sweep of the home-and-home series, something they had never accomplished.

The rivalry had, over the years, developed into a blood feud. And a well-chronicled battle of wits between Landry and Redskins coach George Allen. In what would be the final match-up of the two heralded coaches, the Cowboys won 14–7, giving Landry an 8–7 edge in the series. Dorsett, pounded unmercifully by the Washington defense, still rushed for 64 yards and scored the winning touchdown.

Dallas was back on track, and the fine-tuning began. And Staubach's earlier gut feeling that the presence of Dorsett would elevate the offense to new heights was fast becoming a reality. Against Philadelphia the following week he ran for 206 yards, breaking the team's single-game rushing record of Calvin Hill by 53 yards, as the Cowboys scored a 24–14 victory. A week later, the offense continued to explode in a 42–35 win over the 49ers. And in the final regular season game, Dallas defeated Denver 14–6.

The Broncos, having emerged as the premier team in the AFC, entered the game with a 12–1 record and were being hailed as the heir apparent to the Pittsburgh Steelers. Their defense was exceptional, and the offensive leader was a rejuvenated Craig Morton, who had put Dallas, New York, and a lengthy history of injuries and misfortune behind him. With a playoff spot already assured, Denver coach Red Miller had opted to have Morton sit out the meaningless regular-season finale.

Another head-to-head meeting with old friend and former rival Staubach would have to wait.

The Chicago Bears, absent from the playoff picture since 1963, visited Texas Stadium as a wild card entry and ran into a Cowboys team clearly eager to flex its muscles.

Pressured all day by the Dallas defense, Bears quarterback Bob Avellini threw four interceptions, three of them picked off by safety Charlie Waters. The fourth interception went to linebacker D.D. Lewis, who also recovered a Bears fumble. Running back Walter Payton could find nowhere to run.

By the end of the third quarter, the Cowboys led 34–0 and ultimately won 37–7 in what was described as one of the most lopsided playoff games in modern history.

So dominant was Dallas that Landry was content to allow the running game to drive the offense. With Dorsett and Newhouse each gaining more than 80 yards, Staubach threw only 13 passes, completing eight.

As the Cowboys prepared to host Minnesota in the NFC championship game, they had arguably emerged as the best team in the franchise's history. The offense, which had so often relied on Staubach and his collection of gifted receivers, particularly in big games, had a balance reminiscent of the Calvin Hill–Duane Thomas days. With Dorsett in full stride, striking fear into opposing defenses, every other aspect of the Cowboys' attack became more lethal. Staubach was suddenly guaranteed additional throwing time only by first faking a run. And in the event Dallas did find itself in third-and-long, it had a quick solution. Despite losing his starting job to Dorsett, Preston Pearson assumed a role that offered yet another explosive aspect to the Cowboys attack. Coming off the bench as a third-down specialty back, he was on his way to a club record 46 receptions by a running back for the season.

Dorsett, meanwhile, claimed a team record of his own, becoming the first Cowboys rookie ever to rush for 1,000 yards.

And Dallas' Flex defense was playing at an equally high level. During the regular season, Harvey Martin had been credited with 23 quarterback sacks.

One superlative seemed to lead to another as Staubach emerged as the NFL's most efficient quarterback.

And from it all emerged a subtle change that the Dallas quarterback welcomed. The spotlight, which had so often focused on him, had expanded greatly as his supporting cast blossomed. Though he would, over the course of the regular season, complete 210-of-361 passes for 2,620 yards and 18 touchdowns, his statistics only blended into the overall picture. Less pressured and more confident in the talent around him, he liked it that way.

In the NFC title game, the Vikings fared only slightly better than had the Bears. With Fran Tarkenton injured and unable to play, the chore of directing the Minnesota offense went to Bob Lee who was relentlessly harassed by Harvey Martin from one side and Ed Jones from the other. Before game's end, Jones had a dozen tackles, one a thundering hit on Vikings running back Chuck Foreman, which forced a fumble that Martin quickly recovered. The Vikings could muster only two field goals as Dallas methodically paved its way to the New Orleans Super Dome and Super Bowl XII with a 23–6 victory.

After spending three seasons with the Giants, Craig Morton had been traded to Denver where his career was been rejuvenated to a point that he was soon to be named the NFL's Comeback Player of the Year. He'd led the Broncos to a 12–2 regular record and had performed well as Denver defeated Pittsburgh and Oakland in the playoffs. He arrived in New Orleans with the distinction of being the only quarterback to start in a Super Bowl for different teams.

And in the week leading up to the game, the media repeatedly questioned him and Staubach about the days when they had been in competition for the starting job in Dallas.

For both, it was an expected yet uncomfortable theme that sportswriters had chosen for their pregame stories.

Even at the height of their battle for Landry's favor, the two had shared a mutual respect, ultimately becoming friends.

"Craig was coming off a tremendous season with the Broncos," Staubach recalled, "and I was happy for him. If anyone wanted to second-guess the decision that led to my staying with the Cowboys and Craig's leaving, they had to admit that it had been good for both of us. The fact we were both in the Super Bowl certainly addressed that so far as I was concerned."

The game plan devised by Landry and his coaching staff was basic and conservative. On offense, the Cowboys would attack Denver's greatest strength, a defense that throughout the season had yielded the fewest yards rushing of any team in the league. Meanwhile, the Dallas defense, aware that Morton was not a mobile quarterback who would attempt to break out of the pocket and scramble to allow receivers time to get open, had a simple objective—constant and relentless pressure.

In the early going, Dallas looked as if it might bow to the nerve-wracking pressure of the moment. In the first five minutes of the game, the Cowboys fumbled three times. On the opening kickoff, Dorsett and Butch Johnson attempted a handoff that was bobbled at the 20-yard line. Dallas, however, was able to recover the loose ball. Tony Hill then mishandled a punt at his own 1-yard line yet was able to fall on the ball. On the next offensive series, Dorsett fumbled as he broke into the Broncos secondary, but center Fitzgerald managed to make the recovery.

Though the media had spent a good deal of pregame time alluding to what it called "Cowboys Cool," the team was hardly living up to its reputation.

In the huddle, the normally stoic Newhouse shouted at Staubach over the domed stadium's thundering noise. "Roger," he said, "you've got to get these guys under control."

While the offense did settle into a grinding style of play, mounting a short drive that ended late in the first quarter with a three-yard Dorsett touchdown run, it was the defense that brought order to the Cowboys. The front four of Martin, Jones, Pugh, and White was relentless, forcing four Morton interceptions in the first half. One set up a Dallas touchdown, another an Efren Herrera field goal as Dallas took a 13–0 lead into intermission.

In the third quarter, after Denver had narrowed the score to 13–3 on a 47-yard field goal by Jim Turner, Staubach broke from the conservative plan. Following a series of runs by Newhouse and Preston Pearson, subbing for Dorsett who had gone to the sidelines with a knee injury, that advanced the ball to midfield, Landry called for a down-and-over-the-middle route Butch Johnson had successfully run against the Broncos in that final game of the regular season. While reviewing film of the game, Staubach had noticed that Denver free safety Bernard Jackson had not dropped into his deep zone on the play, opting to help defend against receivers breaking across the middle of the field. As the team prepared to break the huddle, Staubach instructed his young receiver to fake the called route, then break downfield on a deep post pattern.

While the Denver defenders closely covered Preston Pearson and tight end Billy Joe DuPree as they cut across the middle of the field, Johnson was sprinting toward the end zone, a step ahead of his surprised defender. Despite playing with a finger that had been broken earlier in the game, Johnson made a sensational diving catch for the 45-yard touchdown.

The Broncos responded to the 20–3 deficit with a dazzling 67-yard kickoff return by Rick Upchurch. With the ball at the Cowboys' 29-yard line, Morton's first pass went directly into the outstretched arms of Ed Jones. With nothing but 70 yards of open field in front of him, the ball slipped from his grasp.

Another interception averted, Denver coach Red Miller opted to pull the battered Morton from the game. And with a scrambling Norris Weese at quarterback, the Broncos drove for their first touchdown of the afternoon.

The Cowboys took a 20–10 lead into the final quarter.

Following a fumble recovery by Aaron Kyle late in the game, the Dallas offense took over at the Broncos 29-yard line. It was time, Landry decided, to deliver the knock-out blow. The play he sent in was "Brown Right, x-opposite, shift, toss, 38, halfback lead fullback pass to Y."

The English translation: fullback Newhouse was to take a pitch from Staubach, fake a run, then throw a pass to Golden Richards.

When the play came in from the bench and Staubach began calling it in the huddle, Newhouse's eyes widened. Just minutes earlier he had applied a generous portion of stickum to his hands and was genuinely concerned that he would even be able to release the ball. "As we broke the huddle, I tried to rub as much of it off as possible," Newhouse said.

As he ran to his left, the fullback saw open field and briefly considered running. Instead, however, he pulled up and lofted the ball into the end zone where Richards waited.

Thus it was a touchdown pass delivered by someone other than Staubach that sealed the 27–10 victory.

Roger, in fact, spent the waning minutes of the game hoping not to have to throw at all. Early in the final quarter he had been hit by Denver linebacker Tom Jackson and suffered a broken forefinger on his passing hand. The injection of Novocaine given to him by the team doctor had numbed the finger.

What pain he felt when the medication wore away was masked by jubilation.

For him it had been a workman, blue collar–like performance. He completed 17-of-25 passes for 183 yards and the touchdown to Johnson. He had consistently connected with receivers on key plays that kept drives alive and had not thrown an interception.

But on this day, the lion's share of plaudits were reserved for the Cowboys defense. Harvey Martin and Randy White were named as the game's co-Most Valuable Players. Safety Randy Hughes, with an interception and two fumble recoveries, wasn't far behind in the voting. The defense's dominating performance forced Denver into the Super Bowl record books in numerous negative categories—most interceptions, most fumbles lost, fewest yards gained, and fewest first downs.

When told that Martin and White had been named as co-MVPs and would each be awarded a new automobile, weary Denver guard Tom Glassic best summed up the day, "Why stop there? Give everybody on their defense a car."

Long after the Vince Lombardi Trophy was presented, awards continued to flow to the newly crowned champions. Martin was selected as the NFL's Defensive Player of the Year, and Dorsett was honored as Rookie of the Year. In back-to-back years, he had played on teams that won the mythical national collegiate championship and the Super Bowl. A dozen Cowboys were invited to participate in the Pro Bowl, Staubach, the NFC's passing leader, among them.

Even before the celebration calmed, Dallas general manager Tex Schramm was forecasting even bigger things to come. A man who attached great importance to historical achievement, he made no secret of his desire that the team he'd nurtured since its infancy would finish the 1970s strong. The franchise's next goal, he said, was to make sure that it would be forever remembered as the team of the decade. To achieve that, Schramm acknowledged, Dallas would need one more Super Bowl victory than the Pittsburgh Steelers who had also collected two Lombardi trophies.

Schramm was looking to the future, already dreaming of a perfect scenario for the next season.

CHAPTER 16

"The Dallas Cowboys are supposed to be undefeated, untied, unscored upon and under orders from NFL headquarters to hold the score down."

Joe Marshall, *Sports Illustrated*

Having played in four Super Bowls during the Seventies, winning twice, the Cowboys' place among the NFL's elite was firmly established. They had evolved into a team of almost embarrassing riches—superior coach, a great quarterback who set the tone for a talented and innovative offense, a defense that had demonstrated just how good it was in humiliating the Denver Broncos, an ideal mixture of youth and veterans—and there was strong evidence they were hungry for more.

Though unspoken, the goal of establishing itself as the Team of the Decade served as Dallas' new motivation.

It seemed only fitting that they would open the season in the spotlight of a Monday Night Football telecast, flexing their muscles in front of a national television audience. The Cowboys responded by bombarding the Baltimore Colts 38–0. Staubach put his remarkable roster of receivers on display as he passed for four touchdowns, one of them a screen pass to Dorsett who turned it into a 91-yard score. Any concern over the injuries the two had suffered in the previous January's Super Bowl were set to rest. Dorsett provided strong notice that the running game was equal to the passing attack of Roger and his receivers. He carried 15 times for 147 yards.

A week later Dallas visited the New York Giants, and again the offense went into overdrive. Staubach threw for more than 200 yards, and Dorsett rushed for more than 100.

Any fears that the Cowboys might suffer the post–Super Bowl letdown so many previous defending champions had experienced seemed unfounded. Certainly the off-season had been one in which players had scattered hither and yon, picking up awards, following the banquet circuit, making endorsement deals, and generally being treated as the celebrities they had become. But the first two weeks of the season served as evidence that the distractions had left no damage.

Then the wheels fell off.

Against the Rams, the Cowboys seemed to be sleep-walking as they lost 27–14. They appeared to have regained some of their footing in a 21–12 win over St. Louis, then lost a defensive struggle with the Redskins 9–5. Midway through the season, they were a 6–2 team that was struggling. The offense, gifted with so many weapons, had become a shadow of itself.

"We were suddenly in this slump, inconsistent and tentative, as if everyone was waiting for the other guy to do something to get things back on track," Staubach later noted in his autobiography.

He was throwing interceptions. Dorsett was suddenly fumble-prone. And the defense was allowing too many big plays.

Even Landry seemed puzzled by the downturn. "I have no magic solutions," he admitted to the press, "just more hard work. We've had other teams face adversity and overcome it. This team has character but up to now it hasn't had to deal with that adversity. Now they do, and we'll see just how much character they do have."

In the privacy of the locker room, veterans were grumbling that the younger members of the team were spending too much time enjoying being a member of the Dallas Cowboys while not putting in the preparation necessary to produce continued success. "Too many players seemed to think that once practice and meetings were over, their work was done," Harvey Martin observed.

It soon became clear that fixing the problem would not come quickly as nagging injuries began to haunt the defense. Martin missed time with knee problems, while Thomas Henderson was sidelined by a severe ankle sprain.

In the following weeks, the Cowboys lost back-to-back games with Minnesota and Miami as the offense was held to 10 points by the Vikings and 16 by the Dolphins.

Soon it was mid-November and the bewildering Cowboys were 6–4. Experts were ready to dismiss them as a legitimate contender for the NFC East title. Another trip to the Super Bowl seemed out of the question.

And injuries continued to take a toll. When backup tight end Jay Saldi suffered a broken forearm, player personnel director Gil Brandt placed an urgent call to a man who had long been a thorn in the side of Cowboys defenders. Jackie Smith, a veteran of 15 years in the NFL, announced his retirement from the St. Louis Cardinals at the end of the '77 season at age 38.

As he listened to the caller explain how badly the Cowboys needed him, Smith decided that someone was playing a practical joke. Only when Landry himself called did the All-Pro tight end realize the offer was for real.

Though at first hesitant, Smith was soon booking a flight to Dallas.

As quickly as the light had dimmed, new hope arrived with a convincing road victory over the Packers. Suddenly the offense returned to life, amassing 537 yards en route to a 42–14 victory. Staubach threw for 200 yards, while the running game featured two 100-yard performances as Dorsett collected 149 and Newhouse gained 101.

The Saints were victimized by the revitalized Cowboys the following week, then Dallas scored 37 points in a surprisingly easy victory over the Redskins.

Suddenly, all was right in the Cowboys' world as they roared through the remainder of the regular season with a six-game winning streak that provided them a 12–4 record, the NFC East championship, and another invitation to the playoffs.

They would face the Atlanta Falcons with a repolished résumé. Despite having thrown 16 interceptions, Staubach countered with 25 touchdown passes and ended the regular season as the league's top-ranked quarterback, a tenth of a point better than Pittsburgh's Terry Bradshaw, and Dorsett's rushing yardage had jumped from the previous season to 1,325 yards, third in the NFL behind legends-in-the-making Earl Campbell and Walter Payton. With all finally in good health down the stretch, the Dallas defense had climbed to the No. 1 spot in the league against the run, allowing opponents an average of only 108 yards per game. Over the final six games, it had held the Jets and Saints to seven points each, the Redskins and Patriots to 10 apiece, Philadelphia to 13, and Green Bay to 14. Doomsday, it seemed, was back.

Then, as they hosted wild card entry Atlanta in the Divisional playoffs, the task again turned difficult. By the half, quarterback Steve Bartkowski had directed the underdog Falcons to scores on each of their first four possessions—two touchdowns, two field goals—to lead 20–13. And Dallas was to play the remainder of the game without Staubach who had been knocked unconscious late in the second quarter by blitzing linebacker Robert Pennywell.

If the Cowboys were to fashion a comeback that would continue their season, it would be under the direction of backup Danny White—and with a great deal of help from the defense.

Midway through the third quarter, White methodically orchestrated a six-play, 52-yard drive that moved the ball to the Falcons' 2-yard line. Then, sprinting to his right, he threw to Jackie Smith for his first touchdown as a member of the Cowboys.

In the fourth quarter, with the scored tied at 20–20, the defense did its part. Stopping the Falcons, it forced a punt from deep in the Atlanta end of the field. The rushed kick netted only 10 yards, giving Dallas the ball on the 30-yard line. Six plays later, fullback Scott Laidlaw, playing in place of Newhouse who was still sidelined with a hamstring injury, burst into the end zone from the 1—his second touchdown run of the afternoon—to seal the Dallas victory.

Despite managing to keep the game close, Bartkowski completed only 8-of-23 passes and was intercepted three times.

As Dallas prepared to visit the Los Angeles Rams for the NFC championship, Staubach assured team doctors that he felt no lingering effects from the blow that had sidelined him against the Falcons. By mid-week he was cleared to play.

The oddsmakers were calling the game a toss-up as both teams had compiled identical records. And while Dallas had struggled in its divisional win over Atlanta, the Rams had been impressive as they eliminated Minnesota 34–10. Though both had road-tested offensive firepower, experts were predicting that it would be the superior defense that would rule the day.

Proving that the prognosticators are sometimes right, the Cowboys and Rams battled to a 0–0 stalemate through the first two quarters. Neither Staubach nor Rams quarterback Pat Haden could consistently move their teams.

The game stayed scoreless through most of the third period until, with less than two minutes remaining, Charlie Waters intercepted a Haden pass and returned it 20 yards to the Rams' 10. It would take five plays, but the Cowboys finally got on the scoreboard when Dorsett scored on a five-yard run.

Minutes later, as the fourth quarter began, Waters got his second interception of the day when Randy White and rookie defensive end Larry Bethea battered Haden just as he released the ball. Haden's hand collided against White's helmet as he followed through on the throw, breaking his thumb.

While Staubach was throwing a four-yard touchdown pass to Scott Laidlaw, Haden was headed to the X-ray room, finished for the day.

With Vince Ferragamo at quarterback, the Rams seemed to gain new life. He quickly connected with Willie Miller for a 65-yard pass-and-run that advanced the ball to the Dallas 15. But with power-running fullback John Cappelletti sidelined by an earlier injury, the Rams soon found themselves in a fourth-and-1 situation. Since time was becoming an issue, Los Angeles opted not to attempt a field goal and instead sent running back Jim Jodat into the brunt of a Cowboys front wall where he was swarmed for a loss.

Still, the work of the Cowboys defense was not done. Midway through the fourth, Ferragamo again appeared to be moving his team to its first score of the day before running back Cullen Bryant fumbled the ball away to Harvey Martin at the Dallas 10.

Dorsett, who had been stopped after only short gains all afternoon, broke for a 53-yard run that moved the offense out of a potentially dangerous position and provided the launch of a third Cowboys scoring drive. By the time Staubach connected on a short touchdown pass to tight end DuPree, the issue was put to rest.

The increasingly flamboyant Henderson provided a final explanation point to the shutout victory as he intercepted a desperate Ferragamo pass in the waning minutes and returned it 68 yards for a score.

During the course of the game, the Dallas defense had forced seven Rams turnovers—five interceptions and two fumbles—en route to the 28–0 victory.

Tex Schramm's dreamed-for perfect storm was on the horizon. In Three Rivers Stadium in Pittsburgh, the Steelers had methodically defeated Houston 34–5 to claim the AFC championship.

Super Bowl XIII not only crowned an NFL champion; it determined which of its proud entries would reign as the premier team of the decade.

Of all the Cowboys looking ahead to the visit to Miami, none cherished the moment more than Jackie Smith. As his new team had advanced through the final games of the regular season, then the playoffs, he had adopted the habit of waking before sunrise. While the rest of his family still slept, he started the coffee, then sat at his dining room table contemplating the unique opportunity that had come his way. "My wife would join me once the coffee was ready, and we would just sit and talk. Here I was, with a chance I'd never realistically thought possible. We would get downright emotional about it."

Only twice during his remarkable career had the Cardinals even made the playoffs, and they were eliminated in the first round both times.

"I wanted so badly to sit down with some of the young Cowboys players and tell them just how fortunate they were. I'm sure some, like Roger and Preston, Cliff and Charlie and Jethro, understood it to some degree. But none of them had ever been on the other side of the fence, never knew how hard it was to begin every new season, trying to regroup one more time while not really having any better prospects than the year before," he said.

For all those years in St. Louis, Smith had dreamed of playing in a championship game. But in truth, it had always been an unrealistic aspiration. "I don't think we ever admitted it to ourselves, but that's just the way it was," he remembered.

Smith had been amazed at the approach the Cowboys took, from the front office to the players, to assure that the team won. "In Dallas, the notion of making it to the top starts with management and filters down to the players," he observed. "In St. Louis, it was just the opposite. Year after year the players would start the idea and try to get it worked up to the front office. It never happened."

It was, he realized, the attention to the smallest of details that helped give the Cowboys an edge. Everything possible was done to make things run as smoothly as possible for the team. Purchase of extra tickets was never a hassle. Team travel was more comfortable and accommodating. Practices ran like clockwork. "It was obvious to me that avoiding even the smallest distraction of players was a priority," Smith said. "Little things were important in Dallas. I was even impressed by the fact they sent out Christmas cards. In the grand scheme of things, it was no big deal. But all those little things add up."

Most important, he saw a more serious attitude among his new coaches and teammates. "I saw more studying, more communicating with each other about game plans. And almost everyone in Dallas was team oriented. The attitude, which Coach Landry had a great deal to do with, was team first, individual performances second."

For the 38-year-old Smith, comfortable in his Johnny-come-lately role as a back-up player, knowing that he would now complete his career by playing in a Super Bowl, the last hurrah of an old warrior had become an almost magical experience.

From the windows of the Braniff charter that was slowly moving toward the Love Field runway, players could still see the milling fans waving banners wishing the Cowboys good luck. The cold Texas winds had done nothing to dampen the enthusiasm of those who remained behind, preparing to count down the days until the kickoff of Super Bowl XIII.

The atmosphere on the plane headed for Ft. Lauderdale, where the team headquartered for the coming week, was loose and cheerful. Members of the Cowboys front office staff who had bit roles in the made-for-TV movie *The Dallas Cowboys Cheerleaders* that had aired the previous evening were chided about their acting debuts.

"Great plot," Staubach observed with no small amount of sarcasm. "I thought I'd never figure out how it was going to end. In fact, I've got a great idea for a story line for *Dallas Cowboys Cheerleaders II* if anyone's interested."

"Sit down, Roger," said *Dallas Cowboys Weekly* photographer Russ Russell, who had played a small role.

There was a lavish in-flight meal, and finally, arrival at the Ft. Lauderdale airport where bands played, a red carpet was rolled out, and TV cameras focused on the deplaning players.

A new member of the front office staff, making her first visit to a Super Bowl, viewed the welcoming hoopla and said, "It's just Monday and I'm already so excited I can hardly stand it."

Super Bowl Week had officially begun.

Careful to chronicle the events that lay ahead, the *Cowboys Weekly* had even assigned a writer to keep a diary:

Tuesday: Picture Day, the first official act of the media circus that had become as much a part of the Super Bowl as the game itself. Before the week is out, there will be something in the neighborhood of 2,000 accredited journalists on hand. Some will file daily reports, some gathering material for magazine pieces (including a female writer fighting over-whelming odds—her assignment was to do a profile of Landry for *Playboy* magazine), others with no real visible reason for being here.

Members of the Cowboys squad, dressed in full game uniform, are on hand at Little Yankee Stadium, the spring training home of the New York Yankees and Dallas' pregame training site. Since Landry had posted no curfew the night before, several players were obviously up at an hour that was not of their own choosing. Fullback Scott Laidlaw, stretched on the outfield grass, peeked up through one open eye at a reporter, grinned, and said, "I'm trying to keep as low a profile as possible."

Out near the left-field fence, players—starters and backups, veterans and rookies—were surrounded by reporters hanging on their every word. Drawing the largest crowd was Thomas Henderson, talking a mile-a-minute. Even as he was speaking with journalists on hand, a call came into the Cowboys headquarters, asking if the flamboyant linebacker would be available to make an appearance on network talk-show host Tom Snyder's *Tomorrow*.

"What I really want to do is host *Saturday Night Live*," Henderson replied.

Wednesday: With Landry still not enforcing any curfew following practice and meetings, the players sampled some of Ft. Lauderdale's night life. Many, the Staubachs included, had quiet dinners at The Wharf, a famous seafood restaurant several miles up the coast. A number of the young, single players stopped in at several local discos.

When a film crew suggested it might be fun to shoot a story in which players were shown judging a wet T-shirt contest at one of the beachfront night spots, discretion ruled.

Players like Harvey Martin, Randy Hughes, and Ed Jones carried cameras wherever they went. "Trying to tell people back home what Super Bowl Week is like is impossible, so this year I'm taking pictures," Jones said.

Earlier in the day, a 45-minute interview session was held at the Bahia Mar Hotel where the team was headquartered. Tables had been set up for each player with what organizers felt would be ample seating. For

Staubach, Dorsett, and of course Henderson, the media demand was greater than expected, and they were moved to an adjacent dining room to speak with the media.

Nearby, a huge tent was going up on the hotel parking lot. Complete with Texas flags waving from its top, it would be the site for the Cowboys' postgame party. "What kind of party is it going to be?" a visitor asked assistant public relations director George Heddleston. "We're planning on it being a victory party," he replied.

Thursday: Three more days and the pressure is beginning to show. During the previous day's workout, running back Preston Pearson takes a fall and feels a sudden pain in his hand. There is silence as he lays on the ground, not moving. In this week, when everything becomes magnified, there is, in Preston's mind, the flash of fear that he might not be able to play Sunday. After trainers check the hand thoroughly, it is determined that there is no serious damage and practice continued.

The press arrives again to repeat questions asked the day before, urging Roger to compare his style to that of Bradshaw's, quizzing Landry on the officiating in the previous Super Bowl meeting with the Steelers. Lost in the furor is the fact fullback Scott Laidlaw has defied the league's must-attend rule and is absent.

Leaving the interview room at noon, center John Fitzgerald says he's going over to the practice field. "Three hours early?" a reporter asked. "It's quiet out there," the Cowboys center explained.

Friday: The crazies have come to town. Throughout the day fans were shoulder to shoulder in the lobby of the Bahia Mar. Pennant and T-shirt vendors were making a killing. Phone lines were so jammed that it was all but impossible to get a call into or out of the hotel. Most of the players, getting weary of the assault of autograph-seekers and well-wishers every time they stepped out of an elevator, retreated to the solitude of their rooms. Even the escape to the practice field, where security guarded against any intrusions, was looked forward to.

Along the streets and beaches, people made it vocally clear which team they favored. A pair of fishing boat operators, cleaning their crafts, stopped to watch the horn-honking traffic go past the hotel, beer bottles and banners were waved by people hanging halfway out of automobiles. "I've got the feeling it is going to get pretty crazy around here before Sunday," one said. "I've never seen anything like it," the other replied.

Saturday: Members of the Cowboys organization were beginning to look like participants in a Chinese fire drill. Phones rang constantly, problems were heard and solved only to be followed by more problems. Transportation arrangements were made for wives wishing to shop or see the sights. Last-minute ticket requests poured in. There were messages for everyone. Ohio State coach Woody Hayes would be arriving at 5:00 PM. Had anyone made arrangements to pick him up? Former Jets quarterback Joe Namath called to ask about meeting someone at the NFL party. Good-luck telegrams were arriving in bunches.

Scout John Wooten, lending a hand with the phones, smiled. "Actually, everything is going more smoothly than it ever has before," he said. "We've learned a lot at previous Super Bowls and have been able to solve a lot of problems before they occur."

For the players it would be the longest day of the week. Impatience was beginning to show. The press no longer had access, curfew was in place, and there was nothing more to accomplish on the practice field.

Unlike his players, Landry was not yet free of interviews. Riding into Miami for a press conference at the league headquarters at the Ambassador Hotel, he had scanned the newspapers and looked over at a reporter who had accompanied him on the trip. "What in the world," he wanted to know, "can you guys ask that you haven't already?"

The reporter shrugged and grinned. "Tom," he finally replied, "what's your favorite color?"

In the days counting down to the kick-off of Super Bowl XIII, the media trumpeted the Dallas-Pittsburgh rematch as if were to be the reincarnation of the O.K. Corral shootout between lawmen Wyatt Earp and Doc Holliday and Ike Clanton's band of hooligans. It was a game that promised everything—the top two quarterbacks in the NFL ready to do battle, and Dallas' Doomsday Defense against Pittsburgh's Steel Curtain.

Landry vs. Noll. Blue-collar Steelers fans against Dallas' big-bucks high society. Draft beer vs. sparkling champagne.

As the teams tossed taunts back and forth, both insisting their team was superior, the build-up had begun to sound more like the frenzied preview of a heavyweight fight than a football game.

Dallas brought its own brand of unprecedented brashness to the debate. Its name was Hollywood Henderson. Despite Landry's admonitions and teammate's urgings, the colorful young linebacker would not shut up. At media gatherings he was a steady stream of outrageous pop-offs and one-liners. Pittsburgh quarterback Terry Bradshaw, he volunteered, was "so dumb he couldn't spell *cat* if you spotted him the 'a' and the 't.'"

At the center of a grandiose stage, Henderson relentlessly worked the crowd. And the media couldn't get enough. The attention the Dallas linebacker called to himself in the days before the game ultimately landed him, not team leader Staubach, on the cover of *Newsweek* alongside Bradshaw.

"Thanks," Roger finally told Henderson during an afternoon practice. "You're taking the pressure off everyone else on the team."

While the Steelers personnel had changed little since the teams met two years earlier, Dallas' lineup was liberally sprinkled with new faces.

Tony Hill had been elevated to a starting position at wide receiver after Golden Richards was traded to the Bears. Billy Joe DuPree had taken over at tight end from Jean Fugett. Pat Donovan had inherited the left tackle job following the retirement of Ralph Neely. Herb Scott replaced Burton Lawless at one guard, and Tom Rafferty had moved into the other, which had previously been occupied by the retired Blaine Nye.

And, it was Dorsett in place of Preston Pearson at the running back position.

Among the linebackers, only D.D. Lewis remained. Dave Edwards had been replaced at one of the outside spots by Henderson, and Bob Breunig had settled in as the play-calling middle linebacker. In the secondary, retired Mel Renfro had been replaced by Aaron Kyle.

And when kicker Efren Herrera had become involved in a contract dispute with management during training camp, his job had been passed on to Rafael Septien.

With the Dirty Dozen coming of age, there had seemed to be little room for rookies, yet there were five first-year players who had made the trip to Miami. Most prominent among the newcomers was backup cornerback Dennis Thurman and promising defensive end Larry Bethea.

It was obvious that the impressive Dallas talent flow had not slowed.

The only team member unhappy by Landry's announcement of the starting lineups was Laidlaw. For the final month of the regular season, then through the playoffs, the five-year veteran had filled in admirably for the injured Newhouse. Feeling he had earned the right to finish out the season as the starter, Laidlaw was disappointed when Landry informed him that Newhouse, his hamstring healed, would return to the starting lineup against the Steelers. "When he told me that, it destroyed a lot of things for me," Laidlaw said. "But there was nothing I could do but sit and be ready in case I was needed."

It explained his absence from the Thursday press gathering. "The way I was feeling after Coach Landry told me of his decision," Laidlaw admitted, "I might have said something I would be sorry for later. The best thing for me to do was just keep my mouth shut for a while and get past it."

Right or wrong, he was a victim of one of Landry's hard and fast rules—a starter might lose his job as a result of the practice-to-practice, game-to-game battle with a challenging backup player but never because of an injury.

A hard morning rain that had greeted early risers on game day had been replaced by a clear blue sky as 78,000 arrived at the Orange Bowl.

On its initial possession, the Cowboys offense was sharp, briskly driving past midfield before the one thing Landry had warned would have to be avoided if Dallas hoped to win occurred. On a reverse, wide receiver Drew Pearson fumbled a handoff from Dorsett and the Steelers recovered.

The play had been one of great promise. Staubach would pitch the ball to Dorsett who, in turn, was to hand off to Pearson. Meanwhile, tight end DuPree was to fake a block, then sprint downfield in anticipation of a pass from Drew. Even as the flanker bobbled the ball, his target was all alone downfield.

Bradshaw quickly took advantage of Dallas' missed opportunity, using a short passing game to move his team into the Dallas end of the field. A 28-yard touchdown pass to John Stallworth put Pittsburgh into the lead.

It would cling to its 7–0 advantage through most of the opening period.

Again, it was the defense that provided the Cowboys the jump-start they needed. Harvey Martin broke through the Steelers offensive wall and got to Bradshaw before he could throw. The jarring tackle resulted in a fumble that Ed Jones recovered. Staubach then connected with Tony Hill for a 39-yard touchdown, and Septien's conversion tied the game at 7–7.

Next to provide the Cowboys with a break was a blitzing Henderson. He delivered a blow to Bradshaw that caused the ball to fly from his grasp and into the arms of Mike Hegman who returned it 37 yards for a go-ahead touchdown.

Generally, in a game of such magnified pressure, teams shake away their jitters after a few minutes of sparring. On this afternoon, however, the tension continued to build with every series of downs. It would be John Stallworth who calmed the Steelers.

Facing a critical third down at his own 25, Bradshaw sent the elusive receiver over the middle in hopes of picking up a first down. The swift Stallworth made the catch and eluded an over-aggressive Cowboys secondary, turning the 10-yard pass into a 75-yard touchdown.

Staubach responded by again confusing the Pittsburgh defense with a play-action passing attack that steadily moved his offense to the opposition's 32-yard line. From there he threw to Drew Pearson who appeared open at the 18-yard line. A split-second later, the first down and all Dallas momentum was eliminated as Steelers cornerback Mel Blount stepped in front of the receiver for an interception.

As halftime neared, the Steelers drove to the Dallas 7-yard line. On the final play of the quarter, Bradshaw rolled out to his right and lobbed an arching throw to running back Rocky Bleier in the end zone.

Pittsburgh would rest with a 21–14 advantage.

Though Dallas dominated the third quarter, it could not muster a touchdown despite once advancing to the Steelers' 10-yard line. From there, however, it would suffer one of the most disastrous moments in the team's history. Jackie Smith, open in the back of the Steelers end zone, let a certain touchdown pass slip from his fingers.

Staubach described the sequence of events in author Peter Golenbock's *Cowboys Have Always Been My Heroes*:

"It was third-and-1 and Landry sent in the play. I realized he was sending in a goal-line play, but I noticed we didn't have the right receivers in the game, so I had to call time out.

"I said, 'Coach, that's a goal-line play.' He said, 'Well, you're right. Go ahead and run it anyway because they'll be in their goal-line defense. Look for your keys, and make sure we get a first down.'

"We had only practiced the play from the 1- or 2-yard line. It was a brand new goal line play put in a couple of weeks before the game. It was a play with three tight ends. One of the tackles was the third tight end.

"On the play, I was to look for Billy Joe, the tight end on the other side, to go to the corner, and I was to come back looking for the fullback out of the flat. The fullback was there strictly as an outlet receiver. What Jackie was supposed to do was get into the back of the end zone.

"When I called the play in the huddle, I said we were going to run the new goal-line play.

"And sure enough, Mel Blount went with Billy Joe to the left, so he was out of the play. The fullback went into the flat and took a defender with him. And Jack Lambert blitzed up the middle. As he was coming in, Scott Laidlaw just cleaned him, actually knocking the wind out of him. Lambert left the game after that.

"And no one was near Jackie Smith, who was running to the back of the end zone, where he was supposed to go. Now if he would have just stopped at the goal line, it would have been perfect. But that's not what he was told to do. He knew his job was to get to the back of the end zone.

"So he was running into the end zone, and I saw that he was wide open. I was seeing the whole thing and saying to myself, 'Oh my God, there is no one near Jackie Smith. No one is even close to him. They let him run free.'

"I released the ball and took something off it because Jackie was not totally turned. He was just starting to turn as I was throwing the ball. I think it surprised him that the ball got to him that fast. I threw it a little bit low, and he kind of slipped.

"And the thing was, he'd never run the play. If he would have stopped at the goal line, he would have been just standing there waiting. It would have been real easy to hit him, and he would have caught it.

"But, see, he was running to the back of the end zone, and I'm getting blitzed. We knew that if Pittsburgh blitzed, it was a perfect play.

"But Jackie was surprised. The ball hit him in the chest, and he couldn't catch it."

Instead of tying the game, Dallas settled for a field goal that narrowed the Steelers' lead to four points. Still, it appeared the Cowboys had taken control of the game. Throughout the third period, Bradshaw, who was facing tremendous pressure from the Dallas defense, had only managed a single first down.

As the final period got underway that the next play that would live in infamy occurred. With just more than nine minutes remaining in the game and Pittsburgh at its own 44-yard line, Bradshaw narrowly avoided a Cliff Harris blitz and heaved a desperation pass in the direction of receiver Lynn Swann. The pass was short, and when Swann reached back in an attempt to make the catch, he tripped over the back of defender Benny Barnes and both players fell to the turf.

As nearby back judge Pat Knight signaled the pass incomplete, fellow official Fred Swearingen threw his flag from the middle of the field, signaling pass interference against Barnes. The Cowboys defender, he ruled, had tripped the receiver.

Barnes argued that he was the one who had, in fact, been tripped. Even Landry, normally a picture of calm and poise on the sidelines, was on the field angrily disputing the call as the Orange Bowl echoed in a chorus of boos. Millions of television viewers watched replay after replay and saw no foul committed.

Nonetheless, Pittsburgh had a first down at the Cowboys 23. Three plays later Franco Harris burst through the middle of the Dallas defense to score. Adding to the frustration was that safety Charlie Waters was in position to hold Harris to a short gain—except for his collision with one of the officials while on the way to make the tackle.

Another game-turning moment awaited on Pittsburgh's kickoff. Planning to kick the ball deep, Roy Gerela slipped on his approach. The result was a bouncing squib that fell into the waiting arms of blocker Randy White inside the Cowboys 20. With one hand heavily wrapped to protect a fractured thumb, the big defensive tackle was unable to control the ball, fumbled, and the Steelers recovered.

Bradshaw quickly attacked the reeling Cowboys defense with an 18-yard touchdown pass to Swann, advancing the Steelers edge to 35–17. After struggling throughout the second half, Pittsburgh had scored 14 points in a span of only 20 seconds.

Short of another Staubach-generated miracle, the game had been decided.

In a hurry-up offense, the Cowboys began driving downfield with less than seven minutes left in the game. From the 7-yard line, Staubach threw to DuPree who muscled his way through two would-be tacklers to score.

Rookie Dennis Thurman covered Septien's onside kick to set up other scoring drive. A 25-yard completion to Drew Pearson and a nine-yarder to Dorsett moved the ball to the Pittsburgh 4, then Butch Johnson gathered in a line-drive Staubach throw for a touchdown. Dallas had reduced the margin to four points. But only 22 seconds remained.

A second onside kick attempt by Septien failed as surehanded Rocky Bleier fell on the ball, allowing Pittsburgh to run out the clock on what was generally considered to be the most exciting Super Bowl game in the still-young history of the championship.

En route to the 35–31 victory, Bradshaw out-dueled Staubach, throwing for 318 yards to Roger's 228. Dorsett won the rushing battle over Franco Harris, gaining 96 yards to the Steelers running back's 68.

When all was said and done, it had, just as Landry predicted to his players in the dressing room before the game, come down to which team benefited from a few big plays. No one needed to be reminded of them: Drew Pearson's failure to get an early game reverse pass off to an open Billy Joe DuPree. The interception by Mel Blount that ended what had appeared to be an almost certain scoring drive. The drop by Jackie Smith in the end zone. Fred Swearingen's call of the phantom pass interference against Benny Barnes. Charlie Waters' collision with a referee that had allowed Harris to score. And, finally, Randy White's untimely kickoff fumble.

Six plays, many felt, denied the Cowboys a third Super Bowl victory.

Even Landry made little attempt to disguise his disappointment. "I'm upset," he told members of the media, "not so much for myself but for the players who worked so hard. This game was the culmination of a decade in which we went to five Super Bowls. We could have been the first to win three, and that would have been a great climax to an era."

And this time, it was not just Hollywood Henderson speaking his mind. Staubach, who had been standing on the Cowboys sideline near the Swann-Barnes play, was asked what he had seen from his vantage point.

"It was some idiotic official throwing a flag when he was out of position to see the play right," Roger said.

While he would not go so far as to label Swearingen "idiotic," even NFL commissioner Pete Rozelle, after reviewing the play, publicly admitted it had been a terrible call.

CHAPTER 17

"What can you say about a guy who has done it so many times?"

Tom Landry

The pain of the loss in Super Bowl XIII faded slowly. Through much of the off-season, many of the veteran players had great difficulty shaking the agonizing realization that an opportunity had slipped away. There seemed to be far less enthusiasm for public appearances, and when members of the media checked in, the few players who responded spoke reluctantly of the loss to Pittsburgh. Instead they dialed up the eternally optimistic football-speak about focusing on the upcoming season, the deep talent pool that remained, and of the need to come together for another attempt at the brass ring.

The interviews, however, often had a hollow ring. True, Dallas looked as if it would return to battle in the 1979 season with its team virtually intact, but it still needed time to put its lingering disappointment aside. Any new sense of urgency and genuine anticipation, it seemed, would have to wait until the call came to travel Thousand Oaks for another training camp.

Still, life went on behind the scenes. The coaching staff plotted new strategies, scouts conferred about another upcoming draft, and slowly the players began drifting back to the practice field for off-season preparation.

General manager Tex Schramm focused on the new horizon, routinely repeating the promise he'd made in the immediate aftermath of the Super Bowl defeat. "We'll be back," he said.

Throughout the NFL community, most people assumed the Cowboys would do just that.

Since the end of the season Bob Ryan and his staff at NFL Films, charged with producing dramatic highlight films for each of the league's teams, had worked toward completion of the Cowboys documentary. After summoning public relations director Doug Todd to a viewing of a rough cut of the film, Ryan suggested the title, *Champions Die Hard.*

Todd immediately rejected it, arguing that it made it sound as if the Cowboys had reached the end of the line. "We're not dead, nor are we dying," Todd said, adding that the team that would soon open a new season was going to be as good, perhaps better, than the one that had appeared in the Super Bowl.

The two men went back to the drawing board, reviewing the film again and again. What each noticed was that it was filled with cut-away shots of enthusiastic Cowboys fans in virtually every stadium the team visited. That, Todd insisted, told the story of what the Cowboys were about. He related stories of fans routinely awaiting the team's arrival in other cities, crowding hotel lobbies where the team would stay, cheering and pleading for autographs, and Todd pointed out that the team-published *Cowboys Weekly* newspaper had among its nearly 100,000 subscribers eager readers in every state in the U.S.

"You've got all this great footage of people in stadiums all over the league waving Cowboys banners and wearing Cowboys jerseys," he said. "We've got a tremendous fan base all over the country."

"How about calling it *America's Team?*" Ryan suggested.

Todd nodded and smiled. "I like it." He phoned Schramm to pass the idea along. Ever the promoter of the team he presided over, Tex enthusiastically endorsed it.

Thus was born a new moniker for the Dallas Cowboys.

When players gathered for a preview of the finished product in late spring, some cringed as the title appeared on the screen. "At first,"

Staubach remembered, "I thought it was a joke and that everyone would have a good laugh, then they would bring in the real highlights film."

While Schramm viewed it as a stroke of genius and the ultimate promotion of the Dallas franchise, players knew full well that an additional weight had just been added to their shoulders. They could only imagine how the Steelers, now owners of three Super Bowl rings, would feel when they became aware that the team they had just defeated for the league championship was given such recognition. Landry felt the same way. "When I saw it," he later reflected in his autobiography, "I thought, 'Oh no. Everybody's going to be gunning for us now.'"

If it caught on—and everyone knew it was an absolute certainty that Schramm and the Cowboys PR machine would make that happen—it would become a motivational tool for every opponent they faced.

In his concern, Staubach had not considered the indirect part he had played in the decision-making process. His persona had contributed greatly—the military background, his strong Christian faith, and the legendary come-from-behind victories he had helped engineer. Had he looked closely he would have noticed that most of those jerseys worn by adoring fans bore his No. 12. The steady rush of fan mail addressed to him had been postmarked from one coast to the other. If he was "Captain America," as some writers had nicknamed him, then it was only logical that the team for which he played should be America's Team.

In time, however, the nickname would not be the perceived target that NFL Films had drawn on its back that was Dallas' prime concern as it moved toward the twentieth season of the franchise's history.

On an early evening in June, a *Dallas Morning News* sportswriter assigned to cover the team answered his phone and heard the baritone voice of Ed "Too Tall" Jones. "I just wanted to let you know that I'm retiring," Jones said. "I've decided to become a professional boxer."

Vaguely aware that Jones had been a Golden Gloves champion in his teenage years back in Tennessee, the writer was still taken aback by the call. "You're kidding, right?"

"It's something I've wanted to do for a long time," the no-nonsense Jones responded.

They talked for several minutes, the writer furiously taking notes about the stunning turn of events, then he wished his caller well.

As he prepared to hang up, Jones asked a question. "Do you have Coach Landry's home number?"

"He doesn't know anything about this?"

"Not yet."

And with that conversation and the following day's headline, the quality of the Cowboys defense took a dramatic downturn.

Jethro Pugh had already retired after 14 years with the Cowboys, 10 as a starter at defensive tackle. Though never an All-Pro or even a Pro Bowl selection, he had been a reliable mainstay. Defensive line coach Ernie Stautner had often called the absence of accolades unfair and unfortunate. "First, he played in the shadow of Bob Lilly and later with guys like Harvey Martin and Randy White. But year after year, Jethro just kept on doing a steady, super job."

The Cowboys' defensive picture became even more clouded during a preseason game in Seattle when safety Charlie Waters suffered a severe knee injury that would require surgery and sideline him for the year.

Adding to the ongoing preseason melodrama was the bizarre announcement that Dorsett had dropped a large picture frame onto his foot, breaking a toe in the process. He was still limping slightly when the regular season began.

Still, the Cowboys got off to a positive start as they ran off three consecutive victories. Each, however, was by a razor-thin margin. With Dorsett unavailable for the opener, the Cowboys managed a 22–21 win over the Cardinals as Staubach directed another of his late-game comebacks, moving the offense into range for a Rafael Septien field goal with just 1:16 left to play. Then, even with Tony back and running well, they could only defeat San Francisco, 21–13. And against Chicago, Staubach had to connect with wide receiver Tony Hill for a touchdown with 1:57 left to lift Dallas to a 24–20 victory. Clearly, things were not hitting on all cylinders.

As feared, the Cowboys defense was struggling in the absence of Jones, Pugh, and Waters.

Against Cleveland, it was the offense that sputtered as the Browns defeated Dallas 26–7.

For the first half of the season, the Cowboys, despite building an impressive record, were puzzling. Dorsett was regularly rushing for 100 yards, and Staubach threw for more than 200 yards in four of the first eight games. His best effort had been a 303-yard day on which he had produced only one touchdown in the lopsided loss to the Browns.

In what had been forecast as one of the glamour events of the season, Dallas traveled to Pittsburgh for a game that promised to determine which team was most likely to collect yet another Super Bowl trophy. The Steelers won convincingly 14–3, with Staubach on the sidelines late in the game. Defender L.C. Greenwood had delivered a hammering blow to the Cowboys quarterback as he attempted to scramble. Knocked backward, Roger's head bounced hard on the Three Rivers Stadium turf and he was knocked unconscious.

It was not until the team charter was in the air that evening, making its way back to Dallas that his head cleared enough for him to ask who had won the game.

Despite the concussion, however, he was in the lineup for the next game.

To earn Dallas a 16–14 win over the Giants, Staubach and the offense had to score 10 points in the final two-and-a-half minutes of the game. Roger threw a 32-yard touchdown pass to Drew Pearson and later directed a hurry-up drive that set up Septien's winning field goal with just three seconds left.

Though they entered November with an 8–2 record, the Cowboys were a team living on the edge. And hidden from the public's attention was the fact they were a team in turmoil.

Since his "notice me" arrival at training camp in a stretch limo, Thomas Henderson had become an endless disruption and constant irritation. Suddenly belligerent, often late for practices, and sometimes sleeping through meetings, he strained the patience of all around him. Hollywood, unknown to Landry and his increasingly impatient coaching staff, had developed a serious cocaine habit. A sideline display during a 34–20 mid-November loss to the Redskins was the final straw.

Teammate Preston Pearson, attempting to get a novelty business up and running, had borrowed the "Terrible Towel" idea that had long been popular with Steelers fans and designed a similar marketing plan in Dallas. A bandanna, featuring the Cowboys insignia, was fast becoming a favorite with Dallas fans.

As time ticked away in the loss at RFK Stadium, Henderson mugged for the TV camera located behind the Dallas bench, waving the bandanna in a misguided effort to promote Pearson's product.

When linebacker coach Jerry Tubbs confronted him about his actions following the game, Henderson cursed wildly at the coach as stunned teammates looked on. If the Cowboys didn't like the way he played, Henderson shouted, why didn't they just trade him and forget about ever getting back to another Super Bowl?

On Monday, Landry called the talented but self-destructive linebacker into his office and informed him he was no longer a member of the team. The response was classic Hollywood. "You can't fire me," he yelled at the coach. "I quit."

Landry's decision created a good news/bad news scenario. In Henderson's absence, much of the tension that had built within the team was eased. Still, his sudden departure served as another damaging blow to the Cowboys struggling defense. Inexperienced Mike Hegman moved into the starting lineup in Henderson's place.

The loss to the Redskins had come in the second game of a three-week losing streak.

Then with three NFC East opponents remaining on the schedule, Dallas came to life. With Dorsett running for 108 yards that would put him over the 1,000-yard mark for the third straight season, and Staubach and Drew Pearson combining efforts for three touchdowns, Dallas was suddenly its old self in a 28–7 win over the Giants.

While the offensive display was welcomed by the sellout Texas Stadium crowd, it was the revitalized effort of the defense that got the loudest applause as it recovered two New York fumbles, picked off an interception, and denied a potential score with its first goal-line stand of the season.

A stretch drive that Landry had insisted would be necessary if the Cowboys hoped to defend their divisional title was underway. The following week they assured themselves at least a wild card spot in the playoffs with a 24–17 win over Philadelphia.

All that remained of the regular season was a visit from the Redskins and, for the 10–5 Cowboys, the math was simple—defeat Washington and they would repeat as champions of the NFC East.

No one thought it would be easy. Dorsett, having suffered a badly bruised shoulder against the Eagles, would be unavailable. Strong safety Randy Hughes was also sidelined with a shoulder injury and would be replaced in the secondary by second-year player Dennis Thurman. And Drew Pearson, still hobbling on a twisted knee that had resulted from a post-touchdown celebration against the Giants, wasn't likely to be a factor.

Few had argued when *Sports Illustrated* crowned the historic Dallas-Washington rivalry the greatest in professional sports. Bad blood had boiled year after year as angry barbs flew from each camp in the days before they would play. Over the years Dallas had hurled accusations that the Redskins spied on their practices, while in the nation's capitol, players scoffed at the wholesome image of the Cowboys. They berated the "tricked up" Dallas offense and its scrambling quarterback and called out several members of the defense whom they considered "dirty players."

It would be more of the same as the teams, both with 10–5 records, prepared to meet in the final game of the regular season.

Dallas players were still fuming over the way the previous meeting had ended. Leading comfortably and near the Cowboys goal line with just 11 seconds remaining, the Redskins had called a timeout to give kicker Mark Moseley time to add an unnecessary and insulting three points to the Redskins margin.

It was that rub-in-the-face decision that became the Cowboys' primary motivational tool as they prepared for the meeting.

For Washington, the stakes were equally high. They, too, appeared on their way to the playoff regardless of the outcome of the game. Only an obscure and long-shot tie-breaker could end their season. In that scenario, even if the Redskins lost, Chicago would have to win their final game by an unlikely margin of 33 points to claim the last wild card spot.

A final touch of sophomoric drama was added during the week before the game when a funeral wreath, allegedly sent by the Redskins, was delivered to Harvey Martin at the Cowboys practice facility. Though most likely a motivational ploy dreamed up by some Dallas fan—or perhaps even a member of the Cowboys coaching staff—everyone but Harvey laughed it off.

Finally, on that bitter Texas Stadium afternoon in December, the greatest game in the history of the famed rivalry played out.

As Dorsett watched, rookie Ron Springs started at running back—and fumbled on Dallas' second offensive play of the day, turning over the ball to the Redskins on the 34-yard line.

Washington hurriedly drove to the Cowboys 3 before Larry Cole sacked quarterback Joe Theismann to stop the drive. Moseley, trotting onto the field amidst a chorus of boos, kicked the short field goal.

The margin would quickly widen after yet another Dallas fumble. The ball was jarred loose from Robert Newhouse, and the Redskins responded with a short touchdown drive.

As the first quarter ended, Washington held a 10–0 lead. And things would only get worse for the out-of-synch Cowboys. Theismann connected with running back Benny Malone on a 55-yard touchdown pass to widen the margin to 17–0.

Then, however, the Dallas offense settled into a 13-play, 70-yard drive that ended with Springs powering his way in for the first Cowboys score of the afternoon. With time running down in the first half, Staubach moved the Cowboys 80 yards for a second touchdown. With only nine seconds remaining before intermission, he completed a 26-yard pass to Preston Pearson for the score, and Septien's conversion whittled down the Redskins margin to three points.

Newhouse scored at the end of a methodical Dallas drive to give the Cowboys their first lead at 21–17 during a third quarter that had settled into a defensive battle.

And as the quarter ended, the public address announcer informed the packed stadium that the Chicago Bears had defeated the Cardinals 42–6, thus achieving the incredible tie-breaker margin necessary to keep Washington's playoff hopes alive. For the Redskins, the task at hand had been simplified—either win the game and advance, or lose and the season was over.

In short order they were back in field-goal range, and Moseley's kick cut the Cowboys' lead to a single point. Then, a Mark Murphy interception at midfield gave new life to the Redskins' comeback hopes.

"I had tried to force the ball in to Jay Saldi," Roger remembered, "and it was intercepted. It was a bad decision on my part. I remember going to the sidelines afterward and telling Coach Landry, 'I blew it.' He gave me one of those 'truer words have never been spoken' looks and turned his attention to the defense."

Two plays later, John Riggins scored to put the Redskins back into the lead.

Dallas was suddenly struggling, its offense was ineffective after receiving the kickoff.

As the fourth quarter got underway, Riggins broke through the Dallas line, cut to the sideline, and went 66 yards for a touchdown that put his team into a commanding 34–21 lead.

For all looking on, Dallas appeared resigned to limping into the playoffs as a wild card entry when only four minutes remained with Washington in possession of the ball.

It was a punishing tackle by Cliff Harris, knocking the ball free from Clarence Harmon, that set the stage for unprecedented Staubach magic.

After Randy White covered Harmon's fumble, Roger stepped into the Shotgun and began moving the Cowboys with deadly accuracy. He threw to Butch Johnson for 14 and Tony Hill for 19. Then a 26-yard touchdown strike to Springs. Dallas narrowed Washington's margin to 34–28, but the clock was becoming as much of an adversary as the Redskins.

Hoping that his defense could fashion a three-and-out stop of the Washington offense, Landry opted not to attempt an onside kick. By the time the Redskins were facing a third-and-2 situation in their own end of the field, just more than two minutes remained. The veteran Cole, who always seemed to play well against the Redskins, tackled the powerful Riggins for a two-yard loss.

Following the punt, Dallas was on its own 25 with 1:46 left to play.

Staubach threw a 20-yard completion to Hill who outreached two Washington defenders for the catch before stepping out of bounds. Preston Pearson was then the target for gains of 22 and 25, advancing the Cowboys to the Redskins 8-yard line with 45 seconds remaining.

Following a first-down incompletion, Staubach had to literally yell to make himself heard over the thundering crowd noise as he called the next play. His primary target, tight end Billy Joe DuPree, was to make his way across the back of the end zone. He instructed Hill to line up wide and go to the corner and, in the event of a likely Washington blitz, "be ready."

Instead of lining up in the shotgun, Staubach took the snap from under center and quickly backpedaled to an effort to avoid an all-out Redskins blitz. Realizing that there would not be time for DuPree to reach his assigned spot, the ball was in Roger's hand for only a split second before he gently lofted it in the direction of Hill.

Hill reached over Redskins cornerback Lemar Parrish to make the historic catch that pulled Dallas into a tie. Staubach, in an uncharacteristic emotional display, jumped into the arms of Ron Springs, hoisting a fist skyward in celebration.

Septien's extra point gave the Cowboys a 35–34 victory.

In the postgame celebration, Staubach called it the "most thrilling 60 minutes" he had ever spent on the football field. Indeed, it had been one of his most productive as quarterback of the Cowboys. He completed 24-of-42 passes for 336 yards and three touchdowns.

Tex Schramm immediately anointed it Dallas' "greatest comeback ever." Even Landry was unabashed in his critique. "That," he told members of the media, "was the most remarkable game we've ever played."

The *Dallas Morning News* viewed the game thusly:

"Move aside, if you please, Santa. Out of the way, Tooth Fairy. Take a backseat Mr. Easter Bunny and all of you other charitable creatures of fantasy and folklore. And kindly make way for flesh-and-blood Roger Staubach, as remarkable a benefactor as any storybook has ever designed.

"On this cold December Sunday afternoon, deep into the season of giving, the veteran Dallas Cowboys quarterback emerged from 60 minutes of emotional ping-pong to win a high-drama race with the clock and present his teammates with their fourth straight NFC Eastern Division title, home field advantage in the upcoming playoffs, and the kind of performance which will one day serve as legitimate fodder for stories to tell the grandkids."

Nearby, the mood in the Redskins dressing room was several notches below somber. "That one little point," observed new Redskins coach Jack Pardee, "took us from division champions to the outhouse."

As the Redskins sat contemplating the sudden end of their season, the dressing room door swung open. Standing there was Harvey Martin, the aforementioned funeral wreath in hand. Washington players looked on in disbelief as he threw it into the room.

The act was the lone tarnish on the stunning victory. The following Monday, at Landry's insistence, Martin sent a telegram to the Redskins' front office and media outlets in Washington, apologizing for his impromptu display of poor sportsmanship.

Days later, after reviewing films of the game, Redskins coach Pardee said, "I went over the game play by play, trying to find out what we did wrong, wanting to make sure it never happened again. My final conclusion was that Roger pulled off two or three plays that made the difference— with sheer athletic ability."

Staubach finally ran out of end-of-the-game heroics two weeks later as the Cowboys lost 21–19 to the Los Angeles Rams in the NFC Divisional playoffs, closing out the tumultuous roller-coaster season.

Early in the fourth quarter, Roger's touchdown pass to backup tight end Saldi had moved the Cowboys into a 19–14 lead. But on this day the last-minute heroics would be authored by Rams quarterback Vince Ferragamo. With just more than two minutes remaining, he threw to Billy Waddy who was running a down-and-out pattern. Dallas linebacker Mike Hegman, playing in the spot vacated by Henderson, managed to tip the ball slightly but it still made its way into the receiver's hands. Waddy raced down the sidelines for a 50-yard touchdown.

In a final effort to rally his team, Staubach and the Cowboys ended their season on a less-than-glamorous note. Scrambling against a blitzing Rams defense, Roger had no receivers open and, in an attempt to ground the ball, threw it in the direction of guard Herb Scott. The surprised Cowboys lineman caught the wayward pass, and Dallas was immediately penalized 15 yards.

During a postgame interview, Roger attempted to inject a touch of levity into the somber aftermath. "Can you believe," he asked, "that my last pass was caught by Herb Scott?"

Reporters collected in front of his locker chuckled as they dutifully recorded the quote. At the time, none picked up on the importance of what seemed to be nothing more than a clever offhand observation.

But by the time the Pittsburgh Steelers defeated the Rams for their second straight Super Bowl championship and their fourth of the decade, Roger Staubach was already close to a decision that would ultimately signal an end to one of the most remarkable careers in NFL history.

CHAPTER 18

*"When you talk about great quarterbacks, Roger has to stand alongside
Otto Graham and Johnny Unitas, mainly because he was such a consistent
performer. And he was great in the two-minute drill, like Bobby Layne in his
prime. I don't know of any quarterback I played against or watched that I'd
rather have than Roger."*

Tom Landry

Time was when National Football League lore was well-littered
with machismo-driven stories of thundering collisions and jarring
hits that left players dazed, confused, or unconscious. There were
more polite descriptions for them back then, masking the grim dangers
and the possibility of permanent damage posed by head injuries.

Before medical researchers created a stark new awareness of the
nature and the effects of concussions, before the league awoke to the
need for rules forbidding helmet-to-helmet contact, a player simply "got
dinged" or "had his bell rung." Some would even get a good laugh with
their strange tales of experiences in Neverland.

The Cowboys were no exception.

Fullback Walt Garrison remembered the time when, unaware that
he had suffered a concussion, he finished a game as the team's leading
rusher despite having no recollection of playing. "From what I've heard,"
he recalled, "I must have been something. I just wish I could have been
there to enjoy it."

205

Then there was the game-winning touchdown pass that quarterback Don Meredith doesn't remember throwing. And the second half of a game Mike Ditka played with Chicago before coming to Dallas wherein he made several spectacular catches he couldn't recall. Or the time receiver Golden Richards finally regained his senses after playing most of a game against the Bears while out on his feet. In the dressing room, after he had regained his senses, he asked teammate Ralph Neely what he had missed. A consummate practical joker, Neely went to great lengths to convince Richards that for some reason he had suddenly pulled down his pants in full view of 60,000 cheering fans. Briefly, the still-addled Richards bought the story and sought out several reporters to ask if they were going to include his indiscretion when they wrote their game accounts.

Doctors call such blackouts a "state of fugue," a period of time during which one is able to continue to function while suffering what amounts to temporary amnesia resulting from a blow to the head.

Early in a game in Philadelphia's Veterans Stadium, middle linebacker Bob Breunig had gathered the Cowboys defense into the huddle and called the alignment for the next play. To this day he doesn't recall doing so. Nor does he remember finally being helped to the sidelines where trainers and the team doctor began asking him a series of questions.

Did he know what year it was? "I'm not sure."

Do you remember the game plan? "I do," Breunig replied, "but I just can't think of it right now."

Outwardly, he looked fine. But an opponent's knee to his head had momentarily frozen time, leaving only rote motions while locking out all rhyme and reason. It was, Breunig admits, a frightening experience.

Even now, quarterback Danny White has no recollection of his first date with wife Jo Lynn. He was in high school then and had invited her out following the annual Dad's Day game. Knocked out in the first half, White was still having trouble getting his bearings when the game ended.

"The only thing I can remember is seeing all the players' fathers wearing jerseys with their sons' names on them. I kept looking at Dad, asking what he was doing wearing that silly-looking jersey. He kept trying to explain it to me, and I kept asking him the same question as if I couldn't hear him."

Still, White played an entire game that he doesn't remember. Same with the party he and Jo Lynn attended afterward. White says there is little of what happened in the entire week previous to the injury that he can remember. It is as if a seven-day span of his young life had been wiped away.

Offensive lineman Pat Donovan experienced similar memory loss after suffering a concussion in his freshman season at Stanford. "After being helped to the sideline," he said, "I was sitting on the bench and started crying like crazy. I couldn't stop for the life of me, yet I had no idea what I was crying about. I didn't even remember being knocked out, yet there I was, bawling my head off and having no earthly idea why. It was strange."

What was even more troubling was the fact that the blow to his head had somehow wiped out all the math he had learned in a course he was taking, forcing the need to repeat the class the following semester.

"The thing that really gets to you in a situation like that," Randy White said, "is that once you do come to, you're aware that something is wrong with you but you aren't functioning well enough to understand what it is. Not knowing what is going on is hard to deal with. It's frightening."

He recalled a Sunday afternoon when, having been knocked unconscious, he returned to the game only to find that he didn't have the slightest idea what he was expected to do in various alignments. "The whole second half I had to go to Bob [Breunig] before every play and ask him where to line up and what I was supposed to do.

"The only thing I remember is that I kept wondering how I was going to get out of the stadium once the game was over. I couldn't get it out of my mind. I didn't remember that we had a dressing room to go to or a bus to take us from the stadium to the airport."

For Drew Pearson, a concussion suffered in that memorable Thanksgiving Day game against Washington was not his lone experience with a head injury.

In a game against Tampa Bay, he was hit with a crack-back block late in the game. Unconscious for a few seconds, he slowly made it to his feet and back to the huddle. He has no memory of catching a pass on the following play. "It wasn't until the following day that I read in the papers that I learned I'd caught one more pass than I thought I had," he said.

Then there was the bizarre postgame scene played out by Cliff Harris and *Dallas Morning News* sportswriter Bob St. John. En route to the stadium, St. John had been involved in an automobile accident during which he'd taken a hard blow to the head. Still, he'd managed to make it to his spot in the Texas Stadium press box before the kickoff. During the game, Harris had been knocked out and helped from the field.

It was Dallas public relations director Doug Todd who later called other journalists' attention to St. John and Harris as they stood in front of the players' locker following the game. Both were simultaneously talking rapidly, neither apparently listening to what the other had to say.

The following day, neither the reporter nor the player had any recollection of the conversation.

In the Staubach household, the subject of head injuries was far from a laughing matter. Increasingly, Marianne was concerned with the possibility of long-term brain damage her husband's concussions might produce. Privately, she had kept close count. Dating back to the 1978 playoff game against Atlanta, he had been forced to leave games with head injuries on six occasions, five of them occurring over the course of the just-ended season.

She waited for Roger to initiate the subject of retirement. "I never asked him to quit," she told author Frank Luksa, "but I was ready for him to retire. Yet I knew if I really pressured him to and he wasn't comfortable with the decision, if he did it 'because Marianne is upset about the head injuries,' he wouldn't be happy. Then it would be a heavy burden to live with."

She was relieved when, prior to the Pro Bowl in Hawaii, Roger told her he had met with Landry and general manager Tex Schramm and informed them that he was strongly considering not returning to the Cowboys for another season.

Should he decide to call it a career, he wanted them to know as soon as possible so the transition could be made smoothly. Danny White, he was certain, was a ready and highly capable replacement at the quarterback position. And the more off-season time he and his fellow players had to adapt to the change, the better.

Staubach, however, wanted to be sure before reaching a final decision. He still loved the game that had been so much a part of his life since he was a kid back in Cincinnati. His competitive urges remained strong; he was still confident in his abilities. And he felt that the Cowboys were still a championship-caliber team. Additionally, hadn't Landry already told him that following the coaching staff's annual postseason there was no doubt he could continue to play at a high level? The list of pluses was lengthy.

On the other hand, as he pondered the pros and cons, he admitted to himself that he had begun to weary of the drudgeries of the game, training camp, endless meetings, travel, and being constantly in the public eye. Additional involvement in the lives of his children, escaping the constant spotlight, and spending more time in the business world were among the things that had begun to call out to him.

He had fulfilled the demands of the last two-year contract he'd signed.

All these thoughts, he knew, were triggered by growing concern over his history of head injuries. Only when that issue was put to rest could a proper and comfortable decision be reached. Thus he went in search of the advice of medical experts.

In February, Roger traveled to New York to consult with famed neurologist Dr. Fred Plum. The doctor had asked that he recall every concussion he'd experienced during his life in football. Going back to high school days, he could remember 20. He described each, from those where the cobwebs had disappeared in just a brief period of time, to those that had left him nauseated, and others that had caused memory loss and temporary lack of feeling in his face and hands.

Dr. Plum recommended that Staubach undergo a series of tests before he rendered any thoughts on whether it would be dangerous for him to continue to play. He also suggested that a second opinion would be wise.

With that he arranged for a battery of tests to be conducted in Dallas' Presbyterian Hospital and recommended that Dr. Phil Williams also examine Staubach, review test results, and offer his opinion.

After a series of X-rays and computerized tests that measured everything from reflexes to impulses to the brain, the doctors independently reviewed the data and offered their recommendations.

Writing later in his autobiography, Staubach remembered Dr. Williams not being unduly concerned about the possible danger from further injuries but that he had told him, "If you retired, it wouldn't be a decision you would regret."

Dr. Plum's evaluation was more straightforward. He had detected what he described as slight neurological changes in the left side of the brain. They were, he explained, extremely minor and probably the cumulative effect of Roger's long history of concussions. His concern, however, was that subsequent injuries could be progressively more damaging. It was his recommendation that Staubach seriously consider retiring.

And with that, the decision was made.

Seated in Tom Landry's office at the Cowboys Valley Ranch headquarters, Staubach informed the coach of his decision. The conversation between the two men whose careers had been so entwined over the past decade was, as Roger expected, brief and businesslike. Ten minutes, maybe. There would not even be a farewell handshake.

As he rose and walked toward the door, Staubach turned back to the man seated behind the desk. "Coach," he said, "what if I come back this year? Would you let me call the plays?" It was something the two had joked about often in recent years.

Landry smiled. "Sure. You can call some from the press box."

"Seriously, what if I come back? If I played again, could I call plays?"

For some, regardless of all their great achievement and high acclaim, unfulfilled dreams die hard.

"No," Landry replied, a finality and firmness in his voice. "We have a system."

CHAPTER 19

"The thing that will always stand out in my mind about Roger is that he never knew when it was over. At the end of the game, even if we were down by 20, he'd be standing there by himself, trying to figure out how we could win it."

Billy Joe DuPree

The game would not allow Staubach to go quietly.

CBS Sports wanted him to offer up his expertise from its TV booth on Sundays, companies with new products to peddle requested his endorsement, and banquet organizers sent invitations and promises of new awards to add to his trophy case. And in the aftermath of his retirement announcement, the flow of fan mail increased rather than decreased.

Seldom did a day go by when some political observer didn't suggest that he would be an ideal candidate should he decide to make a run for Texas governor, a seat in the U.S. Senate, or mayor of Dallas. For a time, it was rumored that he was in line to become the next Secretary of the Navy.

Charities found him eager to lend a hand. Included among the lengthy list of non-profit and civic involvements were the roles of national chairman for the American Diabetes Association and Easter Seals. Though he is silent on the subject, a number of former teammates turned to Staubach in times of financial difficulties.

The list of Staubach's accolades is lengthier than one might imagine.

In 1983, he was inducted into the Dallas Cowboys Ring of Honor and received the Walter Camp Football Foundation's Man of the Year award, both previews of his sport's ultimate recognition. In 1985, immediately after the required five-year waiting period had expired, Staubach was unanimously voted into the Pro Football Hall of Fame. In 2000 he was awarded the NCAA's Teddy Roosevelt Award, given annually to a former collegiate athlete who had gone on to establish a national reputation as a distinguished citizen, joining a list that included political luminaries like Ronald Reagan, Bob Dole, George Bush, and Dwight Eisenhower. A year later he became the first recipient of the Davey O'Brien Legends Award. If someone had a trophy to pass out, it seemed, Staubach was the man they wanted to give it to.

As the Cowboys organization neared its 50th anniversary in 2009, the *Fort Worth Star-Telegram* and *Dallas Morning News* conducted polls to determine the 50 all-time favorite performers in the team's colorful history. In the *Star-Telegram* poll, restricted to players only, Staubach was the easy winner. In the *Morning News* voting, Tom Landry finished first with Staubach a close second.

And all the while, he was thriving in a new arena. During much of his playing career, he had spent off-seasons working for the Henry S. Miller Company, learning the ins and outs of the Dallas real estate business. By 1977 he and partner Robert Holloway had formed the Holloway-Staubach Corporation, a commercial real estate brokerage firm. Four years later, it evolved into the internationally successful The Staubach Company. With its namesake in the role of CEO, the Dallas-based company would ultimately expand to include more than 1,100 employees with more than 70 branch offices throughout the United States.

As he achieved success in a new arena, his fellow realtors added Executive of the Year citations to his lengthy list of recognitions.

In 2008, the man whose largest seasonal paycheck as a Cowboy was $230,000 sold The Staubach Company to Jones Lang LaSalle, one of the world's largest real estate brokers, for $613 million. Part of the monumental transaction was the request that Staubach remain as a member of the firm's board of directors.

Forty years after his rookie NFL season, his ties to Dallas and the Cowboys remain. When current owner Jerry Jones purchased the team and unceremoniously dismissed Landry after 29 years as the team's coach, former players, Roger among them, were openly bitter. In time, however, it was Staubach who quietly made efforts to calm the dissent between Dallas fandom and its brash new owner. They were, after all, still the Dallas Cowboys, even if much of the style and class of the '70s glory days seemed forgotten.

When Landry died in February 2000, it was no surprise that Staubach was called on to deliver the eulogy. In a sense, he was saying a final goodbye to a remarkable time in Dallas history. Original team owner Clint Murchison was gone, soon too would be Tex Schramm. Roger had affectionately referred to Landry as "the nuts and bolts of the Cowboys, the man who wears the funny hat" during his retirement announcement. Of those who had played the most vital roles in the creation of the perfect storm of the '70s that had finally lifted the Cowboys and the city of Dallas to such remarkable heights, only Staubach remains.

Today, at age 68, he has more time to spend in the company of fast-growing grandchildren and to occasionally lunch with old teammates and friends. He still stays in shape for an occasional game of hoops or pass-touch.

And it is still Roger to whom others reach out. When Dallas city fathers and other north Texas community leaders decided to make a bid to host the 2011 Super Bowl, he was the man asked to chair the committee that would make its pitch to the National Football League.

"There was really only one person whose presence, aura, or mystique represents football in north Texas," Jones, architect of the billion-dollar Arlington stadium where the game will be played, told Richie Whitt of the *Dallas Observer.* "He was the obvious choice to be the leader of this pursuit because his entire career has been about leadership and getting the job done."

Ever the good ambassador, Roger Staubach agreed to take on the job—and scored yet another victory.

FINAL THOUGHTS

THE LIGHTER SIDE

"He can play until he's 40 because he doesn't know what a hangover is."
Sonny Jurgensen, Washington quarterback

Were all the words written about Roger Staubach over the course of his remarkable career laid end to end, they would likely reach a distance far greater than all the football fields on which he ever played. And the profiles have covered similar ground: determined athlete; dedicated Christian, father and husband; record-setting master of the come-from-behind win; the constant award-winning, and the Captain America image that has often caused him private cringes despite the fact it was justly earned.

Still, in endless efforts to provide the reader with a broad canvas portrait, we have all—big shot national magazine writers to those of us who toiled as beat writers for local dailies—fallen short of the mark on at least one count.

For the most part, we have failed woefully to shed proper light on the Staubach sense of humor.

Perhaps it's because we have become so narrowly focused on his stoic game-day image, his dedicated involvement with the Fellowship of Christian Athletes, his "Father Knows Best" family life. How could one so dead-on poised and well-grounded have time for jest and frivolous behavior?

But the truth of the matter is that Roger is a funny guy. It's just that the humor he favors is not the didja-hear-the-one-about-the-two-guys-sitting-at-the-bar? type. Rather it is richly subtle and broad, the punch lines often directed at himself and delivered in the most deadpan manner. Staubach is, for lack of a better description, a thinking man's comedian. Which is why his humor has occasionally backfired and been misunderstood. Roger has never learned that too many of us get the joke only when the teller himself bursts into teary laughter accompanied by a resounding *bah-boom* from the guy on drums.

"I know that I've long had the image of a straight, goody-goody sort of person," he admits, "and I can't honestly say I regret it. Basically, that's just what I am. I'm proud of being a Christian, a family man, things like that. But there are a lot of people who think that because you don't fit into the swinging image, you go around with a frown on your face all the time.

"And when you do say something in jest, some people simply can't take it for what it is meant to be.

"For instance, I had this magazine writer with me one afternoon when I was going to pick up my dog at the vet's office. I said something like, 'Boy, this is one of the things I really love to do,' and he took me at my word. I was talking tongue-in-cheek, but his story came out saying that 'one of the great pleasures in Roger Staubach's life is driving down to the vet to pick up his dog.'

"Boy, I'd like to think that my life is a little more exciting than that."

Reporters have often been the target of the unique Staubach humor. There was the time, for instance, when a writer approached the Cowboys quarterback to inform him that snow and bitterly cold temperatures were forecast for an upcoming Sunday game against the Green Bay Packers. Roger pondered the news silently for several seconds, then shrugged. "Well," he finally responded as he walked away, "if that's the case, I'm not playing."

Once quizzed about why he had never bothered to have the pinky on his throwing hand—the one that made an ugly 45-degree turn at the top knuckle—surgically repaired, his answer was quick and to the point, "If I did, I couldn't get into handicapped parking spots anymore."

And how about the radio guy, visiting the practice field in the off-season in desperate search of some new angle? "Roger," he asked as he extended his microphone, "what can we expect of you when the new season gets underway?"

"A couple of things," Staubach quickly replied with a straight face. "I'll have this massive chest and will be wearing my hair shoulder-length."

Even Tom Landry got a good-natured jab now and then. Standing next to Landry during a long ago sideline timeout, Roger impatiently waited for the coach to provide him with the next play. Landry, arms crossed against his chest, looked skyward for several seconds before finally giving his quarterback instructions. As Staubach prepared to reenter the fray, he turned back at his coach and grinned. "You know," he said, "I always wondered where some of these plays came from."

Or how about that afternoon at the practice field when Landry wasn't particularly pleased with the way Staubach was running a certain quarterback roll-out and offered to demonstrate?

Landry moved behind the center, took the snap, and in a limping gait, showed how he wished the play to be run. "Now try it like that," Landry instructed.

Roger nodded, took the snap, and perfectly imitated the route—and the limp—his coach had used in his demonstration.

Even Tom had to smile.

There were times over the course of their unique relationship when Landry briefly got the upper hand only to prompt a quick Roger comeback. When his coach was inducted into the Pro Football Hall of Fame, Staubach delivered the introductory speech. (Earlier, Landry had done the same for Roger when he was inducted.)

Staubach was feeling good about the speech he'd given until after the ceremony when Landry began his jesting yet deadpan critique, "You should have said... and mentioned... and maybe elaborated on..."

Roger listened intently before finally responding. "Coach," he said, "we're both retired now. Don't you think it's about time you quit sending in my plays?"

Staubach's favorite target is most often himself. After being introduced as the guest speaker at some forgotten banquet he attended with Landry, Roger approached the podium and for several seconds stood silent. Then he apologized. "I'm sorry," he said, alluding to his long-standing battle with the Cowboys coach over his calling plays. "I was waiting for Coach to tell me what to say."

One summer evening when all the training camp practices and meetings at Thousand Oaks had been completed, I had finally judged it a proper time to ask that he sign a copy of his just-published autobiography, *First Down, Lifetime to Go*.

"Be more than happy to," he said. "Here's what you do: Call my attorney and tell him what you have in mind and let him know exactly what you want me to write. Then, if everything's okay at that point, he'll get in touch with my secretary. She'll in turn set up an appointment for you. I'm sure it won't be any problem at all."

And with that he walked away, leaving the book unsigned—until later that night when he knocked on my door, a wide grin on his face, pen in hand.

It was during the drudgery of the Cowboys' training camps that Staubach was often at his mischievous best.

Like the time he decided on a plan that would break teammate Tom Rafferty of the habit of nightly stopping into his dorm room and munching from a bowl of mixed nuts until it was empty. Before Rafferty's next arrival, Roger secretly sprinkled bits of dry dog food among the almonds and peanuts and eagerly waited for his offensive guard to drop by. Rafferty, true to form, hungrily emptied the bowl before taking his leave.

Only later, when he stopped in again to inform Staubach that he wasn't feeling too well, did the trickster fess up. "Gosh, Tom," he said, "maybe we'd better get you to a vet right away."

Captain America, it seems, had a particular fancy for veterinarian jokes, whether anyone got them or not.

Most often, his humor was and is of the self-deprecating kind, the sort that might even leave the punch line to someone else.

En route to Super Bowl XII, the Cowboys had managed a 16–10 victory over the Philadelphia Eagles. A 33-yard scramble had been a key factor in preventing what, for much of the afternoon, appeared to be an Eagles upset in the making.

Seated on the team bus outside Veterans Stadium, awaiting a trip to the airport and home, Staubach was informed by team public relations director Doug Todd that his run had been the longest of his Cowboys career.

Roger didn't even smile. "Frankly," he said, "I was amazed that anyone was able to catch me. I don't know who it was who made the tackle, but he must have been some really fast dude. In fact, I wouldn't be surprised if the game films don't show that it was one of those illegal off-the-bench tackles or something like that."

Todd, quite the quipster himself, replied, "Truthfully, Roger, it was the first time in NFL history that 11 players from a defensive unit were credited with simultaneously making a tackle. They *all* caught you. There's talk that the ball you carried might end up being displayed in the Hall of Fame."

Staubach loved it. It was his kind of humor.

And finally, when rumors spread that he was considering retirement, the repeated concussions the primary reason, a *Washington Post* medical writer had phoned his secretary, Roz Cole, to request an interview. "Tell her I can't talk now," Roger said, "because my head's bothering me."

It was *Sports Illustrated* that first published this anecdote: On the day he announced his retirement, the switchboard at the Cowboys offices received a number of calls from gruff-voiced "fans," each insisting that if Staubach retired they would immediately cancel their season tickets.

When the switchboard operator answered yet another call, fully expecting the same ticket-cancelation threat, she heard a familiar voice. "Hi," the caller said, "This is Roger. I was just wondering how many people have phoned to cancel their season tickets so far."

The operator burst into laughter. "That was *you* making those calls?"

Roger confessed. "Aw, I was just killing time before the press conference," he admitted.

Even when he'd met with teammates to let them know he would not return for another season, the straight-arrow Staubach left them laughing. "Yeah, I'll miss training camp tremendously," he said. "I'll miss the booze and the broads. Breaking curfew... the nude beaches..."

Bah-boom.

THE BEST OF TIMES

"Roger Staubach had great belief in his ability to win. That's why he led us out of so many games in the final two-minute period and won the game for us."

Tom Landry

The memorable games in which Roger Staubach played during his 30-year football career have already been revisited in some detail on earlier pages. Yet aside from his obvious delight over the '79 win against Washington and the Super Bowl victories, there has been little attention paid to Staubach's own evaluations, a personal sorting of his best of the best.

While he hedges a bit, insisting that it is impossible to rank their importance in numerical order, these are the dozen games that he most fondly thinks back on.

They are listed here in the order in which he discussed them.

St. John's Eagles vs. Assumption Junior High (eighth grade): "When I was in the seventh grade, we didn't win a game. Then in the eighth, we went undefeated. I was a halfback and a flanker then. Assumption had an outstanding team, and we were scared stiff because they were favored to maul us. The game was a really big deal. I remember Dad even took off work to come see it. We won 21–20, and I was able to score all three of our touchdowns. I ran back the opening kickoff for one, caught a 50-yard pass for another, then ran for the other. It was one of the most thrilling games I ever played in."

Purcell High School vs. Elder High School: "It was my first year as the starting quarterback. We had no running plays for me, but in the third quarter I told the assistant coach that I thought I could run against their defense. He said okay, so I faked a power sweep and went down the sidelines for an 80-yard touchdown. We won that one 21–14 in a come-from-behind effort. Elder was an outstanding team with a quarterback named Steve

Tensi, who later played at Florida State and later with the San Diego Chargers and Denver Broncos."

New Mexico Military Institute vs. San Angelo Junior College: "It was our homecoming game, and we'd lost only once that season, to Tyler Junior College. With four minutes to go, we were down by two touchdowns. It wound up a lot like that Cowboys-Washington game in '79. We scored, got the ball back, and started driving again. I got knocked out, went to the sidelines for a couple of plays, then came back in and threw a pass to the 1-yard line. Then I sneaked the ball over and we won 35–34."

Navy vs. Army (sophomore year): "The Army-Navy game was always such a big thing, a major event. Throughout my career I never had any trouble sleeping the night before a game—except when we played Army. That year we won 34–14 and I had a really good game, running for a couple of touchdowns and passing for two others."

Navy vs. Army (junior year): "We won that one 21–15, and they were on our 1-yard line when the game ended. The game was delayed a week because of the assassination of President Kennedy. At one point we went ahead 21–7, but they went right down the field in the fourth quarter and scored. Then with six minutes left, they got the ball again and drove to the 1 before the game ended."

Navy vs. Michigan (junior year): "We won 26–13, and I had a really good day passing, hitting 14-of-16. There is one play that stands out in my mind. I took off on what wound up being a 30–second scramble during which I retreated until I was 25 yards behind the line of scrimmage. I finally got off a pass for a one-yard gain."

Dallas vs. Miami, Super Bowl VI: "That win [24–3] took a lot of pressure off a lot of people, players and coaches alike. It got the 'can't win the big one' burden off a very good team's shoulders. The defense was the big thing for us that day, playing a near-perfect game. For me, it was just nice to be in the dressing room of a Super Bowl champion for the first time."

Dallas vs. San Francisco, 1972 Division Playoff: "I had been injured early and came into the game late for Craig [Morton]. Actually, I had gone into the playoffs thinking about the next year. It was a game when things didn't go too well, and I got to play in the second half. We scored 17 points and came back to win 30–28. Actually, it was a win we probably didn't deserve, but it was a memorable comeback and we were glad to take it."

Dallas vs. Pittsburgh, Super Bowl XIII: "In the second half of that season, we'd gotten our act together and won eight in a row. I thought we had the better team so it was a great disappointment that we lost 35–31. I guess people are always going to remember the pass to Jackie Smith that was incomplete in the end zone. People seem to forget that it wasn't the greatest pass I'd ever thrown. It's just so unfortunate, but there's no way you can call one like that back."

Dallas vs. Washington, 1979: "That one was wild, one of the most exciting games I ever played in. It was also one of the craziest. Both teams scored in bunches. They jumped out to a 17–0 lead, then we came back, then they came back. Then we came back again. The fact they had beaten us in Washington earlier in the year and that the game decided the NFC East championship made our final comeback to win 35–34 even more enjoyable."

Dallas vs. Minnesota, 1975: "That one was a game everyone in the world thought we were out of. We were behind, had no timeouts, [center] John Fitzgerald was out with a bad elbow, and we were looking at a fourth-and-18 situation. Drew [Pearson] beat Nate Wright for a first down, and when he came back to the huddle, I asked if he could go again. He said he was too tired so I told him to rest. I threw incomplete to Preston on the next play. Then Drew said he was ready and beat Wright again. I under-threw the ball, but he still caught it to score and put us ahead 17–14. The silence in the stadium was unbelievable. The only downside to that day came later when I learned that [Vikings quarterback] Fran Tarkenton's father had died during the game. That took some of the edge off the win for me. I felt really bad for Fran."

Dallas vs. Denver, Super Bowl XII: "To be in the Super Bowl with Craig Morton was special in light of all we'd gone through when we were both competing for the Cowboys quarterbacking job. Playing indoors at the Superdome was an experience. I remember [Robert] Newhouse yelling at me early in the game, saying that I had to get the team under control. I told him, 'House, I'm having enough trouble getting myself under control right now.' Again, that was primarily a defensive game. But there's no greater feeling than winning a Super Bowl, a wonderful feeling of having accomplished something special."

AFTERWORD

Since that long ago summer when we first met on the old Dallas Cowboys practice field—me a long-shot free agent hoping to make a place for myself in the NFL, him already an established star and team leader—Roger Staubach has played a special role in my life. And I'm not just talking about the eight years we spent together as teammates, the excitement of last-minute wins, or even Super Bowl championships.

Rather, I'm talking about the admirable things I saw in him that went far beyond athletic ability, things I've been borrowing from through much of my adult life: His courage, work ethic, loyalty to family and friends, laser-vision determination, and absolute refusal to accept defeat.

I hadn't been in Dallas long before I realized that if I dedicated myself to trying to do things the way Roger did, I too might have a chance at success. I watched how he worked, and how he dealt with coaches, teammates, and the media. I took note of the fact that he arrived at the practice field early and stayed late. I was amazed by the study habits that made him such a keen student of the game. Later, I watched how he related to people in the business world. I told myself I was going to try to do things the same way.

So yes, I owe the guy. I cherish the fact that for a special time in our lives, I was his Sunday afternoon "go to" receiver. Even more valued are the lessons I learned from him. During the time I've known Roger, he's been an encouraging friend, a great teammate and, most important, a shining role model.

As you look at his athletic career, from his schoolboy days to the Naval Academy and then with the Cowboys, it is easy to assume Roger was one of those rarely blessed individuals simply born with that magic gene that makes athletic success easy. Guess what? That isn't the whole truth. Sure, he had God-given talent, a keen instinct, and an obvious love for sports. But the fact of the matter is that Roger Staubach had to work long and hard to become a Heisman Trophy winner, a Super Bowl MVP, and a Hall of Fame inductee. He was never the biggest or strongest or fastest. He reached great heights by being an incredible competitor—the guy who never thought a game was lost, regardless of what the scoreboard said.

I think often of that Sunday when we were to play the St. Louis Cardinals just after Roger's mother passed away. He was devastated, naturally, but insisted on playing, not letting his teammates down. And on that afternoon he was spectacular, once again proving himself to be not only physically tough but incredibly strong mentally, as well.

And once his playing days were over, he simply applied the same work ethic and mind-set to becoming a successful businessman.

On the day he announced his retirement, I opted not to attend the formal press conference. He had already met with members of the team earlier in the day to tell us of his decision, so I opted not to go out to Texas Stadium. It would have been too hard. And frankly, I didn't want to be seen crying in public.

Roger Staubach, the friend and teammate I had bonded with so many years ago, meant that much to me. And he still does.

—Drew Pearson

Drew Pearson was a three-time All-Pro wide receiver for the Cowboys, was picked to the NFL's All-Decade team for the 1970s, and is the author of the bestselling autobiography, Hail Mary.

REFERENCES

The library of books already written by and about the Dallas Cowboys is extraordinary, perhaps rivaled only by the literary attention given the New York Yankees over the years. Part of the process of jumping into the publishing parade with this retelling of Roger Staubach's remarkable career was to review what others have written. Each, in its own way, was of valuable assistance, and when another's recollection has been used, a conscious effort has been made to give due credit.

Staubach, Roger with Sam Blair and Bob St. John. *Staubach: First Down, Lifetime to Go.* (Word Books, 1974).

Staubach, Roger with Frank Luksa. *Roger Staubach: Time Enough to Win* (Word Books, 1980).

Gergen, Joe. *Roger Staubach of the Dallas Cowboys.* (Scholastic Books, 1972).

Towle, Mike. *Roger Staubach: Captain America.* (Cumberland House, 2002).

Landry, Tom with Gregg Lewis. *Tom Landry: An Autobiography.* (Harper Collins, 1990).

Perkins, Steve. *Next Year's Champions.* (World, 1969).

Perkins, Steve. *The Dallas Cowboys: Winning the Big One.* (Grosset & Dunlap, 1972).

Klein, Dave. *Tom and the 'Boys.* (Zebra Books, 1990).

St. John, Bob. *The Landry Legend: Grace Under Pressure.* (Word Publishing, 1989).

Luksa, Frank. *Cowboys Essential.* (Triumph Books, 2006).

Sham, Brad. *Dallas Cowboys: Colorful Tales of America's Team.* (The Globe Pequot Press, 2003).

Golenbock, Peter. *Cowboys Have Always Been My Heroes.* (Warner Books, 1997).

Whittingham, Richard. *The Dallas Cowboys: An Illustrated History.* (Harper & Row, 1981).

Guinn, Jeff. *Dallas Cowboys: Our Story.* (Summit, 1996).

Stowers, Carlton. *Journey to Triumph.* (Taylor Publishing, 1982).

Martin, Harvey. *Texas Thunder: My Eleven Years with the Dallas Cowboys.* (Rawson Associates, 1986).

Pearson, Preston. *Hearing the Noise: My Life in the NFL.* (William & Morrow, 1985).

Garrison, Walt with John Tullius. *Once a Cowboy.* (Random House, 1988).

Stowers, Carlton. *Dallas Cowboys: The First Twenty-Five Years.* (Taylor Publishing, 1984).

Stowers, Carlton. *The Cowboy Chronicles.* (Eakin Press, 1984).

St. John, Bob. *Tex: The Man Who Built the Dallas Cowboys.* (Prentice Hall, 1988).

St. John, Bob. *We Love You Cowboys.* (Sport Magazine Press, 1972).

Donovan, Jim, Ken Sims, and Frank Coffee. *The Dallas Cowboys Encyclopedia.* (Citadel Press, 1996).

Hayes, Bob with Robert Pack. *Run, Bullet, Run.* (Harper & Row, 1990).

Lilly, Bob with Kristine Setting Clark. *A Cowboys Life.* (Triumph Books, 2008).

Wright, Rayfield with Jeannette DeVader. *Wright Up Front.* (R. Wright Enterprises, 2005).

Henderson, Thomas with Frank Luksa. *In Control.* (Thomas Henderson Publishing, 2004).

Morton, Craig and Robert Burger. *The Courage to Believe.* (Prentice Hall, 1981).

Garrison, Walt and Mark Stallard. *"Then Landry Said to Staubach..."*. (Triumph Books, 2007).

Housewright, Ed. *Game Changers: The Greatest Plays in Dallas Cowboys Football History.* (Triumph Books, 2009).

Taylor, Jean-Jacques. *Game of My Life: Dallas Cowboys.* (Sports Publishing LLC, 2006).

Pearson, Drew. *Hail Mary: The Drew Pearson Story.* (Zone Press, 2004).

Freeman, Denne H. and Jaime Aron. *I Remember Tom Landry.* (Sports Publishing, 2001).

Stowers, Carlton. *Cotton Bowl Classic: The First Fifty Years,* (Host Communications, 1986).

Clary, Jack. *Navy Football: Gridiron Legends and Fighting Heroes.* (Naval Institute Press, 1997).

ABOUT THE AUTHOR

Award-winning author/journalist Carlton Stowers has written more than two dozen books, many sports-related. *Marcus,* which he co-authored with Hall of Fame running back Marcus Allen, was a *New York Times* bestseller, and his work had been anthologized in *Best American Sports Writing.* He is also a two-time winner of the Mystery Writers of America's Edgar Allan Poe Award. A native Texan, he's been writing about the Dallas Cowboys since their Cotton Bowl days.

INDEX

M

N

Townsend, Brad, 64
Trinidad, 14
Truax, Billy, 87, 92, 95, 122
Trull, Don, 28
Tubbs, Jerry, 5, 198
Tulane Stadium, 100
Turner, Jim, 171
Tyler Junior College, 221

U

U.S. Military Academy, 24, 27
U.S. Naval Academy, 17, 34
U.S. Senate, 211
Unitas, Johnny, 14, 34, 82–84, 139, 205
United Press International, 39
University of California, 44
University of Cincinnati, 10
University of Houston, 108
University of Illinois, 139
University of Maryland, 20, 33, 45
University of Miami, 28
University of Michigan Wolverines, 30, 44
University of Minnesota, 21
University of Pittsburgh, 22, 45, 163
University of Southern California Trojans, 23–24
University of Tennessee, 64
University of Texas, 31, 34, 38, 40
University of Tulsa, 47, 118
Upchurch, Rick, 172
USS *Forrestal*, 21

V

Veterans Stadium, 141, 206, 219
Vietnam, 54–56
Vince Lombardi Trophy, 173
Virginia Military Institute, 32

W

Waddy, Billy, 204
Wagner, Mike, 150
Walden, Bobby, 149
Waldrop, Ken, 37
Walker, Doak, 62
Walker, Malcolm, 49

Walter Camp Football Foundation, 212
Ward, Al, 106
Warfield, Paul, 12
Warren High School, 12
Washington Post, 219
Washington Redskins, 79, 91–94, 96, 110–11, 113–14, 121–23, 126, 131–34, 140, 161, 167–68, 176–78, 198–203
Washington, Mark, 83
Washington, Vic, 112
Waters, Charlie, 1, 98, 159, 165, 168, 179, 191–92, 196–97
Weese, Norris, 172
West Coast, 44, 99
West Texas State University, 80
West Virginia, 29
Westmoreland, General William, 27
White House, 104
White, Danny, 128, 152, 154–55, 160, 178, 206, 208
White, Jo Lynn, 206
White, Randy, 138, 146, 151, 158, 165, 171, 173, 179, 191–92, 196, 202, 207
Whitt, Richie, 213
William and Mary, 21, 29, 43
Williams, Dr. Phil, 209–210
Woolsey, Rolly, 138
Wooten, John, 185
World Football League, 128–129, 134, 152
World Hockey League, 128
Wright, Nate, 144, 222
Wright, Rayfield, 97, 104, 128

X

Xavier, 10

Y

Yale, 64
Yearby, Bill, 44
Yepremian, Garo, 103

Z

Zloch, Bill, 58
Zorn, Jim, 140, 152